Darcy White, Chris Goldie (eds.)
Proximity and Distance in Northern Landscape Photography

Image | Volume 171

For Jared and Theo

Darcy White is Principal Lecturer in visual culture at Sheffield Hallam University.
Chris Goldie, formerly Senior Lecturer in media and cultural history, is now an Honorary Research Fellow at Sheffield Hallam University.

Darcy White, Chris Goldie (eds.)

Proximity and Distance in Northern Landscape Photography

Contemporary Criticism, Curation and Practice

[transcript]

Bibliographic information published by the Deutsche Nationalbibliothek
The Deutsche Nationalbibliothek lists this publication in the Deutsche Nationalbibliografie; detailed bibliographic data are available in the Internet at http://dnb.d-nb.de

transcript Verlag | Hermannstraße 26 | D-33602 Bielefeld | live@transcript-verlag.de

Cover layout: Maria Arndt, Bielefeld
Cover illustration: © Temporal Wandering, Tracy Hill, Artlab Contemporary Print Studios, University of Central Lancashire 2016, from the series *Matrix of Movement.* All worldwide results reserved.
Typeset by Justine Buri, Bielefeld
Printed by Majuskel Medienproduktion GmbH, Wetzlar
Print-ISBN 978-3-8376-4950-5
PDF-ISBN 978-3-8394-4950-9
https://doi.org/10.14361/9783839449509

Printed on permanent acid-free text paper.

Contents

Preface and Acknowledgements

The essays in this collection have their origins in papers presented at a conference held at Sheffield Hallam University on 2nd and 3rd July, 2018 – *Northern Light: critical approaches to proximity and distance in northern landscape photography.* This was the second conference organised by Sheffield Hallam's photography research group addressing critical landscape issues, and as with the 2016 event it was accompanied by an exhibition of photographic work. The 2016 conference and exhibition also provided the foundations for a collection of essays – Chris Goldie and Darcy White (eds.). *Northern Light: Landscape, Photography and Evocations of the North* – published by transcript Verlag, and we are now able to continue our critical project with this volume. We would like to acknowledge the contributions of all who participated in our most recent conference and exhibition, without whom this publication would not have been realised: those who presented their research or showed their work, the academic and technical staff from the university who gave their time and skill in the organisation of the event, and student volunteers from BA Photography, whose assistance throughout the event was vital.

This book would not have been possible without the generous support of Sheffield Hallam University's Art and Design Research Centre, the Department for Media Arts and Communication and in particularly the latter's Head, Geff Green, whose help has been invaluable. The Centre for Practice as Research at the University of Gloucestershire has also generously supported this publication. We wish to especially thank Angus Pryor, Head of Arts, and Andrew Bick, Chair of the School of Arts Research Steering Group, who have been unstinting in their support and encouragement of this publication.

Introduction

Darcy White and Chris Goldie

The essays in this collection discuss the northern landscape from different perspectives but across a range of contributions a number of distinct themes are addressed, all of which can be framed through the concepts of proximity and distance and the relationship of these to the theory and practice of landscape photography. To juxtapose proximity and distance is not to suggest that one is necessarily superior to the other in providing a view of the world and of the reality of landscape. In general, one emphasises the primacy of direct, embodied experience in the perception of place, the other advocates a distant, detached, critical point of view, but they coexist, with neither having the capacity to replace the other, both are valid although mutually exclusive. As Christopher Norris argues in his account of Derrida's deconstruction of both structuralism in its objectivist form and the phenomenology of presence, these are "two different orders of thought which can never be reduced to each other's terms but which nonetheless cannot be assumed to exist in self-sufficient isolation" (Norris 1991: 50).

Photography has, nevertheless, a particular relationship to the direct, embodied and perceptual because, as Norman Bryson argues, it is a *deictic* art. *Deixis* encompasses both the description of an event and the circumstances of describing it: a photograph "is the product of a chemical process occurring in the same spatial and temporal vicinity as the event it records" (89). This process is one of immersion in which the light sensitive surface of the camera bears the traces of the field to which it is exposed; an existential bond between the photograph and that which it represents, the image being less a depiction of a place than its extension. Such an emphasis on photographic process as part of a continuum with its subject must inevitably extend to the photographer herself and her mode of being in and seeing the landscape, hence the significance within much recent landscape photography of walking, a practice within which the proximity of space and the unfolding of an event in the course of time are inseparable.

It is unsurprising, then, that the practice of landscape photography has in recent years placed an emphasis on direct and lived experience, and that it has done so by drawing upon concepts from the phenomenological tradition and its more recent iterations within post-structuralist theory. Landscape photography's affinity with phenomenology can be identified in a number of themes and concepts recurring throughout this collection: temporality as a way of conceiving place as an ongoing event rather than a static, fixed, mapped and preconceived location; perception as multisensory and embodied rather than purely visual; a questioning of objectivity and the transcendental point of view.

Because this collection is concerned with photographic representations of specifically northern landscapes – with their own history of being conceived and represented through painting, literature, cultural narrative, memory – to advocate the primacy of direct experience without regard to more distant or detached representations of place would not be desirable, however. Such representations are a significant albeit contested aspect of the identity of places, which is particularly evident in essays with an historical dimension, those chapters where the focus is on the relationship of the present to cultural memory, contributions exploring the framing of landscape images through their dissemination in different material forms such as book illustrations and postcards, video and social media, and in the practices of curation. The North, as several accounts suggest, is a place enfolded in histories originating in the past but realised in the evolving cultural narratives of the present; every 'present' involves remembering and experiencing narratives of the past differently.

Both the direct experience of the present and the histories with which it engages are sources of knowledge, however, and when northern landscapes are considered from such a dual perspective it becomes clear that the relationship between the proximity of direct experience and the conception of place from a distant perspective is nuanced and complex. By focusing on contemporary criticism, curation and practice these studies of northern landscape photography aim to address the complexities of reading and interpreting a field of historically evolving representations whilst engaging with the challenges of contemporary practice.

However, it is impossible to understand the notion of the proximate in respect to the distant, without engaging with the new technological and material realities of life and travel. John Tomlinson (1999) argues that accessibility alters the way in which the distant is perceived. In the 21st century the relative affordability and ease of travel over large distances is responsible for creating a new relationship with far-off places – where greater accessibility effectively brings such places closer. For Tomlinson this increased "connectivity" through ease of travel is merely an empirical fact, whereas he employs the term "proximity" as a metaphor to account for the ways in which the distant is increasingly experienced as relatively close. In this way greater accessibility creates a feeling of proximity.

Beginning with the work of contemporary practitioners, it is quite evident that there has been a shift towards a more experiential approach to landscape photography and that aspects of 'northerness' are associated with this development, particularly where environmental degradation through climate breakdown is the issue of concern. As has been suggested, the character of landscape photography as a material practice does lend itself to a phenomenological understanding, and if the latter's conceptual framework isn't necessarily explicit in all of the following group of contributions it does have an underlying presence.

The emphasis on temporality and of 'being in' the landscape is demonstrated in several essays in the collection but particularly in the work of three practitioners – Olaf Otto Becker, Aileen Harvey and Tracy Hill – each of whom present contributions where their own work is central and where they perform the role of participant-observer. In the interview with Olaf Otto Becker, Julia Peck refers to how Becker's work has changed in recent years, from representing "an untouched landscape to recording traces of how we shape the landscape". Becker's work photographing the Arctic over many years is very well known, as is his more recent efforts to chart environmental degradation in the Global South. Becker's interview is revealing of the importance of a temporal dimension for the evolution of his work. When Becker began photographing the Arctic he also recorded how its landscape changed: firstly by capturing images of the contemporary landscape of hydroelectric plants and dams rather than pristine and apparently timeless views of waterfalls, for example; then through the production of sequences of images in which, through rephotography, the shrinking of glaciers could be observed over a period of years. Subsequently, this approach became part of a dedicated project. Becker returned to Iceland ten years after publishing *Under the Nordic Light* (2005), in order to supplement the book with photographs of changes: "I visited the same places and I waited for the same light conditions and I used the same framing of the image. And I even made portraits after 10 or 11 years to show how we experience time".

Although a very different type of landscape photographer, Aileen Harvey shows a similar but more theoretically inflected concern with photographic time. Her essay proposes links between the "snapshot" as an "everyday object" and "drawing and writing" – considering all of these as "inscriptions" – all *deictic* arts as Bryson would define them. Harvey's own practice and that of other artists she cites responds to the "changeable and liminal qualities of landscape specific to northern latitudes: such as seasonal shifts in light, littorality, weathering, and deciduous woodland". Whilst acknowledging that notions of the photograph as document or evidence are powerful, her essay suggests that photography allows for a relationship of "continuity and proximity" to landscape. This is achieved by activating the temporal dimension of photography and drawing, allowing walking to provide a structure able to grasp place, not as singular and static but fluid and changing; a landscape irreducible to an objective, distancing visuality, allowing for the influence of "visual qualities" such as "colour, shape, scale, tone, and intensity of light", but "also volume, texture, movement, heft, smell, moisture, warmth, taste, sounds". Following Donna Haraway she argues that "our way of seeing the world is a matter of positioning – and that positioning is mobile, fluid, and active".

Becker's landscape photography can also be understood as having a time-based character associated with the material processes of the medium. This is evident in the dependency of his images on his own protracted presence in the landscape, and the traces of that temporality recorded in the photograph. The image from *Under the Nordic Light*, '60 Minutes Dettifoss', captures the limited duration of the tourist gaze, referring to the average period of time spent by visitors at Iceland's Dettifoss waterfall, whilst Becker is also aware of the time involved in making composite images. Harvey, similarly, discusses the different moments in the photographic process, arguing that the "single instant" of capture or exposure should not detract from the duration of the construction of an image, while its content arises from different "making activities", each with its own "footing in time".

Tracy Hill – in "Matrix of Movement: Post-industrial Wetlands of the North West" – bases her essay on her own art practice, specifically two projects, *Matrix of Movement* (2016-19) and *Haecceity* (2018). The art works within these projects are created through the appropriation and repurposing of data collection technologies but the centrality to her work of direct experience of landscapes through walking is clear. The aim of the projects was to challenge historic perceptions of some forms of northern landscape as wasteland, which she does by exploring the tensions between preconceived notions of landscape – formed through conceptions of the picturesque or through the dislocating and distancing perspective of mapping – and landscape perceived experientially and intuitively. She argues that an embodied experience, the practice of walking, can realise the values of place not recognisable through a distant and ordered perspective. She explores these ideas through her art work's engagement with the precariousness of wetland environments in North-West England, responding to them as liminal landscapes and aiming to recover these "forgotten ways of seeing", recognising what went before but also its relationship to the present.

This challenge to preconceptions of landscape involves redefining and exploring the notion of place, which several essays in the collection also attempt. Aileen Harvey argues that "place is not an object, not a static, clear-cut thing. A place has no edges. It surrounds, moves and alters". Tracy Hill follows John Agnew (1987) in suggesting that place be understood as a meaningful location through three vectors: as having a clear sense of "where", as a setting for social relations and as the site of subjective and emotional attachment. As with Harvey and Becker, the primacy of temporal experience is central to her landscape work: "representational traditions of mapping do not lend themselves to the transitory nature of wetlands", she argues, so "what is needed is a system of temporal mapping", or a form of spatio-temporality, forsaking the distant perspective of the purely visual and striving, through walking and the "physical interaction of touch", towards the multisensory, and through this forming new knowledge.

Darcy White's essay is also concerned with space, understood – following Massey – as composed of "fluid and multivalent elements", as "in a constant state of being made". In contrast to the emphasis on the photographic medium's deictic character advocated by Bryson, White proposes – through a study of commercial landscape images associated with cookery books of the Nordic region – that landscape photography plays a role in envisioning geographical space. As with Becker's repudiation of a pristine and timeless landscape in favour of producing images containing people and signs of historical transformation, White offers a critique of landscape imagery devoid of human activity. These 'stripped-out' and almost abstract images evoke notions of a 'pristine', 'wilderness' landscape and have the effect of reinforcing specific political geographies within which the nordic territories are still and unchanged, denying the ethnic diversity of its populations and the complexity of the globalised world.

Mikko Itälahti's essay is an historical account considering the significance of place within 19th century Finland, exploring literary and photographic images of Finnish travel landscapes, and juxtaposing the spatial immediacy of premodern travel to the detached and disembodied visuality typical of the railway era. There are, therefore, thematic continuities between Itälahti's essay and the preceding ones. For those whose earliest experiences were of coach or sleigh journeys railway travel was initially perceived as alienating and 'placeless'. Finnish landscape photographers would eventually foster a greater cultural acceptance and familiarity with the railway, however. Itälahti argues that even though the landscapes of modern travel involved separation and distance, railway photography tended to mitigate the loss of sensations of actuality, of truly 'being there', through its capacity to re-evoke the foreground eradicated by the industrial revolution. By the beginning of the 20th century, the railway itself was elevated to "the foreground of the landscape, echoing the romantic trope of picturesque roadside views and evoking, visually, the proximity of the old premodern roadside". A more optimistic vision of the railway could even present it, now, as "a harmonious component of a modern cultural landscape".

In an important historical study based on painstaking archival research – "Polar Expeditions: A Photographic Landscape of Sameness?" – Elizabeth Cronin and Jessica Keister argue that as soon as photography was viable it became an integral part of journeys to the Arctic. Images from expeditions appeared in numerous publications as well as being an important component of "lecture tours, and lantern slide extravaganzas", and some of these form the basis of an album of photographs held in the Photography Collection at the New York Public Library. The album, however, shows little regard for the original context of the photographs, but "highlights instead the universal event of the far north: heroism in a harsh environment, ice cliffs, hut interiors, polar bears, sled dogs, native populations, and scientific responsibilities". This fascinating essay then proceeds to discuss the album's distinct layers of meaning: the event each photograph depicts; the history of these images as material artefacts; and the broader meaning of the album as an exercise in "categorization and organization". Cronin and Keister give a detailed discussion of the history of the album, noting that curatorial interventions have been prevalent and arguing that changes in its material characteristics have had a significant impact on how it has been understood. Their exploration of the album as material artefact is both a history of curatorial practice – the once extensive use of retouching, earlier practices of "collecting, organizing, and synthesizing" – an account of these images as objects of consumption, their physicality giving some indication of the audience for whom they were intended, and an intriguing discussion of changing views of the Arctic.

Cronin and Keister's archival work provides an insight into the role of landscape photography in establishing the meaning of place, not simply in the choice of subject matter and point of view but in terms of the materiality of images, their intended audience and the form of their organisation and dissemination. This focus on the materiality of landscape images, particularly when illustrations in books aimed at particular readerships, is comparable to White's discussion of the phenomenon of Nordic cookery books in which lavish illustrations of sparse, pristine and purportedly timeless northern landscapes address their readers' "hopes and fears, ideas and values", constructing and confirming conceptions of "Nordicness" rather than being guides to food preparation.

The insights of Cronin and Keister are paralleled in other essays in this collection with an emphasis on the archive. Anne Wriedt's essay is based on work with photographs by Knud Knudsen, contained in the picture collection of the University of Bergen library. Knudsen's photography is considered in the context of a transitional moment in the evolution of Norway's landscape. In the late 19th century landscape photography played a crucial role in the formation of Norway's national identity. During this era landscape photography redefined the nation, producing images within which the physical and topographical features of Norway were emphasised. The production and dissemination of these images occurred in a period of growing modernity involving: the building of the railway infrastructure and the mechanisation of coastal and inland passenger shipping; the growth of tourism; the commercialisation of photography and its development through new forms of distribution and mass circulation; and the transformation of the photographic medium through new technology. The essay considers how Knudsen's landscape imagery developed in these contexts as well as the extent to which his images were drawn from earlier depictions of the Norwegian landscape. Wriedt shows how the consolidation of Norwegian national identity occurred in relation to the appearance of now familiar landscape images, and that Knudsen was at the forefront of these developments, but that these images framed their subject in new ways as their audience changed, culminating in the emergence of the tourist postcard as the most significant means through which they circulated.

Wriedt's emphasis on the material form of the postcard, the wider dissemination of Knudsen's landscapes – and the relationship of these to the development of tourism in the 19th century indicate the significance of travel, an aspect of the discussions of both Itälahti and Cronin and Keister, in the former case the landscape of the railway journey, in the latter the polar expedition. Tourism as discussed by Wriedt is a particular form of travel, but in essays concerned with the contemporary landscape travel and tourism are still present, albeit in novel and sometimes virtual forms. Whites' essay considers the Nordic territories in relation to the forms of mass migration typical of the global era, but the landscape images of the books she discusses also constitute a distant, tourist gaze in which the complex realities of places are subordinate to an unchanging, timeless vision. Ease of travel and distribution has also changed the relation of the local to the global, particularly where local practices impinge on people and places elsewhere in the world. Such factors are explored by Becker and White in their respective discussions of environmental degradation.

Furthermore, new technologies of recording visual information, and then disseminating it via the Internet – perhaps instantaneously – facilitate new ways of experiencing distant places in relation to the local. Meaning that in some ways places that once seemed at a great geographical distance are now experienced as more proximate. However, this new relationship with the distant is not necessarily an easy one and may instead create feelings of unease or incongruity about a given, far-away place. Lena Quelvennec's analysis of digital recordings of the aurora borealis addresses these issues.

Quelvennec considers how landscape images produced in the context of tourism transform them, preserving some of the meanings and effects that would have been evident in their forerunners whilst intensifying others, as well as producing new ones. Quelvennec is concerned with the contemporary tourist experience and recognises tourism as now involving both a physical presence and a virtual element, which she explores through tourist recordings of the aurora borealis and their subsequent dissemination as YouTube video as well as the relation of these to older representations of wilderness spectacle. If the image of northern wilderness reached its apogee in 19th century narratives of heroic exploration, hardship and remote landscapes, there is still a connection, she argues, between this vision and the contemporary tourist gaze. Tourists seeking a direct experience of the northern lights are still under the influence of wilderness narratives. The key aspect of YouTube recordings of the phenomenon, however, is immediacy: experience is recorded in 'real time', there are opportunities for viewer feedback, and in the technical production of the images there is an emphasis on movement and speed. The author compares a 19th century painting of the aurora borealis to the most recent developments in photography, film, video and online distribution, and is able to identify significant continuities in these representations of northern wilderness, whilst forms of observation associated with the tourist gaze have also evolved, in particular she identifies a symbiotic relationship between real and virtual tourism through the functioning of social media. What is quite evident from Quelvennec's image analysis is that Barthes' "reality effect" remains a powerful element in northern wilderness tourist landscapes.

Nicky Bird's "Ghosting the Castle: the case of (re)landscaping in a Northern place" is a discussion of a project she undertook, to investigate issues of heritage, the archive, memory and "layered histories" in Helmsdale, a fishing village on the North-East coast of Scotland. Bird's project involved archival research, oral history, and an engagement with images from the past through rephotography. Archival photographs are shown to have significant meaning within people's narratives: they "prompted memories and knowledge" of heritage sites, but this is not a matter of simple recollection because "heritage" – in a quotation from Raphael Samuel – "is continually shedding its old character and metamorphosing into something else". And in fact the connections people made to different landscape photographs were diverse and sometimes uncanny, bringing distinct conceptions of the past into a relationship with present-day concerns. The essay is particularly interesting in its efforts to investigate received ideas about the meaning of 'North'. If some standard approaches to northerness imply remoteness and a lack of connectedness this is very much a distant perspective, a view from outside; when places are viewed from within, the landscape is more complex, something revealed through photography-based memory work. There are several aspects to this work, however, involving not simply recovering the past but "mediating the memories and knowledge of others". A key element of this research involves gaining knowledge of the history of the photographic materials in the archive. It is also vital to understand the location itself and its people. Finally, of critical importance is the production of "collaborative photo-based artworks that respond meaningfully to place and people", in which rephotography has a significant part.

In Tim Daly's essay – "The North as a fantasy playground: re-evaluating the literary influences in the landscape photography of Raymond Moore" – Moore is recognised as working outside of the observational, documentary category so significant in Britain in the 1970s and 1980s. Paradoxically, perhaps, it was this lack of interest in the mainstream of documentary photography that framed his images of northern England and informed his interest in places such as Silloth on the Cumbrian coast. This was a distinctly unpicturesque vision of northern England with a focus on the unexceptional environment of places in a "kind of limbo land"; they were a "depiction of inanimate objects in the quasi-surreal landscape of concrete, tarmac and pebbledash". Moore's representations of "an unpeopled terrain" communicated a sense of "loss and decline", combining the "sublime and the banal, making the commonplace both recognised and mysterious". Moore was drawn to bleak, derelict landscapes, "liminal spaces and deserted edgelands", and "had a fascination with the nondescript in a social landscape, overlayed with his own sense of entropy...".

Moore's orientation towards some versions of English surrealism – Daly compares him to 1930s artist Paul Nash – is particularly interesting because it was also given a northern character: as his work became more focused on northern England "it took on a deadpan and poignant undercurrent", thus it could be suggested that his work promoted an English northern landscape aesthetic. He did this partly through the activation of a literary sensibility in his work – particularly the influence of Arthur Machen – and significantly through the influence of the "literal, deadpan style" of American photographers associated with the New Topographics show, who represented a "social landscape physically and spiritually depleted, released from romantic and picturesque concerns".

Across the range of essays contained in this volume, issues of place and space, proximity and distance are prominent. As a whole the essays demonstrate that notions of northerness rooted in an earlier era and represented in the landscapes of the 19th century have continued to have an impact since, even when the aim of these different discussions is to question received ideas about place and its conception in visual and literary representations of the North, whether in historical case studies or contemporary practice. An important strand throughout is one exploring the extent to which framing and reframing of northern landscape images both preserves and consolidates older, historic meanings whilst intensifying and transforming them. The subject and point of view of a landscape image is important but its source and conception lie outside of the field of depiction and these frame the image in numerous ways; the image, consequently, is never static and stable and is historically malleable.

References

Norris, Christopher (1991): Deconstruction: Theory and Practice, London and New York: Routledge.

Tomlinson, John (1999): Globalisation and Culture, Oxford: Polity.

In conversation with Olaf Otto Becker

Julia Peck

This interview with Olaf Becker took shape over three conversations in 2018. The first part of the conversation was held on 3rd July at a conference at Sheffield Hallam University – *Northern Light: critical approaches to proximity and distance in northern landscape photography* – during which there was the opportunity for an audience Q&A. The conversations have been edited together, and audience questions have been acknowledged.

Julia Peck [JP]: Olaf. Hello.

Olaf Becker [OB]: Hello!

JP: It's a real pleasure to be able to talk to you today about your work, and I thought I would start with a general question. Can you tell us how you became interested in photographing Iceland and Greenland?

OB: I started taking photographs in Iceland after I took photographs in Germany, and the landscape in Germany is shaped by agricultural use, and I was looking for a landscape that was really untouched. I was interested to see landscapes shaped by nature, just by nature, really without any influence by humans and so I started to travel to Iceland for the first time in 1999. I was working on a project about waterfalls in black and white, and I was just interested in the movement of water. I took photographs of waterfalls, one after the other in the way that Bernd and Hilla Becher did with their photographs of industrial buildings. And I took the photographs in black and white with an 8 x 10" camera, and also by a 12 x 20" camera. However, I could not fail to notice that we were shaping the landscape even there.

So I realised that on the one side there is untouched landscape, and on the other side we were shaping the landscape, even where it was before untouched. And so besides the waterfalls I started to take some photographs in colour of power plants, of buildings, and of dams, and hydroelectric power plants, and so on, and when I came home and I looked at my photographs I felt that the photographs of the waterfalls in black and white, looked like they were made centuries ago, and I thought this is not the way I should be working. And I realised that it is more interesting to see the photographs of what is happening now and how we use the landscape to make electricity and things like that. And so I continued going to Iceland and I changed the topic of my work and I was more interested to report the traces of how we shape the landscape in an area where you can still find untouched landscape and where the landscape is used.

I was travelling for four years to Iceland and I took a photograph in 1999 of a glacier and in 2002 I visited this glacier again and I saw there was already a change, that the glacier had retreated, and I asked the people in Iceland, "what has happened with the glacier?" and they said, "it's because of global warming; there are a lot of glaciers, they shrink and everything is melting." And then I thought, well, this then is an interesting issue and so I decided to continue with the next project in Greenland. And I went to Greenland to document the shoreline because if all the glaciers will retreat in Greenland, then the Greenland shoreline will change first, and then because of the rising water the shores all over the world will change. So I thought I would go to Greenland to work on the project to show what's happening on the west coast; this was the reason that I went to Greenland for the next project, *Broken Line*.

JP: That's a great introduction to your work. Thinking about the fact that you shifted from the idea of an untouched landscape to recording traces of how we shape the landscape, one approach that has been mentioned in the discourse around your work is the idea of documentary, with Gerry Badger (2007: 9) in particular describing your work as lyrical documentary. How do you see your work relating to the documentary traditions?

OB: For me, I'm interested in documenting something I see, something I witness. But I wanted to create pictures in a way that it's not only documentary, for me it is important that you feel something with this image, so the sublime in the landscape is important for me. And it's important to tell a story with a single image, but also to tell a story with a series of images. I'm more interested to find connections between things so at the moment I am working on a European project and I tried to find connections between different countries and landscapes. So I have tried to show with my images relationships between humans and nature.

But there are two important things when I make a picture. Firstly, I'm very interested in the single image. That is, the single image has to be successful and tell a story, but the single image should also be a part of a larger story. And the next thing, is to feel the location, like travelling with a small boat over a period of four or five months, being there and feeling the landscape. The one part is being there and feeling it and then the next part is framing it after I have the feeling that I understand something. And then I have in my mind the whole story that I want to tell and what I want to show finally in my book or in my exhibition. But the single image is always very important for me.

When I take a photograph about melting rivers, on the one hand it's a document about this river in this moment, but on the other hand, because the shape of the river will vary after a few days, it is not important that the image looks exactly like that river, tomorrow or later. You can find thousands of similar rivers every summer on the ice. So, it is a document of an example that is happening a lot.

JP: *Under the Nordic Light* first came out in 2005 and then you went onto *Broken Line* and *Above Zero*, so what brought you back to Iceland in 2011 and 2012?

OB: The publishers were very interested to republish my book *Under the Nordic Light* and he said it would be good if you can add some new photographs, because we want to have a new edition and I said, "I'm not interested, that project is finished, and I don't want to continue with that." But then after a while, I thought that "why not?" and I decided to travel again to Iceland and when I was there I went to the places where I had already taken photographs in 1999 until 2002, and I thought it was interesting to document some places after a period of 10 years. Sometimes I saw a lot of change and sometimes I saw nothing, no change. And so I visited the same places and I waited for the same light conditions and I used the same framing of the image. And I even made portraits after 10 or 11 years to show how we experience time.

In the book there is a portrait of two young boys and when I met them the first time they were 14 and 15 and of course 10 years later they were 24 and 25. I took the photograph of them in the same place with their motorbikes and the landscape, ten years apart. And I visited other places where I took photographs of glaciers in 1999 and then ten years later, and you really see the difference with what happened with the ice: there is no ice any more. And I also took photographs of some landscapes in the highlands after 12 years, and you get the feeling that it's just another photograph five minutes later. So, with a lot of these photographs you don't see a change, but at some places you see a very clear change, and the reason is always us: we produce this change in landscape and so this is also the subtitle of the book: *A Journey Through Time.*

For me, it was a great experience to see how change can be different and I had an opening at the museum of photography in Reykjavik (May 2018) about my work in

Iceland and Greenland, and I took photographs of these places now, where I had been in 1999 to 2002. And there are definitely changes. Some of the houses that I photographed in 1999 and 2011 are not there anymore. I took a photograph again of the two boys, and they are now 30 and 31 and they have families, and so I decided to include their wives and their children in the picture. I can tell a story about an island, about a period. I have observed something and this is the kind of poetic documentary that I am doing. So, it's not just showing something, I put things in relation to each other.

JP: Of course the big thing that happened between the first episode of your work in Iceland, and the second episode of your work was the 2008 economic crash. How do you think that economic crash affected Iceland and its landscape?

OB: Yes, I took photographs of houses in the construction area and a lot of families were not able to finish building the houses because they ran out of money, and even the workers were not able to pay for the materials for the houses. So I took photographs in 2011 and 2012 of some houses, and there was virtually no difference because the people were not able to continue to build the houses. The funny thing was that in 2011 I took a photograph of one house with no roof, and in 2012 I went again to this place and there was still no roof, and this year I went again to this place. And the house now has a roof and people live in the house, and I knocked on the door and I asked them if I could take a photograph in the place where I had stood before. Now it's their living room, with furniture, and with a young boy preparing himself for an exam at the University. At the moment when I started the project I did not know that would happen. But for me, it is interesting to see and I am curious about change so there are new photographs every time when I come to Iceland and I follow up what is happening there.

JP: Thinking about your interest in human traces and the human relationship with the land, you've also been interested in how indigenous cultures live in the landscape. Can you tell us a bit more about that, especially in relation to the Greenland photographs that you've done.

OB: During my trips in Greenland, I travelled from one settlement to the other, going north on the West coast. When I was there I thought it was interesting for me to take photographs of how the people live now, while there is the global warming and the landscape is changing. I did not want just to show the glaciers, and the mountains, and the shore, because people also live there. They are different from us, but they live now in a similar condition to us. They have TVs, computers, mobile phones, and potato chips. Twenty or thirty years ago they did not have these things. In the summer the Inuit live outside the house so, in the pictures of the houses, you can see there is a table in front of the house and the children play and a lot of things are out of the house that should be inside in the house [fig. 1]. It looks a little bit like a mess there, and it was interesting for me because the tools tell us something about the people. So yes, I realised that it was necessary for me to take photographs of it.

Figure 1: *705 Nuussuaq 07/2006* by Olaf Otto Becker

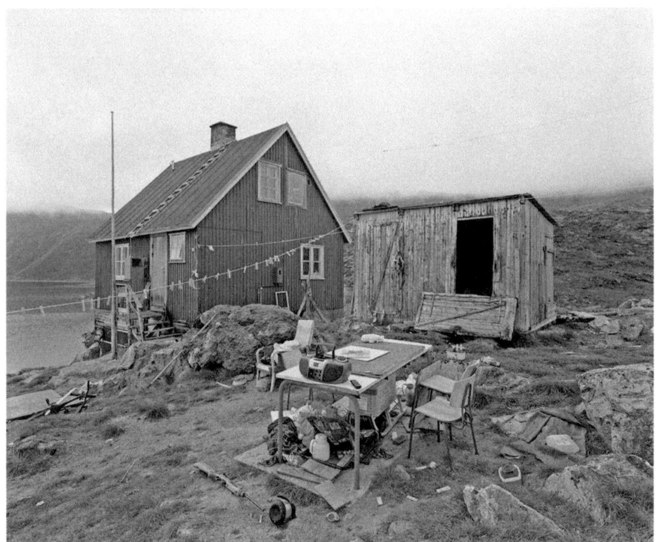

JP: In Iceland, you photographed a few children who grew up to become adults and you also had, every now and again, a person working in the landscape, but for the Inuit, in Greenland, you didn't do that. You had the houses and the signs of how they live and work, but not the people. Can you tell us why people don't feature in your Greenland photographs?

OB: In the Greenland photographs, there are photographs of the scientists in the landscape and there are photographs of the tourists visiting the glacier. And I only take photographs of people if they have a connection with the landscape. The tourists in Greenland, for example, they try to understand global warming while they are walking on the ice field but they cannot understand it (fig. 2). They are looking for something but they are lost in this landscape with their questions about global warming. And the scientists are in the landscape working in the fog, to find out something about the global warming. And this is my experience also with the scientists, they said to me, every time when they return to the ice cap to download the measurements of a whole year, they are surprised about the results because they are different to what they expected. And so the scientists are working in the fog, they are connected to the landscape, but the photographs are not portraits of the people, it is about the relationship of people to the land.

Figure 2: *Point* 660 08/2008

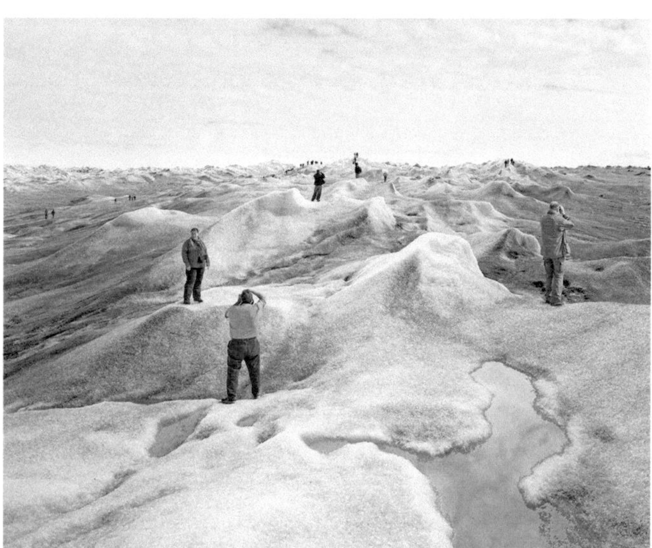

JP: The Inuit, of course, have a relationship to landscape but that will be a very different one to the scientific one, that wasn't something you wanted to photograph?

OB: No.

JP: Do you have a reason? I'm sorry to press you on this point, but do you have a reason for not wanting to photograph that relationship?

OB: I could show the relationship of the Inuit only in that way that I could see, that their lives are outside in the summer. They really enjoy that it is warm and that there is light for 24 hours but when you see the Inuit working they are small dots in the landscape; they are hunting for seals or they are on their fishing boats. It would make sense to take photographs whilst they are hunting but I didn't have a good feeling about showing that. I am more interested in the traces that we leave in the landscape and if a hunter kills a seal there is no trace in the landscape. It is another interesting issue that they kill a seal to eat it, but we go to the supermarket. We lost the relationship between the animal and how we eat it. It's really a great difference if you go fishing and you eat your own fish, or if you buy it in the supermarket. But this is not a topic that I want to represent with my photographs.

JP: Recent work that you've shown in London demonstrates a return to Ilulissat in Greenland. Can you tell me why you've returned to that particular site? Are you undertaking an update to *Broken Line* and *Above Zero*?

OB: I had to return to Ilulissat several times because I was doing some work for *New York Times Magazine* and they sent me there to document the work of NASA and other scientists and I spent some additional days there just to take some new photographs. While I was there I noticed again the beauty of icebergs in water, and this is very rare at the moment, when the water is like a mirror, without movement. And I saw that it is so visually strong, these single icebergs reflected in the sea, they are beautiful sculptures, and they are an answer for what we are doing here on the world. So there is also, in one way, hope. Even if we destroy the world, nature is able to create something beautiful. I decided to do just a series in the way that the Bechers' did, they took photographs of industrial structures and so I thought I would do something similar with these icebergs because they are beautiful and I realised that if you communicate something with beauty the people will place it in their living room, and when they place it in their living room, it will be on their minds.

JP: In the conference we have been talking about the north, and although we have covered different countries, we have focused a lot on Northern England. You've looked at the far north and the Arctic north, but you've also looked at the idea of the global north as well, and I think this really became telling when you started working in Indonesia on the topic of deforestation. So what led you to switch from the global and Arctic north as a subject, to the global south?

OB: I was interested in the traces we leave here on Earth and even on the ice cap you will not find direct traces of people, you find only indirect traces, like the melting rivers. And in the south, you can see that we directly change the landscape. I visited some areas where deforestation was happening and this was very well organised and within only a few years they cut down a huge area of primary forest (fig. 3). Then they plant acacia trees for the paper industry, and the acacia trees are harvested every seven years, and they say it's green paper. But nobody is reporting on the deforestation of primary forest before the plantations existed.

I went to Borneo, and when I was young, for me, Borneo was always a dream of untouched primary forest, and when I went to Borneo I drove about 2000 kilometres to see what happened with the forest there. I saw palm tree plantations: palm trees planted by big companies, and there were only a few areas with primary forest left, where it was too difficult to plant palm trees. And I was really frustrated to see that, and to see that we need forest resources, but it's more that we want to earn money in a fast way. And I talked to the people there and I realised that the local people are not responsible for the deforestation, the deforestation is well organised by global stock listed companies. And they do it because they can earn money with it, and the responsibility is divided between many people, so that in the end nobody is responsible. And this is going on as long as the politicians will not introduce regulations and strict control. My feeling is that it will go on until the last tree has gone.

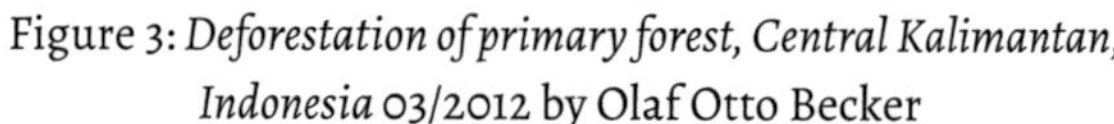

Figure 3: *Deforestation of primary forest, Central Kalimantan, Indonesia* 03/2012 by Olaf Otto Becker

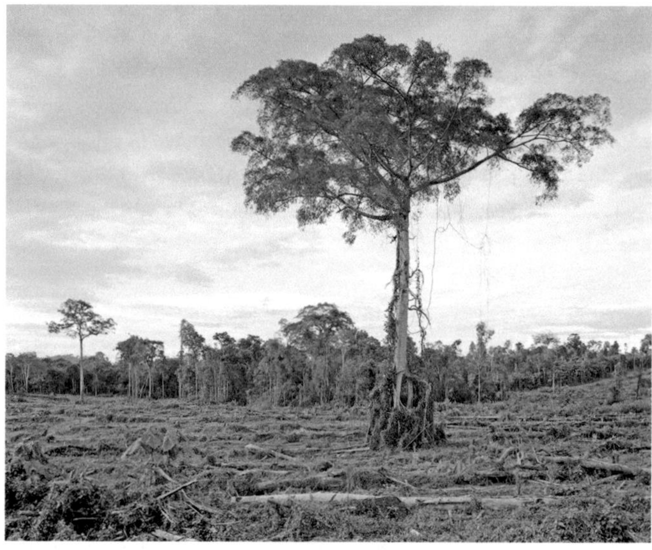

JP: One of the things that I'm interested in is that it is easier to depict deforestation than it is to depict glacial retreat and I think this connects to a whole range of tropes that we're very familiar with in environmental photography. Is this a problem that fascinates you as a visual artist?

OB: There were a lot of reasons to work on the retreating glaciers. One is that the change that I can show can be very beautiful but when you show deforestation it can look like a battlefield. It can be also interesting, and you can see a lot of things and it is something that you are not used to seeing. It is because we are surprised about what you can see there, we can see trees cut down, lying around. In the book *Reading the Landscape*, there are three chapters, and in the first chapter I show untouched primary forest because we can only miss things that we came to know, and in the second chapter I show deforestation of primary forest and in the third chapter I show how we use nature now in mega cities. Trees are now decorating business buildings, and in Singapore I photographed artificial trees in a botanical garden. They put plants from all over the world in one large garden and they teach the people how nature can be, but this is not nature if you put plants together from all over the world. And the same plants that I found in Indonesia, in this area where I took the photographs of deforestation, you can find some of these plants now in China in new megacities. They use it for their gardens, and they do not care if these plants will not survive long in these strange surroundings. So, in the third chapter it was important for me to show that we have already lost the connection to nature when we use plants in megacities.

JP: Do you receive feedback from your viewers of your images in relation to climate change and changing human behaviour? And if not, what are you hoping for when people look at your work?

OB: When I do the work I always think about that. I have the feeling that this is important for me, but I am also concerned about whether it will be important for somebody else. And if I have the feeling that something I want to say could also be interesting for other people then I take the photograph. And I am very happy when I am at an opening and people tell me something about what they feel when they are looking at my images and they experience exactly what I felt when I took the photograph. And then I'm really happy about that. If I choose a topic I always think, it has to be relevant to me, but not only to me, to all of us.

JP: You've previously talked about travelling to places and how this contributes to global warming. And, in *Reading the Landscape*, in the text that you wrote, you acknowledge that the way you live, and many of us live, is part of the global economy. And I was wondering is this something that you find frustrating, or do you feel you're negotiating this in a creative way?

OB: Yes, in one way it's very frustrating because I don't know how to change it. And, as I said, we are part of a system and even if you don't want to be part of the system, you are part of the system. If you buy something you already participate in the system and if you plug in your computer to get electricity, you are part of the system, and if you fill your car with petrol, you are part of the system, if you listen to the radio you are part of the system, so you cannot avoid it. You cannot leave the system. We have to understand that even small steps are important and I already observe in the whole world everywhere that the consciousness about environment is different to 10 or 20 years ago. Everybody who is educated wants to change something. But we have the problem that the capitalistic system wants to earn money, and they don't care about responsibility. There are a lot of problems we have to solve together but we are not able to communicate because we have different cultures, we have different languages, we have different possibilities of understanding because we have different educations. We have different problems. Some people in the world have the problem of not having sufficient food or a place to sleep, but we don't have this problem.

Audience: Your photographic practice uses a large format camera, and I'm wondering whether you have a strong sense of connection with the pioneer photographers.

OB: Yes. At the beginning, the 8 x 10 camera was the only camera I could use when I wanted to show a lot of details. Now it has changed. We can use digital cameras and we can use stitching techniques so that you can use 80 photographs, and stitch all of them into one very high-resolution picture, and you can get a higher resolution picture than you can get with 8 x 10 camera. But the other thing with an 8 x 10 camera is that you put the camera on a tripod, and you have to work slowly, you have to think about what you are doing, and this is a good way to work.

And now I have changed, and I don't use the 8 x 10 anymore, I use a digital camera. So sometimes I shoot 100 photographs, each with 40 or 50 million pixels and stitch these images together to make one image with a very high resolution. When you stitch together 80 photographs you have to imagine the image before it is made. And so I see the landscape like a painter. I really enjoy spending time in museums to study how the painters captured landscape: how they get the depth in the landscape, how they make a composition and the use of light. I try to find the position in the landscape where I get the depth of the picture. And then, light is also very important for landscape photographs. Sometimes I am at a position where I would take a photograph, but the light is not good. Then I have to return to that place when the light is in the condition that I want to have it and sometimes I wait, two, three hours in one place, just to get the right light, or I return another day. I remember a lot of great moments when I was just waiting for the right light for the picture.

JP: I'm really fascinated by the fact that you're stitching images together or using masks, especially when you're photographing landscapes that have a lot of people in them. You must be photographing lots of sections of the image more than once, so of course you can choose whether a tourist is present or not in that particular area.

OB: Yes, right. I have been creating a picture of the Giant's Causeway, and it is an area that attracts thousands of tourists. The interesting thing was, I need to have areas in the picture where there is nobody, but at this place, thousands of people come every day. At every square meter you can take a photograph of people during the day, but to create a picture it is good to have some places where there is nobody. And so I can decide which parts of the picture are filled with people and which are not. But every person that is in the picture, has been exactly in that place, so I did not place the person there, they have been there, exactly in that position.

With this process I have the ability to tell stories. Some groups are acting in a special way and some people take photographs like selfies, and other people they pose for a photograph. Other people are just there, sitting, looking around or waiting to leave. So there are hundreds of small stories in the picture and I can control it, but it's challenging and it's not a picture I can finish quickly. So I work on the picture, then it comes to a point where I think I don't like it any more so I stop it, and one month later I work again on the picture I realise that when I do it this way, the image will become better.

JP: The images that are really fascinating from that point of view are the images of Point 660 in Greenland (fig. 2) because, for me, they're gently humorous. The people are arranged so beautifully over the glacier tongue and it really says something about the performance of being a tourist, and the performance of photography. Combined with the information that the tourists spend very little time there, just...

OB: 20 minutes.

JP: 20 minutes! Which I find incredible as they've travelled so far to spend only 20 minutes in this landscape.

OB: Yes, it's just coming to the point, and then that's it. And so this is a very stupid way to observe something. So, they just go to the point and take a photograph and that's it, and then they leave. It's a way of consuming landscape.

JP: So is that particular image a composite image?

OB: The funny thing is the *New York Times* wanted to publish this image and I sent them the file and then they realised that the image was manipulated and they wouldn't publish it. I explained that I had ten negatives, each 8" x10" and only 20 minutes to make the shot. I did not know what would happen when the tourists arrived and I tried to find the best place for my camera because once it is in position, I cannot move it. So I took altogether 10 photographs from the same place but with different arrangements of the people, and the final version was a combination of three images. But the *New York Times* said they could not publish it, and I offered to do a rescan just of one negative and then they published it.

And then, at the end I thought, there was no need for a manipulation because the one photograph (fig. 2), the one where the couple is in the foreground, this image is much more strange than the invented image and so I feel, sometimes, it is better not to alter a picture. And when you change it, you really have to do it very well because it's so complicated. It's very difficult, because I have a problem with inventing something, and this was the reason that I stopped painting.

JP: This is really fascinating, because earlier you talked about the Iceland project and the second version, the subtitle of which is *A Journey Through Time.* To find out that your images are composites that are obviously made over time makes some of your images a journey through time.

OB: Yes. So there is one image in *Under the Nordic Light* '60 Minutes Dettifoss' (fig. 4) where you see tourists, and I took that photograph over 60 minutes. And 60 minutes is exactly the time that people stand there before they go to the next location. So the photograph '60 Minutes Dettifoss' is a composition of that which happened during 60 minutes at that place.

Figure 4: *60 Minutes Dettifoss,* by Olaf Otto Becker

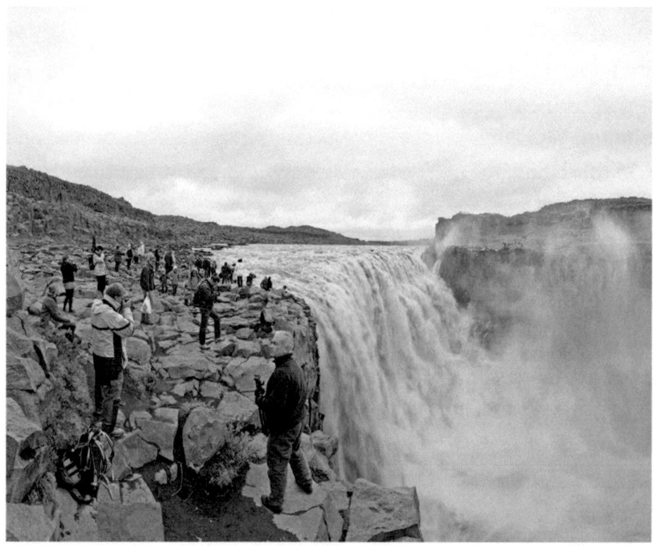

JP: I can see time is particularly important in *Under the Nordic Light,* but across the different bodies of work you've made I think you treat time as something that's incredibly complex and it's not just about objective changes that can be detected through visual change. In *Under the Nordic Light,* you're creating a disciplined record that captures both human time and geological time, but in *Reading the*

landscape time is different. You set the scene of the time of the primary forest, its creation and continued existence, but then there is also the time of the accelerated modernity of the forest, where the forest is being destroyed and used for resources; this latter time is different because the pace of change is faster. So, I was thinking about how in *Under the Nordic Light* and *Reading the Landscape* what you're doing is moving from a slower understanding of time, geological time, then human and social time, to a faster time through modernity and accelerated consumption. I was wondering whether that's something that you've given much thought to?

OB: Yes, this is right. When I took photographs, when I came to the same place in *Under the Nordic Light* after ten years I could not see any change. And then I get the feeling that the second photograph, taken ten years later, shows the same area just one day later. With the photographs of waves on the beach in one way I was joking with time because I came to the same place where the waves come every minute, again and again, and I came to the same place with the same framing and of course you cannot expect something else other than what you can see five minutes later.

In other areas I revisited the same place ten years later and there is no change, and then you have the photographs of houses that disappear over a period of ten years. And then you see the big change with these glaciers over a period of ten years. So, this for me, shows that some changes can happen very fast and the cause for that can be our activities, but if you have a volcano and there is an explosion of the volcano, or another disaster then even the Earth or nature can change things within minutes and it does not need the time of ten years to change something. So, I am fascinated that change can happen fast and it can happen over a long period and everything is related to our observation and the time we have to undertake the observation. And with the rainforest, of course, it seems to be always the same and we see the beauty of primary rainforest, but the change of the primary rainforest happens every day. But for us, if you only look casually, you don't see many changes, yet there are thousands and millions of changes every day in a rainforest. But what we can see very easily is the disappearance of the rainforest. The rainforest may have changed every day but this does not destroy the rainforest, and this is less relevant for us, and the relevant change of a rainforest is that there is no rainforest anymore. But when we destroy the rainforest, there is an end of something that had been in development for millions of years and now this development of this part of nature has come to an end.

JP: I also want to ask you about time and memory. In *Under the Nordic Light* you reported feeling unsettled when, after a period of ten years, there were no changes.

I was wondering if you had ever continued to think about how unsettling it can be to come back to a place and see the absence of change.

OB: For me it was a strange feeling when I came to a place and there was no change, because I experienced, during ten years, a lot of change. And then when I come to the landscape and I see there is no change, then I question, where is the time that I have experienced? It was very strange for me to experience that. Normally, you would expect if you experience a lot of change in your life you will be able to see external change, and when I come to a place and after ten years I can't see any change, then the experience of how I feel time is passing is disturbed. It is very difficult to experience this, and then I can say I feel doubt about our measurement of time, so the measurement of time is always to do with our lifetime and with our experiences and if we would live in a world without any changes we would lose, very probably, all orientation in time. If there are not a lot of changes we have the feeling, probably, that everything is very long lasting and when we have a lot of changes, then life is full of experiences and probably it seems a very long life. So, these are things that I'm thinking when I'm returning to locations again and again. It's also stranger for me when I return to Iceland when I see the two boys with their families and I am a witness of their lives, even though they are not my family.

JP: You're probably very familiar with the word 'uncanny' and I wondered whether you ever thought that the lack of change could be an uncanny experience? I'll relate it to a specific image in *Under the Nordic Light*, a pair of images that you made around Dyrafjörõur Bay. You took two photographs of a coastal area, nine years apart, and they are both taken in glorious sunlight. And in the captions for these images you said "How am I to perceive a panorama when I know that the left half was photographed early in the morning in 2002 and the right half at the same time of day in 2011? Purely as a matter of outward appearances the two linked images could have been taken on the same day but as soon as I know, however, that there are nine years between, I begin to question my sense of time for the moment of observation" (Becker 2011: 155). And I guess the thing about the uncanny is the notion of repetition. Something that is uncanny is meant to be deeply familiar to us but at the same time there is something about it that is very unsettling.

OB: Yes, this is very strange. When I think about the differences in the diptych, where the left side was made in 2002 and the right side was made in 2011 and there was the same weather, and there was the same level of tide in the water, you come to doubt what you see and what you can recognise, so you question whether you can trust your sense of observation. But on the other hand I waited for the same weather conditions and I knew I could not expect vast change, so I was prepared that I would find something like that. But for me, the images are an important part of the book because I want to question whether we can trust our observation. I can say all my observations are made during my period of time and I would probably need more time than the time that is available to me. For me, the doubt in my own observation, and the doubt that a reader of my book will also feel, is necessary because we have a limitation to observe something completely. So we can only observe that what we are able to observe with our senses. And all the things that I look at are limited by the possibilities of my observation.

So, my framing is limited by my lifetime and I am curious about my experience of seeing how things change during my lifetime but during my lifetime a lot of people are also here on this Earth, so it is a story that belongs to me, and all the other people who are around me, and who are interested in what is happening, such as climate change, and deforestation, and so on. I am documenting something about our time, about my limited time here on Earth. I am fascinated to come to know what is happening around me, and in Iceland, over a period of twenty or thirty years. I don't how long I will be allowed to continue with this work because the work will finish with my death. But during this period I can represent something through the observation of one lifetime, and this also shows a limitation of what we can be aware of.

With grateful thanks to Olaf Becker for his generosity and for permission to reproduce his photographs.

Bibliography

Badger, Gerry (2007): "Take Me Back to the Frozen North: The Greenland Photographs of Olaf Otto Becker." In: Olaf Otto Becker, Broken Line, Ostfildern: Hatje Cantz, pp. 8-11.

Becker, Olaf Otto (2005): Under the Nordic Light, Cologne: Schaden.

Becker, Olaf Otto (2007): Broken Line, Ostfildern: Hatje Cantz.

Becker, Olaf Otto (2009): Above Zero, Ostfildern: Hatje Cantz.

Becker, Olaf Otto (2011): Under the Nordic Light: A Journey Through Time, Iceland 1999-2011, Ostfildern: Hatje Cantz.

Becker, Olaf Otto (2014): Reading the Landscape, Ostfldern: Hatje Cantz.

Polar Expeditions: A Photographic Landscape of Sameness?

Elizabeth Cronin and Jessica Keister

On Saturday, March 7, 1896, arctic expedition leader Frederick George Jackson described the contents of the six sledges he and his crew were preparing for an upcoming journey. In addition to one bag of biscuit (18 pounds), a fur coat (5 ½ pounds), and an "odds and ends bag" (34 pounds), the nine-foot six-inch Sledge Number One included a "hand camera and case" (7 pounds) and a "half plate camera, etc., in case and stand" (22 pounds) (1899:453).

This degree of detail is found throughout Jackson's published account of his expedition, *A Thousand Days in the Arctic,* and was standard for the genre. Every object was itemized, every day was chronicled, every variation of temperature and pressure was noted, and all was preserved for posterity. While much of this information had valid scientific merit, readers were more eager for tales of heroism from this hostile and foreign environment; publication was standard for both successful and unsuccessful expedition leaders. Not limited to books, post-expedition information dissemination would regularly include magazine articles, lecture tours, and lantern slide extravaganzas. Photography was an integral part of this process; almost as soon as the discovery of photography was announced people began transporting cameras and photographic equipment on their travels to the Arctic and elsewhere.

The Photography Collection at the New York Public Library holds an item that confounds all aspects of this exhaustive practice of documentation – an album of photographs given the rather inattentive but specific title of *Arctic Exploration, being a collection of photographs of Arctic regions and explorers.* Its date is listed as 1890s-? The album is in essence a mini photographic archive, yet it contains very little identifying information and has almost no regard to organization. It creates one experience by collapsing various expeditions and timelines, eliminating any specificity of their original documentary functions. Separated from geography, time, and distinct narrative, the album highlights instead the universal event of the far north: heroism in a harsh environment, ice cliffs, hut interiors, polar bears, sled dogs, native populations, and scientific responsibilities. Although each arctic expedition is singular all are presented as nearly identical, the result stresses the reality of an arctic experience and landscape more than individual voyages.

As a conglomeration of images put together in a material three-dimensional object, the album is more than its depictions. It has three distinct layers of meaning. The first and most obvious layer is the descriptive content of the photographs. Each image is recorded from a moment in time and these moments tell parts of a story, that of arctic exploration. Inextricably bound up with these stories is the objects' history as physical artefacts. This second layer speaks to the photographs' lives before they were pasted into the album; namely, the photographs were used in making the photomechanical reproductions found in published books and printed media of the time. Looking at that function illuminates the role that photography plays in our understanding and treatment of arctic exploration and the northern landscape. The final layer of meaning revolves around the album as a piecemeal collection of images. It is an artefact of categorization and organization. It reconciles the contemporary practice of dissecting collections with a past imposed amalgamation of images. An examination of all of these layers provides answers as to why such seemingly random assortments are important. As a whole, the *Arctic Exploration* album shows us one way in which our treatment and perception of arctic photography has shifted with the passage of time. It speaks to our changing expectations of the Arctic and how that influences vision and a choice of imagery.

In order to understand the *Arctic Exploration* album and its contents, it is first necessary to provide a brief overview of photography in the Arctic. Soon after the invention and announcement of photography in 1839, photographs of the polar north were desired. During expeditions in the 1840s and the early 1850s, photography was planned for and attempted. The technology, however, did not work favourably with the climate or arduous journeys. The earliest extant imagery stems from the mid-1850s, but it was not until Isaac Israel Hayes' 1860 expedition that the most successful series of images was produced. Without having a professional photographer on board, Hayes taught himself the technique with the aid of books and despite what he rightly characterized as serious disadvantages, he managed to obtain "some views characteristic of the rugged beauties of the Arctic landscape" (1867: 46). Hayes' photographs were translated into woodcuts and then engraved as illustrations in his book *The Open Polar Sea* (Fig. 1). The photographs were also published and distributed by T.C. Roche in the form of albumen-silver-print and glass stereo-views. This format allowed for them to be more widely distributed and seen in slide lectures.

Figure 1: *Tyndall Glacier, Whale Sound*

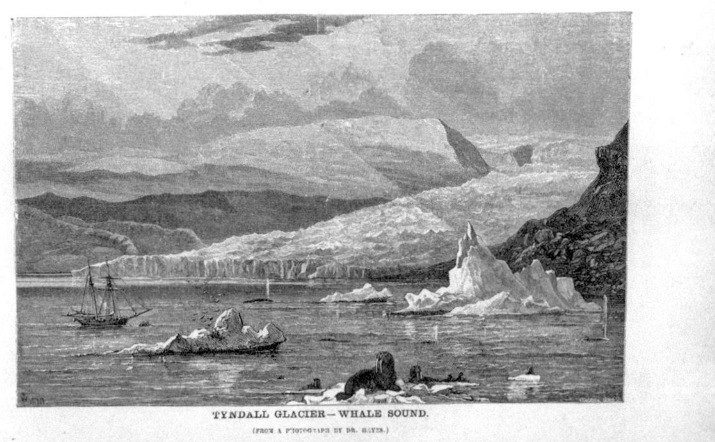

The best known 19th-century photographs of the Arctic are those that were eventually published in William Bradford's *The Arctic Regions* (1873). In 1869 the Boston-based professional photographers John L. Dunmore and George Critcherson accompanied Bradford, who was a painter, on his artistic expedition and produced hundreds of glass-plate negatives.[1] These negatives were converted into positives on both glass and paper supports. In announcing the forthcoming publication of *The Arctic Regions*, the *Art Journal* lauded it as most instructive and claimed the admirable photographs were as "wonderful as geological studies" (1872: 241). This praise suggests that for an amateur the photographs in their veracity appear to be as accurate and valuable as scientific measurements. When the volume was finally published in 1873, it measured 25 x 21 inches and was lavishly illustrated with 141 albumen silver prints (Figure 2). The individually inserted photographs gave new credence to Bradford's paintings because they validated the artist's technical skill and vision. The photographs became primarily known through Bradford's stereopticon slide lectures in the U.S. and Britain. He continued to awe audiences with his "Bradford Recitals" well after the book appeared (cf. Potter 2007).

For Dunmore and Critcherson as well as others, using the wet-plate collodion process of photography aboard a moving ship was no easy feat. In order to overcome technological limitations and still relay as dramatic an experience of the Arctic as possible, some of the photographs produced for Bradford's *Arctic Regions* were composites. Negatives were combined and altered to produce what Brad-

1 The 1869 expedition was his seventh. Critcherson accompanied Bradford photographing on his 1863 voyage along the Labrador coast. Also, aboard the ship on the 1869 voyage was Isaac Israel Hayes.

ford must have felt was a more accurate view of the experience. Scholar Adam Greenhalgh points specifically to plate 82, "Nearer View of the Polar Bears," in which the polar bears were cut from a separate photograph and pasted onto another landscape and then re-photographed as the composite image (2003: 80, 86). Hand-drawn additions and retouching also enhanced the photographs. Common at the time, these minimal interventions did not detract from the truth value of the photographs (cf. Fineman 2012).

Figure 2: William Bradford, *The Arctic Regions* (detail)

The Arctic Regions. 63

combination such as one rarely sees, that I did not feel inclined to sleep, and, long after my companions had retired, I remained on deck alone sketching the midnight sun in its various phases, in connection with Wilcox Point and the Devil's Thumb, although the latter object was so far away that it was impossible for me to distinguish its outlines clearly.

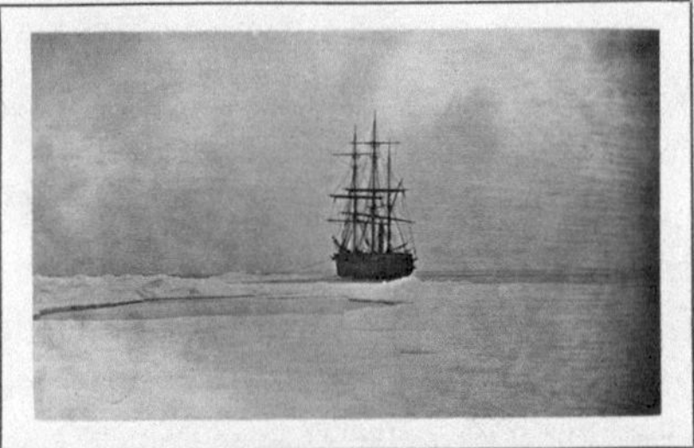

No 79. The "Panther" moored to the heavy Hummock Ice.

While completing a sketch, my attention was attracted by some objects moving on the ice between us and the land, which, as they drew nearer, proved to be a polar bear with two cubs. They were attracted doubtless by the smoke and smell from the galley, where the fire was kept burning night and day, that the

Interventions are prevalent within the *Arctic Exploration* album. Scholars Elizabeth Edwards and Janice Hart argue in their book *Photographs Objects Histories* that the material characteristics of photographs have a profound impact on the way the images are "read" (2004: 2-3). Materiality is especially apparent in contained micro-collections which are institutionally housed within a box or an album such as the New York Public Library's *Arctic Exploration*. This album, a micro-collection of arctic imagery, is what Edwards and Hart would call a "synthetic object": its order and logic was impressed upon it, thereby creating a new physical entity. Disparate photographs were arranged and pasted into a nondescript album with seemingly little forethought. To modern viewers especially, it is a dubious organization scheme and difficult to understand. Edwards and Hart would embrace this illogic because it does not fit in with current practice. They argue the inconsistency of synthetic objects is precisely what makes them so fascinating (ibid: 49). To understand the organizational structure behind the *Arctic Exploration* album and how it was meant to function we must first take a look at its genesis, how it is contained and what its contents are.

The volume was officially catalogued into the Library's collection on June 7, 1926, and it was likely assembled shortly before being accessioned. The New York Public Library's bindery, a precursor of the modern conservation lab, would often put together albums by collecting loose prints and photographs related to a theme. The rationale was practical: loose prints could be lost or damaged, were easy for an unscrupulous reader to pocket, and were inconvenient to serve to researchers. Furthermore, by amassing objects related to the same subject, the reader benefits from finding many sources in one place. The uncommonly thick boards and heavy grade bookcloth all point to a construction date of around 1925. The textblock structure, the brown starched buckram exterior, and NYPL oval stamp are also typical of the Library at the time. The resulting album itself lacks any inscriptions except those that had been previously written on top of a few photographs. The album only has its given title and its call number. Assigned a KBM+ classmark, the Library placed it among books under the subject heading "Arctic Exploration and Polar Research; General and Miscellaneous Works."

The album was transferred to the Photography Collection at some point after 1980. Its new home within a medium-specific collection removed the album from its analogous subject. The album's original catalogue card, which was later transcribed into the digital catalogue, contains scant information; though to a learned librarian the card is slightly more revealing. The title labels it a distinct collection and a descriptive note indicates the collection is "mounted in scrap book." The first subject heading on the card was originally listed as "Arctic Regions-Photographs" but at some point, someone crossed out photographs and wrote "Views." This erroneous correction was presumably made because many of the photographs in the album do not actually look like photographs.

In total, the album contains 237 photographs and prints. Most of the photographs, approximately three quarters, are printing-out paper silver gelatine prints. They show men on skis and on sledges. There are huts, animal specimens, polar bears, and sled dogs. They depict barren rocky landscapes, icy crevasses, and ships. Almost all are heavily reworked, with extensive overpainting, masking, and drawn and collaged elements. Expedition photographers understood that the arctic light, as well as the climate, made it challenging to create a satisfactory photograph. Rudolf Kersting, a photographer on an 1891 expedition to Greenland, describes the difficulties as follows:

> The rocks are of a color which, like the color of grass, will absorb rays of light, while the water, the ice, the sky, and the snow will reflect them. Therefore, in exposing

for light objects, the dark ones will be under-exposed; and vice versa, exposing for darker objects, the sky, ice, and snow will be so much exposed that they will melt into an opaque mass on the negative. To be certain at all, one should have a good dark room, and develop some plates daily to enable him to keep in touch with the quality of light (1902: 237-238).

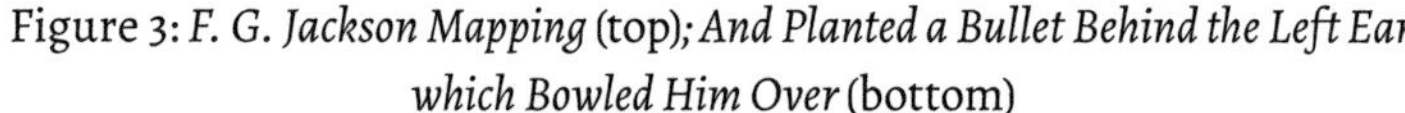
Figure 3: *F. G. Jackson Mapping* (top); *And Planted a Bullet Behind the Left Ear which Bowled Him Over* (bottom)

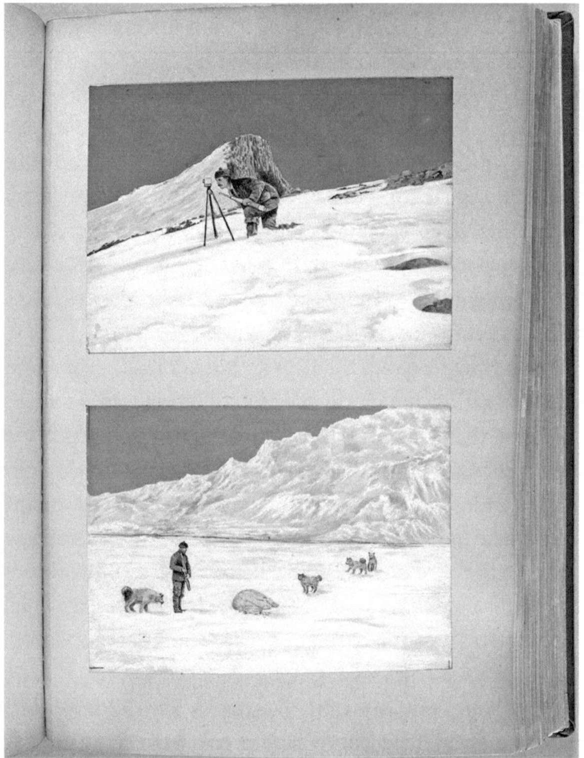

The *Arctic Exploration* album is remarkable in that it includes two pairs of what might be termed the "preliminary photograph" and the "improved positive" (Newman 1874: 66-67). The preliminary photographs appear seldom. They are tiny, lack detail, have limited tonal ranges, and are in poor condition.

Figure 4: *In Difficulties*

They were most likely made on-site, in the Arctic. Despite being surrounded by ice and snow, water was a luxury for polar adventurers. As Frederick George Jackson wrote, "Photography is carried on under difficult conditions here, and even after a negative has been successfully obtained, every drop of water used in developing and washing has to be obtained from melted snow" (1899: 562). Procuring water was no doubt tedious but light was an even more significant factor. The limited availability of good light tested the skill and patience of photographers like Jackson in the Arctic. With overcast skies and the sun starting to shift towards winter, it took Jackson all day to print-out photographs, tone and fix them (Jackson 1896: September 23). Ice, mist, and occasional snow-squalls also obscured the glass of printing frames and exacerbated the process (Jackson 1896: September 20). These environmental factors point to why the preliminary photographs with their low contrast were most likely printed in Franz Josef Land.

The improved positives, on the other hand, were most likely printed later. They reproduce the same images as the preliminary photographs but they exhibit considerable retouching. They are frequent within the album and quite a bit larger. To the untrained eye the level of retouching on the photographs is quite surprising; they are so extensively modified that upon first glance, they are barely recognizable as photographs. Many, notably the two-page panorama, straddle the lines between photographs, paintings, and assemblages. These photographs were never thought of as final works in themselves: they were transitional objects, intermediate phases between negative and illustration, between the Arctic and the final consumer product. As "improved positives" they were destined to be re-worked into the production of an illustrated book or magazine. Their intended discursive space was their life as a halftone reproduction in a magazine, newspaper, or book.

Bradford had to rely upon albumen prints being pasted into his luxurious *Arctic Regions*, but by the mid-1880s the halftone printing process had been perfected and became an inexpensive replacement. The halftone solved the challenge of mechanically reproducing a photograph. The difficulty had been in converting the continuous tone and gradations of a photograph into a series of dots or lines. The object to be reproduced in halftone form was placed in front of a large process camera and a halftone screen was put in direct contact with the negative or at a specific distance determined by the screen resolution. Made of intersecting lines on a transparent support, the halftone screen created evenly spaced apertures of equal size. The light passing through the screen broke the continuous tone of the original into a series of regularly spaced dots. This halftone negative was then exposed onto a metal plate sensitized with dichromated gelatine. Areas of gelatine exposed to light would harden while unexposed areas would remain soft and water soluble. After exposure the plate was washed and etched, the hardened gelatine acting as a resist. The plate would then be proofed, mounted into the printing chase and inked. Highlights were tiny dots, using little ink, and shadows and other areas of high image density were large dots, using lots of ink. The plate could be edited or modified as any ordinary etched plate.

The success of a halftone depended on the contrast of the image: photographs with more contrast and a wider tonal range reproduced better. Obtaining a high contrast was a consistent, known problem when it came to reproducing photographs of the Arctic. John Dunmore, one of the photographers on the 1869 William Bradford expedition, complained, "My great trouble, while away, was reflected light. Everything worked flat, and I could not force the negative up – the stronger the bath the flatter the negative" (1869: 414). The improved positives within the *Arctic Exploration* album were retouched to increase the contrast and extend the tonal range. The silver gelatine printing out paper prints in the album were common and relatively inexpensive prints to produce and thus were ideal for "improving."

The most striking areas of retouching in the album are the red and pink skies added to several photographs, which increased tonal contrast and visual interest in darker grey and night skies. During the retouching process, while highlights were lifted and details intensified, the skies were masked out with a mixture of iron (III) oxide and zinc white (Pozzi and Basso 2019).[2] The resulting reds worked as masking because of the light sensitivity, or lack thereof, of late 19th-century

2 Scientific analysis in support of this project was carried out at the Department of Scientific Research of the Metropolitan Museum of Art by Associate Research Scientist Federica Pozzi and Research Associate Elena Basso. This research was made possible by the Network Initiative for

photography emulsions. These emulsions were orthochromatic, meaning that the sensitivity of the silver halides extends only into the green/yellow wavelengths and not into the red wavelengths of the electromagnetic spectrum. However, the most effective wavelengths are blue/violet and ultraviolet, or UV; the red and pink absorb the UV light. No light from these areas is reflected back to the halftone negative; the silver remains un-activated and is washed out during processing. The resulting transparent skies print as areas of high image density, as shadows or night skies.

The *Arctic Exploration* album also contains unaltered photographs and prints. Thirty-one albumen photographs reproduce sketches made by chief scientist Emil Bessels and chief engineer Emil Schumann during the 1871 Polaris expedition to Greenland. Because their attempts at photography had failed and they abandoned ship, Bessels and Schumann resorted to making rudimentary pencil sketches, which were then used as the basis for creating paintings and woodcuts (Loomis 2000 [1971]: 335).

Figure 5: *Situation of the Polaris*

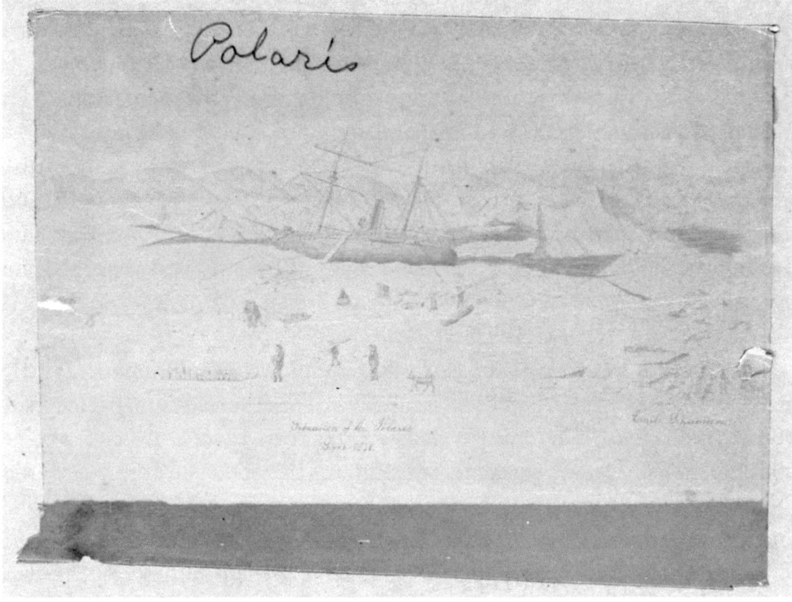

The sketches were photographed so that they could be more easily disseminated. These photographs have faded considerably and lack clarity but they speak to the

Conservation Science (NICS), a Metropolitan Museum of Art program. Support for NICS was provided by a grant from The Andrew W. Mellon Foundation.

public appetite for images from the polar north. Their photography preserved the story telling of the journey just as much as it allowed for its dissemination.

Eight images in the *Arctic Exploration* album relate to the 1881-1884 Lady Franklin Bay expedition. Two albumen photographs document the crew and below them, on a separate piece of the paper, the sitters are identified by handwritten notations. The photographs are stamped on the recto: N.Y. Pub. Lib. Gift of Harper Bros. The photographs, however, did not appear in a Harper Bros publication; instead, they were reproduced in *Three Years of Arctic Service: an account of the Lady Franklin Bay* published by Charles Scribner's Sons (Greely 1886: 40-41). Other various nonphotographic prints in the album are all stamped Scribner Gift. The Library stamped individual loose photographs and prints to acknowledge the donor as well as to keep track of the different sources. At least one of these drawings, but maybe more, was made after a photograph. Most of these halftone reproductions of etchings, drawings, and paintings appeared in a *Scribner's Magazine* article detailing the Peary Relief expedition of 1892 and in A.W. Greely's book *Explorers and Travelers*, also published by Scribner's the following year. That many of the photographs and prints in the album appeared in Scribner's publications explains the presence of three non-arctic prints in the album: St. Anthony's Falls in Minnesota, a buffalo head, and a monkey. They were illustrations in *Explorers and Travelers*, which markedly devoted four of its fourteen chapters to Polar exploration.

The pages with the improved positives – the majority of the photographs in the album – do not contain any stamps indicating a specific publishing house. In one of the photographs, however, the name of the ship Windward is visible. The British explorer Frederick George Jackson had sailed the Windward to Franz Josef Land. Harper and Brothers published his 1899 book *A Thousand Days in the Arctic* and it reproduces the improved positives found in the album.[3] At least 124 of the photographs found in the *Arctic Exploration* album are the basis for the 203 halftone illustrations in *A Thousand Days in the Arctic*.

Jackson was an accomplished explorer who had made a 3000-mile sledge trip across Siberia and whom the Royal Geographical Society and newspaper magnate Alfred Harmsworth sponsored to explore Franz Josef Land.[4] His book is an account of his experiences during this expedition's three-year stay, from 1894-1897. In it he recounts his constant battle with the conditions that make photographing in the Arctic challenging. Like Hayes, Jackson was distinctive in that he acted as the primary expedition photographer himself and did not bring along trained photographers. Unlike Hayes, though, and other explorers before him, Jackson

3 Curiously, none of these photographs or pages with them are stamped to indicate that they were a gift from Harper Brothers.

4 The expedition is known as the Jackson-Harmsworth expedition. Harmsworth owned the *Daily Mail* and later the *Daily Mirror*.

was quite an avid photographer. He carried a hand-held Frena No. 2 camera containing a pack of forty cut films but often resorted to using a half-plate stand camera instead because he found the results were more satisfactory (Jackson 1895: September 3; 1899: 448, 457-458). Jackson considered photography to be "of the greatest importance in an undiscovered country such as this" and he wrote a substantial amount about his photographic pursuits (1899: 458).

The physicality of *A Thousand Days in the Arctic* provides significant information as to the intended audience and especially when compared to William Bradford's large and richly bound *The Arctic Regions*.[5] *A Thousand Days in the Arctic* is meant to be hand held. Its simple cloth-covered case binding was the most common style for books mass produced during the 19th century. As the size of the reading public grew and the number of publishing houses increased, the functional and economic case binding was the one of choice (Diehl 1965: 40). The educated middle class and the armchair explorer would no doubt have been attracted to the book, which combines some higher-end detailing with economical materials and inexpensive means of production. The cover has a three-colour illustration based on one of Jackson's photographs and an embossed faux-gilt title, and the upper edge of the textblock is gilded and the text is printed on a smooth white clay-coated paper. These upmarket details distract from the thin book cloth covering the exterior of the case and lack of endbands. The thickness of the over-900-page volume is also too great for an easy case binding structure, and could eventually lead to serious structural failures of the binding. The average reader of *A Thousand Days in the Arctic* would likely not have known or cared about a lack of end bands or a thinner book cloth, but they would have been enticed by the cover and imposing thickness of the tome. Similarly, a brief 1899 review of the publication was impressed by its physical details, noting that, "[t]he work is well bound and well printed [...]" (American Geographical Society of New York 1899: 395).

Print historian Michael Twyman, in a discussion of the development of the graphic book during the 19th century, suggests that a public accustomed to the spectacles of dioramas, large fixed panoramas, lantern slide shows, and other theatricals would have expected to feed their desire for visual stimulation through illustrations in books (1994: 139-142). The numerous graphic elements found in *A Thousand Days in the Arctic* – charts and maps as well as photomechanically printed images – were certainly prized by the American Geographic Society of New York's reviewer, who concluded, "[...] the Maps and Illustrations are excellent" (American Geographical Society of New York 1899: 395).

---

5 *A Thousand Days in the Arctic* is 23 x 16.5 x 5.7 cm while *The Arctic Regions: Illustrated with Photographs Taken on an Art Expedition to Greenland* is approximately 63.5 x 52.4 x 6 cm in size. *The Arctic Regions* has a full leather tightback binding over six false raised bands. The covers and spine are gold stamped and the textblock printed as black and red letterpress on a thick wove paper.

The book notably included a panorama, in the form of a five-page fold out view. Jackson's halftone panoramic photo-reproduction is the condensation of large panoramic paintings which were already established as part of Victorian popular visual culture (Potter 2007: 44-45). Photographers, similarly, had long been stitching together photographic positives into panoramic views. Bradford's *Arctic Regions* contains a centrally placed two-page panoramic photograph of a glacier extending into a fiord above the water. In discussing photographs from Count Hans Wilczek and Wilhelm Burger's 1872 arctic expedition, photography historian Monika Faber points out that panoramas had also been favoured in geological expeditions because they provided a quasi-exhaustive survey of the surroundings (2008: 17).[6] 360-degree photographic panoramas had become extremely commonplace by the mid-1880s (ibid: 18). It is therefore not surprising that Jackson also desired such an encompassing view.

In 1896 Jackson spent several weeks working on his multiple-negative view of the coast of Cape Flora. Though early versions of specialized panoramic cameras such as the Cirkut Camera existed in the mid-1890s, any delicate camera mechanisms would become unreliable in the cold temperatures as lubricants solidify and glass and metal components contract. Jackson instead relied upon his half plate and hand cameras. His excursions out to the iceberg to select a pivot point for the camera stand were almost always exhausting and sometimes treacherous. The ever-moving tide and ice were a regular source of difficulty, as were the unstable weather conditions, as he details:

> [December 19th, Saturday] I seized this opportunity to complete my panoramic views, and taking the camera out to the berg, I set it up again, and took three negatives, which now completes the series. The ice has still further broken up near the berg, and I felt a little uncomfortable while I was out there lest it should continue this process of disruption while I was on it, owing to the fast running spring tides, and the swell the wind has set up.
>
> I ski-ed six miles backwards and forward to change the dark slides at the end of each hour, and did not finish until after 2 A.M. After all my pains and some risks run, I hope I shall get satisfactory results (1899: 580).

6 Wilczek and Burger's trip was a part of a two-year long Austro-Hungarian North Pole Expedition. This expedition included one made in 1873 by Julius von Payer and Karl Weyprecht, who reported finding and naming Franz Josef Land in honor of their emperor.

To Jackson, the risk to life, limb, and camera must have been worth the result. The completed panorama is one of the most striking visual elements of *A Thousand Days in the Arctic* and certainly of the Library's *Arctic Exploration* album.[7]

Figure 6: *View to the Westward from near the Flag-Staff on Cape Flora*

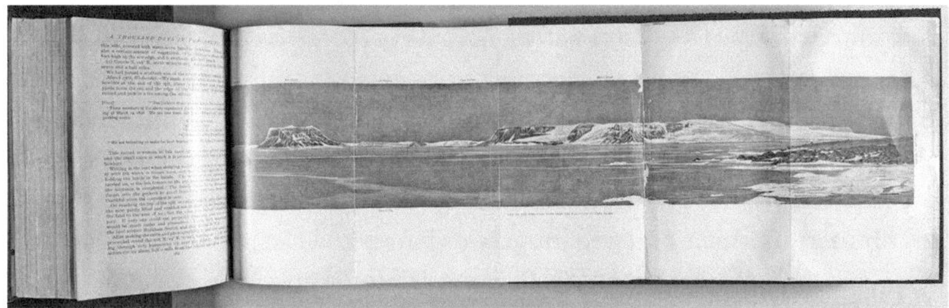

While the published halftone is monochromatic, age, and innate chemical instability have combined to give the photographic original a composite of warm green, red, and violet tonalities with painted black shadows and bright white highlights. Eight individual photographs form the album's panorama: six individual, heavily retouched silver gelatine printed-out paper prints form the landscape while two larger pieces of photographic paper serve as the sky. The horizon line of rock and ice formations is carefully cut and the retouching applied with care and delicacy. It is clear that Jackson was not the only individual to invest significant amounts of time and effort into the production of a panoramic photograph: remarkable skill went into perfecting this "improved positive".

Though significantly smaller in size, Jackson's panoramic illustration would still provide the reader with an expanded skyline, providing in a small way the illusion of the experience of being there. The broad horizon and encompassing view would be familiar to readers and perhaps expected in a book of this nature, especially for a place that the vast majority of people would never visit. The size and weight of *A Thousand Days in the Arctic* and the length of the print both necessitate resting the book onto a surface before unfolding the view. Similar to a full-scale panoramic painting, the reader is required to move his head in order to view the image and only in drawing back from it would he be able to see the entire view. This haptic experience plays to the reader's curiosity and allows him to "partake" in the vastness of the landscape.

The subjects Jackson photographed and reproduced in *A Thousand Days in the Arctic* depict the exoticism of the foreign land (vast plains of ice, glaciers and

7 The panoramic photograph as published in *A Thousand Days in the Arctic* is approximately 70 cm in length. The photographic original, in the New York Public Library scrapbook, is 77.5 cm (79 cm including the secondary support).

crevasses of ice, and native peoples), man's struggle in the severe north (hauling equipment on sledges and the conditions in which they lived), the heroism of the explorers (killing dangerous bears, standing atop mountains of ice), and the scientific purpose of the extended sojourn (discovery of new species and documenting unusual geological formations).

To an extent, the photographic subjects matched the public's expectations of what the Arctic was like. In the early 19th century there existed a craze for tales of the Arctic, in large part because of the British explorer William Parry's 1819-1820 expedition. Parry published an account of his voyage in 1828, that included seven engravings, three of which were maps. Later, Sir John Franklin's disastrous 1845-48 expedition to find the Northwest Passage and the subsequent search for him and his party (128 men) renewed the public's horror and fascination with the harsh polar landscape (cf. Brandt 2010). Their expectations grew mostly out of textual accounts such as these and the engraved and woodcut illustrations in the press. The pencil sketches from the Polaris depict much of the same imagery: a ship moored (and sinking) in the ice. The visual images in books were often fantastical and they, in combination with theatrical culture, created a polar frenzy.

Figure 7: *Fantastic Appearance of the Pack*

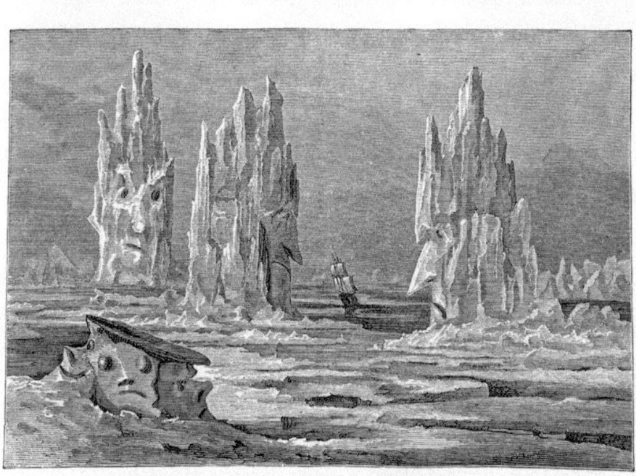

In explaining the motives for such dangerous and difficult explorations, a reviewer of one of Bradford and Hayes' lectures, listed the most mysterious phenomena in nature such as the "fitful splendor of the northern lights, the theory of terrestrial magnetism [...]" and "the grandeur of the midnight sun" (New York Herald 1870: 7). He then commented that these, "fascinate the lover of the romantic and sublime." The historian Huw Lewis-Jones explains that polar explorers themselves contributed much to this culture as they were eager to profit from curating their own heroic image regardless of whether or not the expedition was successful (2017). Thus, books chronicling their journeys were critical to furthering their images and careers as well as the expeditions.

Scholars have remarked how the visual image, and especially the photograph, has swayed the way in which the Arctic has been collectively and subjectively imagined (King/Lidchi 1998: 11). Yet, their examinations tend to be only about specific voyages without looking at a larger context. Before the 1880s, if the public had seen original photography from the Arctic, it was likely from Bradford or it was overpainted with colour as many lantern slides were. Once the halftone became feasible and commercially viable, the appearance of Arctic photography in book form was possible. With ample illustrations and detailed maps, Jackson's book sated the reader's visual curiosity but they did less to spur the imagination. The experiences Jackson had were believed in part because of the tangible proof of photography, regardless of how they appeared in print. The masking, retouching, and drawing of the photographs all made the images clearer and more digestible for the consumer. They were produced so that the public could believe in these real moments, captured and validated by the medium of photography. As Jackson wrote in his book, "There is nothing like a photograph to convince people" (1899: 467). It is our belief in these reproductions that reflects our desire to partake in these lived moments from afar. They fulfil our expectations of the barren and exotic land, the glory of science, man triumphing over nature, and the noble struggle involved in doing so.

A review of *A Thousand Days in the Arctic* in the *New York Times*, noted that the illustrations from photographs by the author were "remarkably interesting and unique" (*New York Times* 1899: BR353). The reviewer does not elucidate any further, but his comment suggests the images were of a kind he had not seen before. Because Jackson's sojourn to the Arctic was so well documented and did not end in tragedy, the photographs as well as the texts served to demystify the Arctic sublime. As Chaucey Loomis suggests, the sublimity of the arctic depended in part on its imagined emptiness and coldness, but by the end of the century exploration itself, which had created the notion, had also subverted it (Loomis 1977: 110, 112). The ever-improving quality of photography and the emergence of the halftone undoubtedly also contributed to this subversion.

Only 27 years after Jackson's account was published, the photographs used to produce the book were placed somewhat randomly alongside other documents from different journeys to make the *Arctic Exploration* album. The haphazard assortment of photographs in the album reflects collective interests and disinterests. It is an album that signals both the desire to organize (keep everything in one easily accessible place) and relativize common tropes (icy landscape and wrecked ship must be the arctic). Copies of the original negatives that were produced for the publication of *A Thousand Days in the Arctic* and other books were then joined into an album that homogenized these individual expeditions into one experience of Arcticness. Nine distinct expeditions became one continuous journey and one landscape. While the earlier published books worked to demystify and categorize the Arctic, the album and its photographs restore an air of this mystery, representing instead a distant and unknown history. The unification of the expeditions, in effect, generalizes the experiences, suggesting that what matters is not the individual expedition, but rather that expeditions to the Arctic happened and were documented.

Created and valued as a visual source of the far off northern landscape, the album became a more or less forgotten object. The photographs lost their original meaning because specifics were not included and the passage of time has distanced the album. Only the most sensational expeditions are remembered, if at all, and the Jackson-Harmsworth expedition is not one of those: they were not the first to visit Franz Josef Land, no remarkable disasters occurred, and they did not even make a serious attempt to reach the North Pole despite having originally planned to. The most memorable aspect of the expedition was when Jackson accidentally found Fridtjof Nansen, who had embarked on his pole attempt three years previously (cf. 1898). As a *Daily News* reviewer of the book wrote, "Everyone remembers the dramatic story of the meeting of Nansen and Jackson in the Polar wilds" (1899: 8). Yet, now, only polar history enthusiasts and scholars know of this remarkable coincidence. Even if the album had named the expedition, it probably still would not stand out as a treasure. Extensively painted-over photographs are not valued as precious objects within the history of photography and yet this album preserves a history of the practice of retouching.

The album speaks to images produced and remade for consumption. Somewhat ironically, the 19th-century images of the Arctic today are easily viewed in another altered form – that of Google Images or Books, Hathi Trust or the Internet Archive. In digitized books, the viewer often does not see the original woodcut, engraving or halftone as is, but rather in an altered view. When the grid of the original halftone screen too closely matches that of the digital image-capturing sensor, the two interact and create a false moiré pattern to appear within the digitized halftone images. These digital images are even more separated from their original source and arguably, they are less engaging to a viewer.

Contemporary imagery of the Arctic, on the other hand, is quite often very impressive and almost exclusively photographic or filmic. It is taken by amateur photographers with excellent state-of-the-art equipment who are participating in adventure travel expeditions or by artists concerned with the acute calamity of climate change. While the photographs from the late 19th and early 20th century especially proved the heroism of men and the triumph of engineering and science, today's photographs of the Arctic still evidence mankind's fascination with the North. They are evidence of our collective mastery over polar conditions. We now have more advanced technology, clothing, and transportation at our disposal, all of which make the journey to the Arctic easier (Brandt 2010: 3-6). Yet, paradoxically at the same time, the photography of the Arctic now is challenging the very pride and science that has made these contemporary visits possible. The Arctic today is still an enthralling site because of its beauty but more so because of the threat of its loss.

Narrative heroism now resides in the animals and unfortunately, to a lesser extent the native peoples as they fight against globalisation and the warming climate to survive. As an example, one only needs to compare how polar bears were photographed and are now photographed.

Figure 8: *I Went Up to Within Eight Yards of Him and Killed Him with One Shot* (top); *An Addition to Our Larder* (bottom)

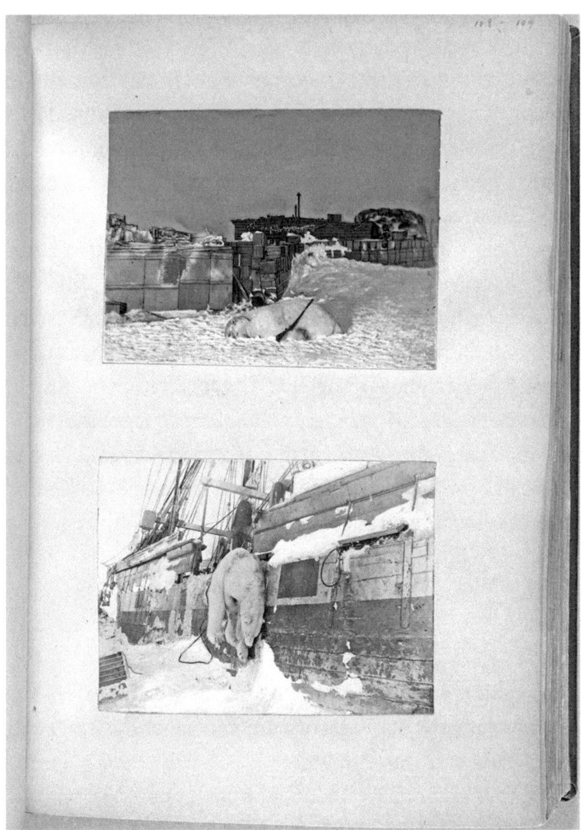

Twenty-three photographs of polar bears appear in the *Arctic Exploration* album. In most photographs the bears are recently shot or about to be shot. A sampling of titles in *A Thousand Days in the Arctic* confirms the fate of all the adult bears: "the dead bear", "I finished her with a shot in the neck", "and planted a bullet behind the left ear which bowled him over", "after breakfast we flensed the bear" and so on. While the men needed to eat the bear meat to survive, there was clearly a natural sense of pride associated with the kill and with being able to care for any remaining orphaned cubs. Two of the cubs which appear in the album were affectionately named Mabel and Benjy. In today's world the polar bear, and especially the cute cub, is almost synonymous with the Arctic and has practically become a mascot for climate change. Most often seen on an ice floe or near the water, the polar bear is very much alive but struggling to remain so in an ever-changing and melting environment. Here too, photography is taken and used to convince people of a struggle, not one of man triumphing over nature's harshness but of the animal and planet's struggle against mankind.

As the photographs in the album have now been identified and more accurately cataloged to represent the specific expeditions from which they came, their significance and use will change. Restoring the original function of the photographs by knowing what they are increases their historical value. Researchers will understand them for their intended purpose. Both the preliminary photographs and the improved positives speak to the life of the physical photographs, from their printing in the Arctic to their eventual reproduction as halftone images in a mass-produced book. They are artefacts of technical innovation and artistic skill. The album, though, remains representative of more than its physical contents. As a synthetic object of common views, it is a micro-collection that marks an institutional past, in which the practice of collecting, organizing, and synthesizing was based primarily on a theme. It suggests an appreciation for simplification and generalizing in order to grasp its contents. The complexity of the *Arctic Exploration* album with all its layers of meaning makes it a fascinating object. It is and will remain a historical record of named expeditions, the process of reproduction, storytelling, and mass consumption.

References

American Geographical Society of New York (1899): [Review of] "A Thousand Days in the Arctic by Frederick G. Jackson." In: Journal of the American Geographical Society of New York, 31/4, pp. 395.

Art Journal (1872): "Arctic Scenery" In: Art Journal (London) 11, pp. 241.

Bradford, William (1873): The Arctic Regions: Illustrated with Photographs Taken on an Art Expedition to Greenland, London: Sampson Low, Marston, Low and Searle.

Brandt, Anthony (2010): The Man Who Ate His Boots: The Tragic History of the Search for the Northwest Passage, New York: Alfred A. Knopf.

Diehl, Edith (1965 [1946]): Bookbinding: Its Background and Technique Vol. 1, New York: Holt, Rinehart, and Winston, 1965.

Daily News (1899): "A Thousand Days in the Arctic: The Story of the Jackson-Harmsworth Polar Expedition" In: The Daily News (London) Tuesday, 16 May, pp. 8.

Dunmore, J. L. (1869): "The Camera Among the Icebergs." In: The Philadelphia Photographer, 6/72, pp. 412-414.

Edwards, Elizabeth/Hart, Janice (2004): Photographs Objects Histories: On the Materiality of Images, London: Routledge.

Edwards, Elizabeth/Hart, Janice (2004): "Mixed Box: The Cultural Biography of a Box of 'Ethnographic' photographs." In: Photographs Objects Histories

Faber, Monika (2008): Infinite Ice: The Arctic and the Alps from 1860 to Present, Ostfildern: Hatje Cantz.

Fineman, Mia (2019): Faking It: Manipulated Photography before Photoshop, New York: Metropolitan Museum of Art.

Greely, A.W. (1893): Explorers and Travellers, New York: C. Scribner's Sons.

Greely, A. W. (1886): Three years of Arctic service: an account of the Lady Franklin Bay expedition of 1881-1884 and the attainment of the farthest north, New York: C. Scribner's Sons.

Greenhalgh, Adam (2003): "The Not So Truthful Lens: William Bradford's The Arctic Regions." In Richard C. Kugler (ed.), William Bradford: Sailing Ships and Arctic Seas, Seattle and London: New Bedford Waling Museum, pp. 72-86.

Hayes, I. I. (1867): The Open Polar Sea: a Narrative of a Voyage of Discovery towards the North Pole, in the Schooner "United States," New York: New York, Hurd and Houghton.

Heilprin, Angelo (1893): "The Peary Relief Expedition" In: Scribner's Magazine 13/1, 3-24.

Jackson, Frederick George (1895): MS 287/1/1, Frederick Jackson Collection, University of Cambridge, Scott Polar Research Institute.

Jackson, Frederick George (1896): MS 287/1/2, Frederick Jackson Collection, University of Cambridge, Scott Polar Research Institute.

Jackson, Frederick George (1899): A Thousand Days in the Arctic, New York: Harper & Brothers.

Kersting, Rudolf (1902): "Photography in the Far North." In Rudolf Kersting (ed.) The White World: Life and Adventures within the Arctic Circle Portrayed by Famous Living Explorers, New York: Lewis, Scribner & Co, pp.231-240.

King, J.C.H./Lidchi, Henrietta (1998): Imaging the Arctic, London: British Museum Press.

Kodak (1999): "Photography Under Arctic Conditions" In: Kodak, October C-9, Rochester: Eastman Kodak Company, pp.

Krauss, Rosalind (1982) "Photography's Discursive Spaces: Landscape/View." In: Art Journal 42/4, pp. 311-319.

Lewis-Jones, Huw (2017): Imagining the Arctic: Heroism, Spectacle and Polar Exploration, London I.B. Tauris.

Loomis, Chauncey C. (1977): "The Arctic Sublime." In: U.C. Knoepflmacher/G.B. Tennyson (eds.) Nature and the Victorian Imagination, Berkeley: University of California Press.

Loomis, Chauncey (2000 [1971]): Weird and Tragic Shores: The Story of Charles Francis Hall, Explorer, New York: Random House, pp. 335.

Nansen, Fridtjof (1898): Farthest North: being the Record of a Voyage of Exploration of the Ship "Fram" 1893-96 [...], New York: Harper & Brother.

Newman, James (1874): The Principles and Practice of Harmonious Colouring, in Oil, Water, and Photographic Colours, especially as Applied to Photographs on Paper, Glass, and Canvas, London: Piper and Carter.

New York Herald (1870): "The Arctic Regions: Bradford's Stereoptic Views and Dr. Hays' [sic] Lecture." In: The New York Herald (New York) December 9, pp.7.

New York Times (1899): "In the Arctic North: Frederick G. Jackson's Account of the Thousand Days He Spent There" In: New York Times June 3, pp. BR353

Parry, William Edward (1828): Narrative of an Attempt to Reach the North Pole, in Boats Fitted for the Purpose, and Attache to His Majesty's Ship Hecla, London: John Murray.

Potter, Russell A. (2007) "The Photographic Artist: William Bradford and the Close of the Panoramic Era." In Arctic Spectacles: The Frozen North in Visual Culture, 1818-1875, Seattle: University of Washington Press, pp. 190-202.

Pozzi, Federica/Basso, Elena (2019): "Results Summary: Arctic Exploration Album (1890s-?) from New York Public Library." The Network Initiative for Conservation Science, The Metropolitan Museum of Art Department of Scientific Research, New York, NY. Unpublished report.

Twyman, Michael (1994): "The Emergence of the Graphic Book in the 19th Century." In: Robin Myers/Michael Harris (eds.), A Millennium of the Book: Production, Design, & Illustration in Manuscript & Print 900-1900, Delaware: Oak Knoll, pp. 139-180.

Verfasser, Julius (1904): The Half-Tone Process. A Practical Manual of Photo-Engraving in Half-Tone on Zinc, Copper, and Brass, 3rd ed. London: Ilffe & Sons.

Wamsley, Douglas/Barr, William (1998): "Early Photographers of the Canadian Arctic and Greenland." In: J.C.H. King/Henrietta Lidchi (eds.), Imaging the Arctic, London: British Museum Press, pp. 36-45.

Whitman, Nicholas (1998): "Technology and Vision: Factors Shaping Nineteenth-Century Arctic Photography." In: J.C.H. King/Henrietta Lidchi (eds.), Imaging the Arctic, London: British Museum Press, pp.29-35.

Memory and the Snapshot: some thoughts on photography, drawing, and writing as inscriptions of Northern landscapes

Aileen Harvey

A snapshot is an everyday object with a particular relationship to our desire to remember, and it also describes a certain idea of photographic time. The dynamic between the snapshot and memory is here taken as a motif, in order to frame some thoughts around my landscape practice: about the territory that photography shares with drawing and writing. Areas of flow between these three artistic methods are discussed in the context of making and thinking about memory: what it is to remember a place, and to want to get it right in certain ways.

The chapter is structured by four ideas: document, time, memory, and the in-between, although these themes will run into one another. The four focal ideas arise from some examples of my work – drawings, and one text piece – that are related to some distinctively *photographic* questions about capturing an experience of place. The works – and so the questions – respond to changeable and liminal qualities of landscape specific to northern latitudes: such as seasonal shifts in light, littorality, weathering, and deciduous woodland.

Bringing these examples together with a selection of works by other artists, the discussion shades in areas of interaction and constructs connections between photographs, drawings, and texts. The aim is not programmatic; rather it is to consider what these methods may do in relation, in counterpoint and parallel – and so how this conceptual space may be used to express something about places and our encounters with them, within my own and other visual art practices.

Document (the snapshot as record)

Many of my drawings and text works stem from a sense that the documentary status of photographs can be problematic. The works often have the explicit aim of creating an alternative record of a landscape experience: one that is to be understood in counterpoint or parallel to the functioning of photographs.

A photograph is a standard of visual evidence – that is its currency in the arena of investigation and proof. The idea of the photograph as a reliably accurate correlate of reality is founded in the theorising of it as directly caused by the event that it represents (by the light reflected from it). However, this causal connection need not lead us to conceive of photographs as perfect, automatic imprints of the facts. We might rather follow Max Kozloff in taking the photograph to be a witness (1987), and accept with that thought all of the possible flaws carried within the idea of testimony: misunderstandings, mistakes, lacunae, and fictions.[1]

Even leaving aside the changes to be made through darkroom methods or editing digital files, a photograph is only accurate in some respects, within limits, and from a certain point of view. Inevitably, any photograph in its chosen framing excludes and leaves open more than it contains. Further, what content it has is distorted – bent, distanced, flattened – by the lens and the single point perspective, and is crucially uncertain, particularly in the matter of colour. The colours in a final print are so radically underdetermined by what is on the negative or screen, that decisions made in printing can lead to several different, equally legitimate (equally convincing) results. Which means that the colours of a photograph are in practical terms indeterminate, and cannot ever be checked against the unrepeatable situation in which the photograph was taken.[2]

This is, of course, to problematize something that in everyday life is unproblematic. As viewers, we are used to these particular distortions within photographs. But what are their unnoticed consequences for our expectations, forgettings, and blindnesses about landscapes? The necessary project of reforming human behaviours towards our surroundings requires a consonant rethinking – and re-seeing – of our relationship to landscape as one of continuity and proximity. Nature as background, as passive, as resource, must give way to an understanding that endows it with moral protagonism and sees ourselves as not separate from the landscape but bodies included within it.[3]

1 Cf. Emerling 2012: 83.

2 The photograph-as-imprint glosses over the mechanics of cameras, and the openings and redirections that happen in the processing and printing of photographs. Photography is more variable in its printed outcomes and their messages than that analysis acknowledges.

3 This endeavour requires, as Val Plumwood has shown, an urgent re-thinking of the dualisms embedded in western culture and philosophy, dualisms which oppose human to natural, masculine to feminine, mind to body, and so forth (1993: 5, 36). Dualist structures of contrastive opposition (culture/nature, active/passive, human/non-human, rational/emotional) are mutually reinforcing, and they foster unacceptable-dangerous-hierarchies and separations (1993: 29, 31). "Overcoming the dualist dynamic requires recognition of both continuity and difference; this means acknowledging the other as neither alien to nor discontinuous from self nor assimilated to or an extension of self" (ibid: 6).

This sense that a photograph can fail as a record of what is seen, and that the failure may be undetectable, led to my series of drawings *River/water/colour.* They might be regarded as attempts to get the colour of water right (or perhaps 'more right'). *East River/Hudson 1405/151005032011* is a watercolour drawing on paper. Two small coloured squares overlap at one edge to form a rectangle: the left-hand square is a midtone olive green-grey; the right is a pale glassy blue-green. They are colour samples of the East River and the Hudson, made where each meets 20th Street, in New York. I mixed the colours by eye, using watercolour paint and the river water collected in a paper cup, and between making the two samples, I walked from one river to the other, across Manhattan island.

Figure 1: *Aileen Harvey, East River/Hudson 1405/151005032011, 2011*

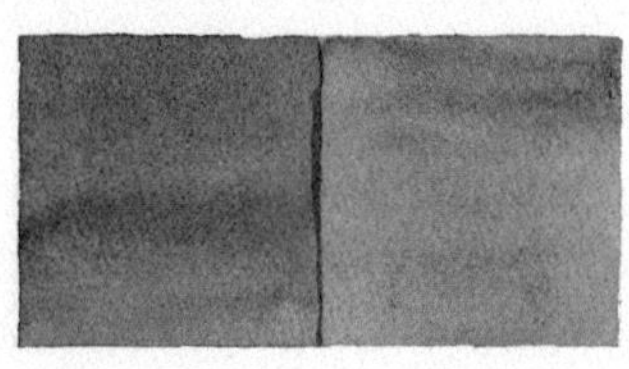

The walking structures the drawing, and it brings geography and my moving body into how the work is understood. As the title indicates, the East River was sampled at 14:05, and the Hudson at 15:10, after walking west, on a day in early March. Given the changeability of water, the sampling is specific to the context. The drawing records the incident light on the water, more than it does a colour that might be considered intrinsic to the river. So the observed colours belong to that low sun, on a clear winter's afternoon, and the lower sun an hour later – in such a way that the sample registers the latitude, as well as the distance walked and my pace, the progress of clouds, the orientation of each river, and my viewing position. Within this, body, terrain and time are co-implicated. The net of contributing elements cannot quite be tidied into alignment with the objectivity that is the usual aim when taking samples.

Although the drawings aim at precision in colour, through their emphasis on the momentary and contextual nature of those colours, the *River/water/colour* series implicitly values subjectivity and transformation. It models a version of accuracy that does not try to be objective. How might that model for accuracy turn out, in other forms and broader contexts? It involves a giving-up on fixed identities, in the hope of bringing representations closer to how people, places and times are interrelated. In inconsistency we find the importance of standpoint. A critical theorizing of landscape benefits from – needs – the feminist insight that we always bring our perspective with us, that our perspective is generative: it makes what we see. Donna Haraway's now indispensable concept of situated knowledges (1988) emerges from a recognition that our way of seeing the world is a matter of positioning – and that positioning is mobile, fluid, and active. The world is not a pre-existing object to be grasped; it arises (reciprocally, multiplicitously, heterogeneously, and provisionally, as Doreen Massey points out [2005: 9]) *in relation* to a perceiver. Thus viewpoint and situation need to be acknowledged, to be openly considered. And so too does the intended audience. Every view is from *somewhere*, made by and for *someone*. The view that claims for itself objectivity and detachment, in fact relies upon denial and the masking of ineliminable subjectivities.[4]

Can we give some content to this idea of accuracy-without-objectivity? It is a wanting to get something right about a place, in a certain way: a way that brings out the irreducible contributions of standpoint.[5] In the context of these thoughts about memory and landscape, the "something" at stake is the telling feature or features of a landscape as it is experienced – it is that which we want to hold on to. This may not be reducible to a set of qualities, but a partial list of concrete possibilities could nonetheless be helpful. It would include visual qualities: colour, shape, scale, tone, and intensity of light. But also volume, texture, movement, heft, smell, moisture, warmth, taste, sounds; all these signify in our grasp of a place.

To return for a moment to photographs, if these listed qualities are often those that matter, those that we want to record, then this opens up further distance between the features central to understanding photographs as documentary, and the ability to be accurate (about the desired things). The aspects of a landscape that are distorted, suppressed or underspecified by most photographs are exactly most of those qualities listed.[6] And the key feature that underwrites photographs-as-documents, their automaticity, functions as a denial of subjectivity; it works against

4 Note that Haraway uses situated knowledges to define "feminist objectivity" (581) – a concept of objectivity that has been rebuilt to incorporate embodiment and the unfinished, the "split and contradictory self" (586). This re-thought objectivity is a "seeing together", through "partial connection" (586). It is "the view from a body, always a complex, contradictory, structuring, and structured body, versus the view from above, from nowhere, from simplicity" (589).

5 The differences between how things are from here and from there, now and then, for me and for another.

6 By "most photographs", I mean those that have the classic single-point perspective and flattened visual field. Note that this is not at all to say that such photographs cannot represent, for example,

the aim of avowing point of view. Further, accuracy itself is in need of some unpacking in relation to these perceived qualities. For a scientific measurement to be accurate is for it to be close to the true value. But we have been talking about mixed, kinaesthetic features where the perceiver cannot be disentangled from the measuring or the measured, and we were also refusing to assert stable, objective values. A place is not an object, not a static, clear-cut thing. A place has no edges. It surrounds, moves and alters; it contours itself around other things. Places have no fixed point of reference; they elude any attempt to pin them down. This creates a problem with giving any useful meaning to 'true value' in this context.[7]

And yet, the wish to be accurate, or true, has a residue that will not go away.[8] It is the question of how to avoid the idealist's dream-world: how to tether our representations to the ground, so they do not become dislocated, mere sensations of the self.[9] A landscape is both material and temporal, and is experienced by bodies, over time. This complex interrelation of land, body and time is integral to landscapes, and to address it requires addressing *both* that essential subjectivity and that physio-temporal rootedness. The desire to document well, to be accurate, without asserting objectivity, might be re-cast as the resolve to ground a subjective encounter in material reality.[10]

In any working medium, this version of the documentary has to be a question of balance: between having some strong basis in the material here and now, and reflecting experience as bodily, in time, and without a fixed point of refer-

---

tactile and kinetic aspects of landscape at all, but they do so indirectly, through inference, the haptic, and routes of association – and so accuracy is not possible (nor is inaccuracy).

7 The problem as I see it is with a truth-to-fact mapping between a photograph and a phenomenon that necessarily escapes from flat, static representations. My point here is indirectly related to Thierry de Duve's characterisation of the snapshot as "an unperformed movement that refers to an impossible posture." Photography's instantaneous arresting of motion means that it cannot show natural movement, but only produce "a petrified analogue of it" (2007 [1978]: 110).

8 I have chosen to discuss accuracy although very similar things could be said about truth, which has a similar role in the idea of the document. Being a more everyday word, "truth" is more flexible than "accuracy". There is, after all, subjective truth, and even a particular kind of truth to be found in fiction. However, these useful ambiguities, together with its long history of philosophical debate, make it too unwieldy to be the focus for this brief discussion.

9 Cf. David Brett's criticisms of romantic solipsism within landscape painting, "in which the ultimate reality… is the sensation of the self within the environment". Such an approach to landscape, he writes, "re-enacts the impulse of appropriation" (1989:16). Also compare again Val Plumwood's point that the other should be recognised as neither discontinuous nor assimilated with the self (1993: 6).

10 See also Liz Wells' discussion of the socio-historic context needed for a "grounded aesthetics", and of the problems with landscape practices that "avoid grounding through emphasis on the formal, the expressive, and the metaphoric at the expense of engagement with particularities of place" (2011: 10, 13).

ence. Approaches to grounding, such as precision and specificity, need openings that point to the transformations, elisions, and lack of consistency entailed by a person's encounter with landscape. As discussed above, walking is one method for providing such openings, in drawings, photographs or texts. Gesture, too, through remaining legible in the work, can function as a remnant of the body's motion, so modifying ideas of the document.

Irene Kopelman's delicate pencil drawings for *Glaciers and Avalanches* were made outdoors, in the Swiss mountains. They are convincingly precise, but their careful outlines register her process of looking, perhaps even more than they conjure a view of a glacier. Drawings like these are read in time: the viewer's eye finds a route across, one that echoes the scanning and tracing of eye and hand as they follow these immense forms. Kopelman's attention to the landscape is palpable; that attentiveness emphasises both her physical presence and the timeline of the making.

Figure 2 and Figure 3: Rhona Eve Clews, *Certain bodies/subtle air and The air is not only an empty space, 2015*

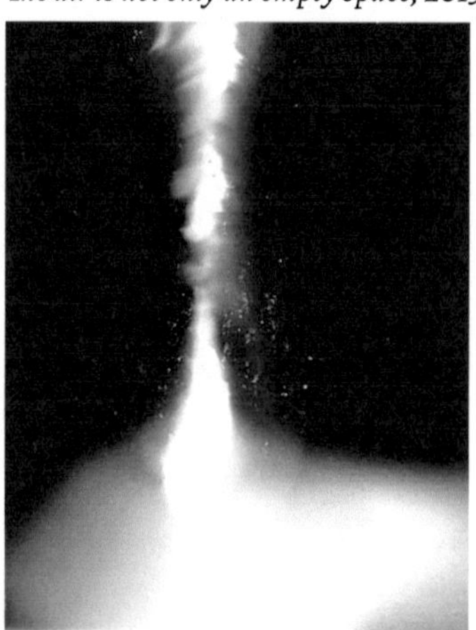

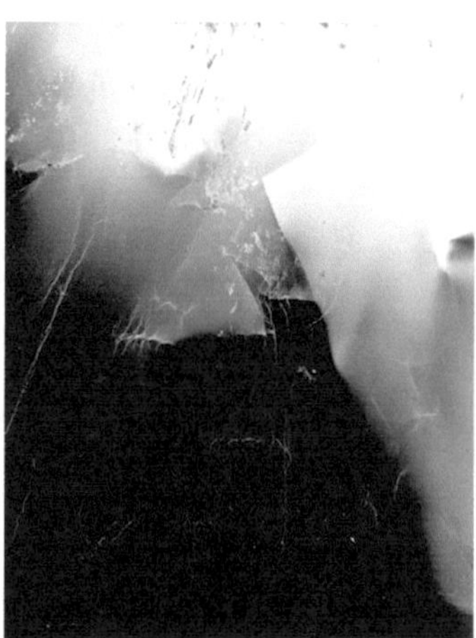

Rhona Eve Clews's photograms of trees scorched by bush-fires, made in the Australian outback, form the series *We overlap but we never touch/Coal is born of the mountain*. On a series of night walks, she pressed and twisted photographic paper against the scarred trees, and struck matches to make the exposure. The paper has been marked by her hands, living wood and firelight. Gesture shapes all of these marks: it is in the scuffs, scratches, compressions, shifts and the bursting light. But it is gesture as *mutual* marking, actions performed together: arm, paper, tree in motion; arm, match, light in motion; darkness pressing back. These movements carry an explosive immediacy into the photograms, while also invoking a complex of past events.[11] Like Kopelman, Clews marks the work with subjectivity, time, and the physical co-presence of artist and landscape – and further, her process makes manifest the active, co-operative character of that co-presence in time. Moreover, the time that belongs to the making of these drawings and photograms is not a simple interval. Clews developed the photograms *in situ*, in an improvised darkroom – in order, she says, "to collapse the gap between making and seeing" – a reminder of the complexities of photographic time.

Time (the snapshot as instant)

If we think of photographic time on the model of a snapshot – the instant of the shutter's blink – that must be modulated by a recognition of duration. There is duration in even the shortest exposure, but also in the photographic process, which inserts itself between the being-there and the created image. These extended timeframes alter the time that can be identified with a photograph; they stretch it out and interrupt it in several ways. A photograph doesn't come into existence as a legible negative or print until after (often long after) the moment it was taken.[12] That separation, however brief, parts final image from event. The visible image cannot be contemporaneous with the event that caused it; it is always in fact *after*, and this necessary pause fractures the time of the photograph. Furthermore, it is not clear that the exposure is the *making* of a photograph, given all of the decisions, excisions, modifications and accidents that occur during processing and printing. Rather, it makes sense for the making to include all of the activity directed at producing and shaping the finished object. This expansion again shifts the signification of a photograph away from a single instant captured, towards understanding it as also constructed, as having content arising from these making activities – and thus with more than one footing in time. Besides this, there is the time of viewing the image, which will have a changing relationship to the times when it was taken or made: an arc that affects how those times are understood.

Such temporal complications affect the idea of the photograph as a document. As a consequence of the interval between event and image, a final print can only be verified against memory. Yet, the photographer generally remembers a segment of time *around* the brief moment of exposure, so the witnessed event is near to, but not the same as, the photographed event. This is disruptive if we interpret the pho-

11 The work records a performance with several protagonists, each with its own history of experience that bears on the collaborative actions.

12 This is the case even for instant photographs, like polaroids. The situation is slightly different for digital, but still there is processing that converts data into onscreen image, and that takes time, if only a fraction of a second. Printing, of course, takes longer and involves decisions.

tograph – the snapshot – as intended to capture the photographer's experience of place. It is as if there were a slight miscalibration embedded in the machinery: aim and capture standing adjacent to one another in time. Then we need to ask: to which event does the photograph refer, and how is it connected to it?

As we know, a photograph is (among other things) an index. It is a sign physically caused by what it represents.[13] Light reflected from the things that are in front of the camera enters the open shutter (over a brief period of time) and modifies the light-sensitive surface to form a picture. Because of this, the photographic image refers indexically to that which lay before the camera, at that time – the event. So far, so good. But the photograph also indexes other aspects of the process: it bears their traces, manifests their physical effects. These aspects include: the lens, the camera, and also, as has been noted by David Campany (2007), the viewpoint, and by Joel Snyder (2007), the light.[14] What leads us (as viewers and in theorising) to focus on the indexing of the *event*, is that the photograph usually also represents that event iconically, by resembling it (in certain respects, that we have learned to recognise) and symbolically, through our learned habits of reading photographs. These ways of being a sign – as index, icon and symbol – align, although they do so to varying extents. Some photographs require interpretation in order to resolve their subject matter, so that the icon is not always a reliable route to the index.

But let us return to time, and to how a photograph refers to time. The exposure of a photograph,[15] that interval of light, renders it an index of that particular moment (with all its mark-making components). However, the *print* is also marked by chemicals, containers and the agitation of them, dust, enlargers and masking frames, among other things, and so the print also indexes their times – the period of making. This is not just a distraction. There are photographic works in which the marks made by the process are not incidental, but are intended to point towards the subject, or one of the subjects, of the photograph (some are discussed here). And, of course, the index is not the photograph's only mode of signifying, so it can refer to times other than the moment of the exposure, through resemblance (consider Jeff Wall's restaging of historical battle scenes) or connotations (for instance, the kinds of *pastness* encoded in contemporary uses of early photographic techniques). As I argued above, there are at least three times that belong

13 Following Charles Sanders Peirce's three-part classification of signs. Signs are analysed as representing objects in three ways: as icon (likeness), index (caused by the referent), and symbol (conventional association) (Peirce 1885).

14 Campany writes that a photograph "is an indication of the presence of a vantage point" (2007: 312). Snyder (2007) argues against the idea that the index is useful in understanding photographs, since the indexing of photographs is promiscuous and settles nothing.

15 Although it is the negative, or a digital encoding, that is directly affected by the exposure.

to any photograph: the taking, the making, and the viewing. These times are, let's say, *mechanically* related to the photograph. And a plethora of further times may be referred to, encoded into the image by the photographer. We might call those times *intentionally* related. And these associations between times re-contour time in the photograph away from a linear scheme: forming jumps, crossings, ruptures, paradoxes, and loops.[16]

In the ongoing undulations of theory, the indexical aspect of photographs has been set up as their essence, dismissed, then reasserted as useful. Michael Leja suggests treating photographs, "like all signs", as mixtures of Peirce's three components, "but ones in which the relative proportion of indexicality is higher than usual" (2007: 206-7). This treatment of photos, he adds, encourages comparison with other visual traditions in which indexicality has a significant role, such as reliquaries or gestural abstract paintings. This is a treatment sympathetic to my interest in teasing out the commonalities between art forms, the areas of overlap and counterpoint that open onto some of the most interesting possibilities of the visual disciplines.

Drawings don't index in the same way that photographs are said to – they don't have the same *automatic* reference to a moment taken out of time. Yet equally, drawings can be primarily indexical. An example may help to activate this crossover area. Roger Ackling's drawings, such as *Voewood,* made with sunlight on found wood, are light-drawings, *phōtos-graphé,* new ancestors of photographs. Focusing the sun's rays with a magnifying glass, he would slowly burn small shapes and lines onto scraps of wood or card. Each shape is an index of the time he worked upon it, a measuring of his attention and of a ray of light. This gathering up of the light-ray marks the end of its long passage to earth; it makes the light solid, palpable as journey and substance. The drawings mark Ackling's time and deep time, the time of the solar system, onto the marginalia of everyday life. In their exploitation of semi-flat surfaces of objects – pieces and parts of artefacts, often not rectilinear – these drawings exceed the image-plane. They therefore sit ambiguously between drawings and sculptures-with-markings, which carry associations with ritual, and with older systems of cosmological understanding.

My group of drawings *Descending Order* refers indexically to the landscape of Assynt. The nine drawings were made using fallen twigs, collected in the woods by the Kirkaig river. Each twig in turn was broken and trimmed into a pen, used to draw the next. The order of the drawings maintains the found order as I came down the path, so as a sequence they suggest the composition of the northern Scottish woodland: the birch on the ridge, the hazel down by the riverside. The

16 Such re-shaped simultaneities can create, as Nancy Shawcross (2007: 210) offers from W G Sebald's *Austerlitz*: "various spaces interlocking according to the rules of a higher form of stereometry, between which the living and dead can move back and forth as they like" (261).

distribution of tree species is visible in the morphology of the twigs,[17] the ink colour, and also in the marks made by the whittled wood pens.

As each stick draws its neighbour, the drawings are interdependent, as trees in a wood are. The drawings represent in several ways: a part standing for a whole, analogy, mimetic resemblance, and the marks made by objects themselves. Each drawing is the direct marks of a stick, but because it is the one pictured in the previous drawing, icon and index are out of step. These two ways of referring to an object – by drawing it and drawing with it – thus tie each image to its neighbours to form an overlapping chain. The dislocation of icon from index is ordinary with drawings (and also happens with photographs[18]); rather it is the sharing of referent between one drawing (as icon) and the next (as index) that attaches the series together.

Figure 4: Aileen Harvey, *Descending order,* 2011

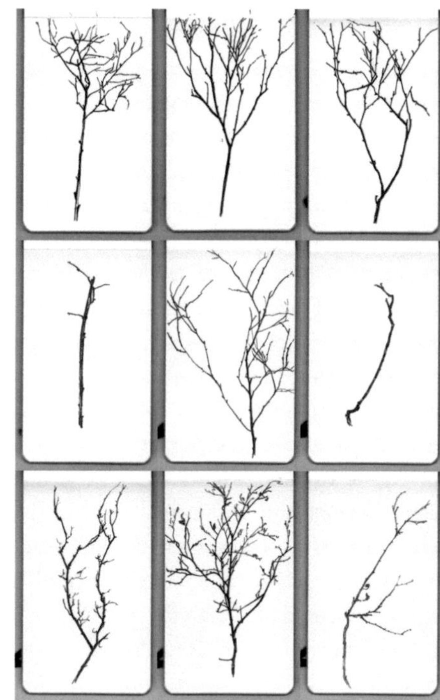

17 The shape of the drawn twigs shows both that birch branches differently from hazel, and that the birches are more twisted, through exposure to wind.

18 A drawing does not in general also index the same object it resembles, though clearly it can do so. A photograph, as I argue above, indexes other things than the view of which it is an icon.

The work borrows materials from the landscape, and also organisational principles – how the twigs are ordered in this place, how and where they grow and fall and are connected. The logic of the series is inter-reliance, both sympathetic and destructive. One stick must become compost so that the next may be drawn. Through these affinities between work and landscape, as well as the shared materiality, the times of drawing and those of woodland are interwoven.[19]

The group of drawings takes up these small things of the landscape, and gives them a role. It asks: what kind of pen does birchwood make, what sort of line? This sense of the landscape as active is part of an approach I have described more fully elsewhere as *dialogical*, in its focus on what happens as an exchange between person and place (2018). The dialogical approach to landscape relates back, too, to my earlier point about the document: that subjective encounters require grounding in material facts. Which is a point about mutual need, a point with two directions: a working process that attends to material specifics also needs the openings of subjectivity, the sense that all facts are partial. Here, a subjective viewpoint inheres in the gaps between the drawings, between the sticks – which are far too few to mimic a wood, even in miniature. Descending order is a fragmentary sequence. Considered in this way, it is a kind of index of the walked landscape, but an index like that of a book. It pulls out extracts, which point to the larger whole. The drawings begin from the concrete particular – these sticks, that day, where my feet fell – in order to form a dotted line that directs attention to the in-between and outside. Such an index indicates that which cannot be included in the pictures, but only gestured towards by the work: the four-dimensional life of the place.

Landscape drawings and photographs can generate images in which both indexicality and iconicity operate significantly. What is the effect of this on the time profile of a drawing? Within observational drawings, the shape of time is variously contoured by three primary processes: encountering a landscape, looking, and making. Perhaps drawings made *en plein air* form one baseline, where being there, observation, and drawing interleave and overlap within a single time frame. But consider the temporal gaps, loops and backtracks inherent in drawings where the resemblance to a place is based on photographs, visual memory, sketches, or collected objects – or arises from accumulated experience (and is thus not traceable to any particular impression or moment).

A series of drawings I have been making with collected earth pigments are concerned with these interactions of visual memory and time. Each drawing begins with a glimpse of a place. This is either a quick visual impression, or a snapshot, of a fleeting detail of landscape: a temporary form taken by water on a mountainside in northwest Scotland. Either way, the looking is a brief and small component of

19 For the drawings, the times of: walking and collecting; drawing and whittling; viewing. For the trees: growing; shedding and pollarding; felling and dying; rotting.

the encounter with the place – a moment spent gazing at a rivulet or a frozen puddle, within a day's climb and descent. A preliminary process of sketching and re-sketching then reduces visual memory or snapshot to an outline of form.[20] The final drawing is a tiled repeat of the outline, drawn on paper using pigments and stream water from the mountainside. Through the repetition of the motif, as a set of small gestures, over and over, the lines alter very slightly, being eroded as they are remembered. Repetition as an ambivalent force is well described by Briony Fer, who calls it "the very ground of consciousness". Repetition, she writes, "is a means of organising the world. It is a means of disordering and undoing." (2004: 2)

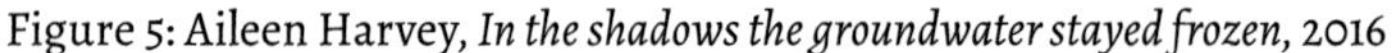

Figure 5: Aileen Harvey, *In the shadows the groundwater stayed frozen*, 2016

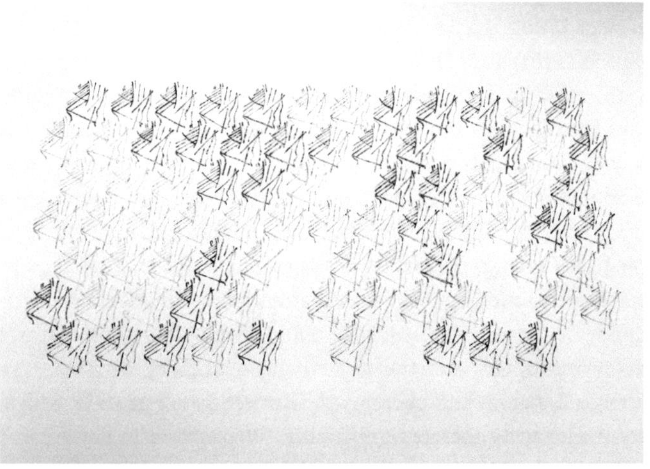

Drawing with repetition offers both construction and warping; it is a parallel for the changes made by memory, and also for weathering. Within the scope of a drawing, there are countable reiterations, and barely perceptible change. The small shifts nudge at an image that has already been thinned to abstraction.[21] The images are in the midst of becoming not-images: patterns, or glyphs. As the image-content is evacuated, the marks come to resemble writing. They seem transitory, their identity unfixed; they may not have finished evolving. Their nature as symbols is not clear. What is more, the motifs are parts of a larger composite something, a wandering

20 The making – both sketching and final drawing – are carried out in the studio, sometimes years later.

21 A side-note on balance: the abstraction of the visual image is a loss of information, a reduction in specificity and context. In compensation, the acknowledgement of a basis in subjective experience is transferred into the narrative content of the titles: *I wanted to call it meltwater, but really I think it was from the rain; and It was a long way down to the first break in the ice.*

shape which in some cases remains incomplete, a process interrupted. Landscapes, they suggest, are not finished, not objects, do not have a resolved shape.

The pigment colours belong to the mountains: pale orange and oxblood sandstone from Liathach; pink stone and dark peat from An Teallach. And the alternation of pigments within a drawing derives from a system, one that – by combining chance with a weighting against changing colour too often – structurally emulates a non-human process, geological or meteorological. Through using these substances, the drawings share the materiality of the landscape. This is partly a way of working between the micro and the macro: applying the forces of water and human reconfiguration to a teaspoonful of land. But it is also an indexical link back to the mountainside, a temporal shortcut that loops the other causal chain that attaches the drawing to the place: the looking, photographing, remembering, waiting, and drawing. The times that contour these drawings are those of physical presence – of the index – and of memory. And also the time of absence: of incompleteness and erasure, the forgotten and the not-yet.

Memory

In the desire to photograph, alongside the thought of an audience, there is a trying to hold on to something, and there is the futility of that. Photographs, especially snapshots, are closely involved in our cultural thinking about memory. As practical reminders, they perform the roles of prompts, corollaries, or affirmations for memories – but they can also shade into substitutes, overwriting and replacing the memories they once supported. The photograph is a frequent metaphor for the workings of memory, memory often understood as an image, one that is taken out repeatedly, that begins to wear and fade. It isn't clear how much insight this metaphor carries. It describes aspects of how we experience memory: the sense that the remembering process itself (like handling) polishes and smudges what it calls up. However, it privileges the visual, whereas memories tend to be all-encompassing and to incorporate a complex of sensations – famously responding with the most force to our sense of smell. Some memory experiences have little visual content, and might be better compared to, for example, finding a familiar object in a pocket with one's fingertips.

Instead, it may be that the photograph metaphor illuminates an *attitude* to memory: the desire for it to have a more solid and reliable form, to be less elusive. Yet there is something tenacious about the comparison. Perhaps the parallel between memory and snapshots is based less in the visual image than in a relationship to the past: a shared dynamic of holding-on and losing. A photograph is (among other things) an index of a moment; it cuts it from the flow of time and gives it image form. And yet that act of preservation is paradoxical. The image is not the moment, and it does not hold the moment still. The photograph, as Roland Barthes observed, represents the moment as both *here* (present to us) and *past* (gone): "an illogical conjunction of the *here* and the *formerly*" (1977: 44) – or in some cases, according to Thierry de Duve, "*now* and *there*" (2007 [1978]: 114).[22]

The dynamic of permanence and impermanence that belongs to photographs is very particular. A photograph appears to grasp a moment, one that has gone. The image seems to fix a lost moment in place, but it cannot do so, not only because of this impossibility of arresting the flow of time in an image – what de Duve calls "the photographic paradox" (2007 [1978]) – but further too, because the image itself is a material object, a thing that decays. In this double failure of the act of preservation, every photograph wears its transience, as a sensation of loss that is more pronounced as time passes. This perplexity about time – the assertion of *here* and the echo of *gone* – is the resonance of photographs; their allure and their poignancy.[23]

Ryan L. Moule's chemically unfixed photographs do something unexpected with time: they fade into obscurity as they are exhibited. Through not completing the printing process, Moule repositions his work in relation to the usual currency of photographs. Instead of preservation, they speak of fragility; instead of clarity and document, doubt and transformation. They do not have the usual hubris of photographs; they do not claim to hold anything still, and they themselves are vulnerable. They exaggerate the materiality of the image. The protection of UV glass, or red safelight, which slows their darkening, also underlines that vulnerability, that process of decline. Each viewer is complicit in the process – witness to an unrepeatable phase of the image and implicated in its condition and meaning. As the prints change, they continue to be made. Their meaning is hooked to the present as much as to the moment when the photograph was taken and so their temporal footing shifts: they refer to now and to then.

A drawing wears its own process of coming into being, but it does so more or less openly. Accumulated marks and areas left undrawn mean that the question of being finished or unfinished can be hard to resolve. A drawing's identity can easily remain fluid: just what it is at this point. Whereas most photographs conceal their made-ness; they project stability and completeness. In these photographs that wear openly their own process of coming into being, therefore, that awareness of flux is the more vivid because unexpected. Writing too tends to seem finished – consider the slightly surprising, irreverent feel of those poetry editions that reproduce older drafts, annotations and revisions. There is a permanence implicit in

22 De Duve's account of the photographic paradox is illuminating here. He locates the temporal meaning of photographs at the junction of two "series": the image-producing and the reality-produced (2007 [1978]: 111).

23 Qualities which individual photographs have in different balances.

the writing down of language, an end to its morphing in speech and thought. In that, it is an analogue of photography – with the diary form, like the snapshot, an everyday expression of the impulse to hold on, to remember.

Figure 6, Figure 7, Figure 8: Ryan L. Moule, *War of the Ghosts; Torn Negative; Fog Variation,* all from Vessels and Vestiges, 2017

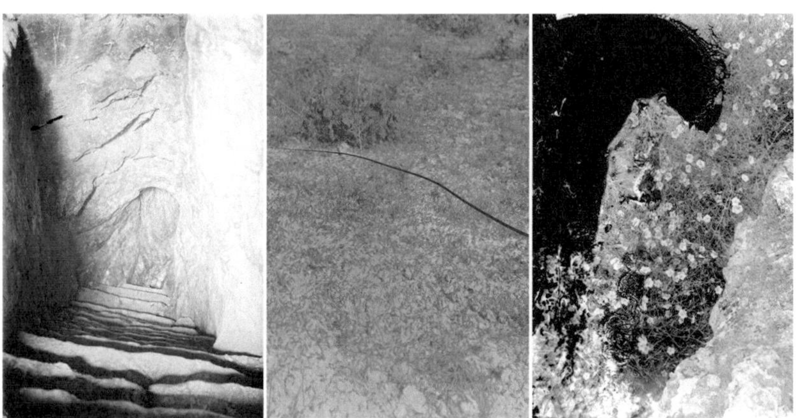

Roni Horn's large-scale pigment drawings are formed from intercut shards of paper. A complex and extended process of cutting, shifting, piecing, and re-piecing builds – or perhaps re-builds – a gigantic, meandering squiggle of saturated colour on an off-white paper ground. However the paper field around the pigment motif is not plain, not empty, but alive with a complicated network of cuts, marks, and writing.[24] Words, numbers, and syllables occur in doubles beside registration marks – so that the marks and notes align (and re-align) the paper sections. The written elements within a drawing are interlinked by playful associations and evolutions; they appear to have a history, an unfolding course like that of a game.

There is an unstable contrast between the dense, snaking currents of varnished pigment and the smaller, fainter annotations in pencil and coloured pencil. Although the pigment dominates, it is the activity of the ground that moves the drawing, and that unifies it, through its breaking and restructuring of the forms. The pigment forms are loose and convoluted, as well as refracted, shattered, and interrupted. Segments seem to be missing; shards of new paper added in. These are not exactly images, rather they are suggestive, in both form and process, of metamorphosis in landscape: eruption, sedimentation, erosion, and schism. The human body is also there. Horn's movements of hand, eye, and thought, over time,

24 For a detailed discussion of this animation of the paper ground, see Briony Fer's essay on the pigment drawings (2013: 8).

are in the erasures, incidental smears, and language accumulated on the surface, in the mix of care and spontaneity – and the full reach of her body is vivid in the sheer size of the drawing. These drawings are thick with tactility. Finger-dirtied, sharply grooved, neatly aligned, textured with pigment, they activate the haptic, making seeing vibrate with touch. By these formal relationships, both landscape and body are implicated in the drawings' processes of dismantling, interspersal, and formation.

The cuts, the marks, the notes, record the progress of a drawing, from intact sheet to this chosen stopping point. Forming a map and mnemonic of fractures and displacements, the drawing dangles the hope of orientation, retracing, maybe even *undoing* – but there is no way back. The grubbiness of the paper, the removed material, the many ambiguities, and the dizzying proliferation of cuts, make that impossible. This final state of the drawing is just a pause in the flow – a pause that punctuates the flow, and so underlines time, alteration, and contingency as the state of things.

Memory, temporary and faltering though it may be, is basic to identity, to the continual work-in-progress that is being something. A landscape remembers, in that it continues to enact its own pasts, in layers, striations and scars. The evolving identities of people and places are best understood not as separate phenomena, but as continuous with one another. Nor should the natural and cultural aspects of either be considered separately: these dualisms mislead. Places and people are inseparable within a reciprocal process of becoming, of forming one another. That process works in part through the sedimentation of memory. Landscapes shape us through our living in them, our accumulated bodily experiences of place. They are a repository of time and recollections (theirs, ours, and others). And they are themselves multiple, contradictory, and continually reconfigured – both materially and in the stories we tell about them. Memory is woven into these natural-cultural dynamics that belong to inhabited landscapes: of stability and alteration, shaping and re-shaping.

It is in thinking about landscape in this way, as a matter of physical memory, that *inscription* makes sense as a term for the common ground between photography, drawing and writing. Inscription connects to the practices of recording and remembering through which the discussion has travelled. Additionally, it offers an escape from the image plane, by conveying the idea of marks that penetrate *within* an object. Such markings transform, rather than lying upon the surface. The active physicality of 'inscription', in contrast with the similar term 'imprint', allows for multiple ascriptions of agency, and therefore for the reciprocity of draughting a landscape and a landscape making its own marks.[25]

25 Even in the formulation "the landscape imprints itself", imprint tends towards an idea of the landscape as inactive, an object that at most leans itself heavily against a surface.

In-between

The experience of being in a place is bodily and motile, and it is an exchange, something that happens *between* people and places. Relatedly, liminal (in-between) states are distinctive of being in a place, not just picturing it. Real experience is blended. It is a meeting point, where senses mix, and self and world are folded together. This fluid combining in time asks to be recorded with methods that share its hybridity, that do not simply picture.

Thinking about images that are not pictures led to my making the text work *Mostly water*. It deals with the in-between: a watery land, and images that exist only in language, in communication. The work is a sequence of eighteen handwritten texts on postcards. The cards were sent to a friend back home, during an 18-day walk along the length of the Outer Hebrides. I wrote one card each day of the journey, and posted it from the first box we passed. On the card's face, where a photograph would usually be, there is instead a written observation relating to water in some form: the sound of the sea, waterlilies, sudden rain, puddles, wet socks, waterlogged ground. Replacing pictures with text, the cards follow the practice of sending picture-postcards, but the written images have a different kind of life from that of a photograph.

Figure 9: Aileen Harvey, *Mostly water 03062010*, 2010

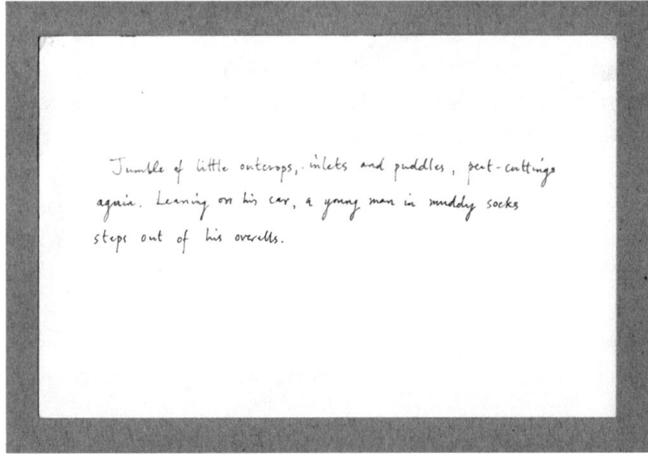

These cards are communicative acts – they form a monologue, admittedly, but it is *for* a particular recipient; it happens between two people. The project considers how experiences of place are passed on, and it reflects the social landscape of the

Western Isles, where the post is so prominent.[26] Water is the focus, because water is the shape offered by the landscape. Maps of the archipelago show more water than land, much of it within the outlines of the islands. And, of course, we humans are mostly water too. In the form of water, Astrida Neimanis writes, we leak into the world and it soaks into us, sharing our substance, participants in a network of hydrological cycles, as "a more-than-human hydrocommons" (2017: 2). Restricting the subject matter of the postcards is a means to encourage quiet attention in the making process – to leave a small gap in which unexpected things can surface. The framework, of water, day intervals, and the post, creates a sequence of systematic extracts. It generates an index, marked by the place and its mechanisms, as well as my handwriting. As with *Descending order,* the sequence is fragmentary. It leaves out more than it includes, pointing to the space-time between and around the cards, between and around the postboxes. Its meaning is networked across the whole sequence; it is not to be found in any one card, but in their repetition with difference. In being mostly water, the cards become less about water, more about noticing other things. Each card narrates something selected from my experience of the landscape – a wet something, each wet in a different way. The texts are descriptive – they emphasise the image-quality of the event – but these being written images, the visual arrives in a composite state, mixed with other sensory aspects, and with stories, thoughts, or social interactions.[27]

Donald Urquhart's *Ornithology* is a set of ten paintings that describe birdsong. Dark grey canvases are inscribed with text in a lighter grey, extracts from an old verbal transcription of the songs of Highland birds – for example: 'a scolding "churr" and an excited "tek, tek".' The painted text is both writing and image, not through creating images from words, but in being an image of writing. The draughting is austere, precise, but still painterly and plainly handmade. In shape the letters resemble short-run typewritten print, suggestive of the source material (a 1920s handbook). These poised formal qualities (citation/worked surface; printed/by hand) reinforce the poetics of the original writing, both warmly colloquial and sharply observed.[28] The paintings depict written words as objects, and they also use the words as symbols, as language. In use, the words invoke sounds – sounds that describe a place in a codified way. They describe an aspect of the aural life of a landscape, and a cultural form of that birdsong within human language and practices.[29] In these

26 Post boxes and small post offices are numerous, and are a key part of life for the more isolated Hebridean communities.

27 This immersion in the world, characteristic of real experience, is made more noticeable by the activity of walking.

28 Cf. Macmillan 1998: no page numbers.

29 That cultural form appears to embrace both folk familiarity and modern ornithology. The texts are transcriptions made with a particular phonetic profile – in which locale is embedded – and

text paintings, nature and culture are not separable. The paintings happen between human language and birdsong, between seeing and hearing, between image and text, and between times (of coining the descriptions and of painting – plus that of viewing). Further, Urquhart has talked about dialogue as a defining relation in his work, which arises through "laying [...] documentation against a more formal aspect of the practice" (2012: 2). This dialogue creates a space for accuracy to combine with sympathy – a movement played out here in the delicate handling of the paint, and repeated too in the (inherited) tone of the text. Within this doubled movement there lies a thoughtful attention to landscape, a stance that is characteristic of Urquhart's practice. Duncan Macmillan describes it as "profound emotional engagement" and "the authority of experience" (1998: no page numbers).

Figure 10: Donald Urquhart, *Ornithology*, 1997

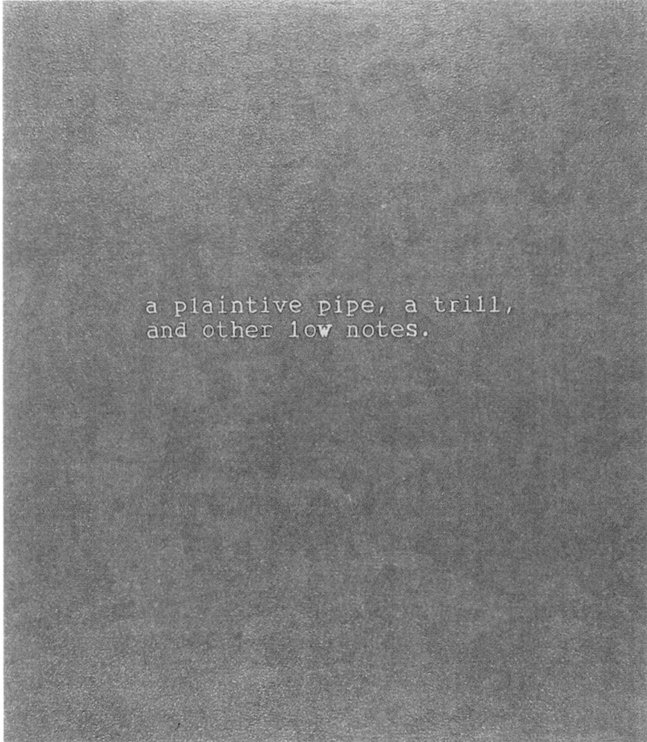

are modified by descriptive elements, which in their anthropomorphic notes („scolding", „plaintive") might seem old-fashioned. In these socio-linguistic aspects, the words have been shaped by a place and a time.

There is something in Urquhart's precise and muted tonality that expresses a receptive quiet – it is the self-restraint of the genuinely attentive. In other works from this period this attention takes the form of complete absorption in observing light and dark in the landscape: shapes and tones shadowed in graphite drawn onto photographs, and repeated in grey painted panels. For me these modes of engagement connect – albeit perhaps only loosely – with a point Elizabeth Helsinger has made about how landscapes work in poetry. She argues that literary landscapes often do not work through visual description, but by evoking the effects of a place on a perceiver. Landscapes, she writes, "shape and pattern [a beholder] through sensation and feeling" (2008: 335). In that spirit too, is a final example: Roni Horn's *You are the weather*, a hundred photographs that record the fleeting expressions of Icelandic weather in a young woman's face. They record near-imperceptible variations and shifts: the precise subtleties that photographs register so well, and that humans are so adept at seeing in other human faces. At the same time, these are photographs of something that is more than physical – something that is also a question of interpretation and metaphor. What is documented here is a phenomenon that blurs inner and outer life: the landscape inscribed in us. Both portrait and landscape, reality and metaphor, Horn's images also demonstrate the continuum of genre, and the artifice inherent in all such categorisation (however useful those categories are).

Conclusion

The sense, to be found in these latter works, of landscape written into us, shading us, patterning us, is a qualification of the thought that places escape from us, are fundamentally unrecordable. Here, perhaps, is a way to think about memory – not as some *thing* that holds events still, but as a tenuous grasp, a movement absorbed. In our flesh, our ambits, our narratives, places alter us, as we reciprocally rewrite them.

This chapter began with ideas traced through works in my landscape practice: thoughts about changeable qualities of place, about photographic (and non-photographic) accuracy, remembering, and the shape ascribed to time. These thoughts offered ways to see a network of overlapping abilities amongst photographs, drawn marks, and words, and so to ask, what can be said with these methods, about places and our encounters with them?

The *River/water/colour* drawings respond to flaws in the notion of the photograph as ideal document, by attempting to record the inconstancy of river colours, the colours that arise between the singular, never to be repeated set of person-place-time. Automatic accuracy does not in fact belong to photographs, and to idealise this model of a transcendent, mechanical eye is pernicious. Far from producing the ideal document, clean of perspective and subjective determinations, automatic accuracy is a way to render invisible those stances, preferences and assumptions that frame every image. Thinking with Donna Haraway's concept of feminist objectivity, we find the need, not only to include positioning in our models of understanding and documentation, but also to become "answerable for what we learn how to see" (1988: 583). This is an active and committed openness to the perspectives of others, human and non-human, and it refines my commitment to a principle of dialogue, to materially grounding the subjective, through her invitation "to join with another, to see together, without claiming to be another" (ibid: 586).

The index, as an approach to making, could be understood as a momentary joining with another, to make a mark – one that is particular, physical, and located in time. The indexical mark may be made by light (as Ackling's pyrography), substance (earth pigments, or the sticks of *Descending order*), or both (Clew's photograms), producing drawings, drawing-writing hybrids, photographs, or activating the marked surface into sculpture. In these indices are made a series of snapshots, isolated moments in which the subjective self (with its mobile positioning) is coupled to the world. These joinings form a dotted line, like footprints and gaps, a metaphor in which we might choose to see the value of balance and grace, and of treading lightly. This principle of balance, of to-and-fro, can be tracked through shifting formats and contexts

The motif of the photographic snapshot in its relation to memory – and to the Western cultural shape of memory – emphasises a dynamic of holding on and letting go. This movement is of course not limited to photographs. In the postcard diary *Mostly water* we find an index of written snapshots that express this same periodic rhythm of memorialisation. The work responds to what happens in-between person and place, as well as to the hybrid liminality of both participants, to the flow-between that joins substances. A serial index, a set of extracts/recordings, is a network that does not contain, yet catches up the outside, the other.

The examples discussed through the course of this chapter are drawings, photographs or texts; they share characteristics – including gesture, indexicality, the urge to document, poetics, fragility, or pronounced materiality. But also, they often take shape *in relation* to other art forms. Within this territory there is overlap, but also counterpoint, exception, qualification, and parallel – not simply ambiguity (is this a drawing or a text?) but reciprocal reshaping that inflects each form in the pairing. This making approach itself can be seen as signifying, as mirroring an attitude to landscape. In these interstices between disciplines – in drawn or written snapshots, in photographic gestures, or text-filled drawings – there is a not-taking-for-granted, a side-stepping of expectations, that expresses fluidity and reciprocity. This in turn, allows the fluid and reciprocal aspects of landscape to be emphasised; it makes more apparent the exchanges, transformations and elisions involved in an encounter with landscape – the fundamental in-betweenness of it all.

Inscription is not the perfect word for these works – it might be better to make a new one up[30] – but the term does make room for thinking of memory in physical terms, and for process and mutuality. Used to speak about photography, drawing and writing, it points towards their shared capacities for texture, movement, and alteration. Capacities, I would argue, that are particularly vivid in the space that is activated between the disciplines. These and related features enable artworks to show landscapes in ways that move beyond such arbitrary limitations as picturing, flatness, fixity and the dominance of the visual – limits which distort landscapes and our relationship to them.

The reflective strategy adopted for this chapter – of exploring lines of argument mainly through my own practice – was intended to help theory and making develop together. As I hoped, exploring this process has led to some degree of the unanticipated in my conclusions both theoretical and practical. It has connected thoughts – about memory and movement – that seemed distinct, and ways of working that seemed unrelated. And it has illuminated questions from different sides. Research has suggested ways that structures of rationality may be shifted towards a feminist epistemology, and I have found openings and routes for developing new work.[31] This is encouraging. It is consonantly clear that a thorough engagement with the central thought-strands of this chapter would require a wider, less personal approach – this would need to be more structured and systematic.

References

Brett, David (1989): "Landscape." In Circa 43, pp. 14-18.

Campany, David (2007): "A Few Remarks on the Lens, the Shutter, and the Light-Sensitive Surface." In: James Elkins (ed.), Photography Theory, New York: Routledge, pp. 304-313.

de Duve, Thierry (1978): "Time Exposure and Snapshot: the Photograph as Paradox." In October 5 (Summer 1978), pp. 113-25. Reprinted in: James Elkins (ed.), Photography Theory, New York: Routledge, pp. 109-123.

30 Or perhaps to borrow one, though neither of these options is always a good idea. However, Gerald Manley Hopkins coined the term "inscaping" to describe the experienced textures of landscape and their expression in poetry, and it might be productive to borrow this invented term, as it does a lot of what I am looking for. Cf. Helsinger 2008: 334-336.

31 In part this has happened through recognising unnecessary circumscriptions of my making – this being the other side of seeing continuities where before the differences dominated.

Emerling, Jae (2012): Photography: History and Theory, London and New York: Routledge.

Fer, Briony (2013): "The Pigment Drawings." In Roni Horn, 153 Drawings, Zurich: JRP | Ringier.

Haraway, Donna (1988): "Situated Knowledges: The science question in Feminism and the privilege of partial perspective." In Feminist Studies Vol. 14, No. 3, pp. 575-599.

Helsinger, Elizabeth (2008): "Blindness and Insights." In Rachel Ziady DeLue/James Elkins (eds), Landscape Theory, New York: Routledge, pp. 323-342.

Leja, Michael (2007): "Index Redux." In: James Elkins (ed.), Photography Theory, New York: Routledge, pp. 206-07.

Macmillan, Duncan (1998): "The Grey Scale." In Donald Urquhart, Grey Weighted Notes, Stornoway: An Lanntair/Edinburgh: Talbot Rice Gallery.

Massey, Doreen (2005) For Space, London: Sage.

Neimanis, Astrida (2017): Bodies of Water, London: Bloomsbury Academic.

Peirce, Charles Sanders (1885): "One, Two, Three: Fundamental Categories of Thought and of Nature." In: Christian Kloesel et al. (eds), The Writings of Charles S. Peirce, Bloomington: Indiana University Press, 1980-2000, vol 5.

Plumwood, Val (1993): Feminism and the Mastery of Nature, London: Routledge.

Sebald, W G (2001): Austerlitz, trans. A Bell, London: Hamish Hamilton.

Shawcross, Nancy (2007): "Seeing is Believing: An Afterword on Photography." In: James Elkins (ed.), Photography Theory, New York: Routledge, pp. 208-10.

Snyder, Joel (2007): "Pointless." In: James Elkins (ed.), Photography Theory, New York: Routledge, pp. 369-385.

Urquhart, Donald (2012): "Interview with Anne Douglas." August 2012 (https://ontheedgeresearch.files.wordpress.com/2013/05/donald-urquhart-interview.pdf).

Wells, Liz (2011): Land Matters: Landscape photography, culture and identity, London: I.B. Tauris.

Distanced visuality, embodied proximity? Literary and photographic images of Finnish travel landscapes from the premodern journey to the railway era

Mikko Itälahti

Overview

This chapter investigates representations of the environmental experience of premodern road and early railway travel in literary descriptions, contrasting them with the aesthetic visions of the early railway in landscape photography. This historical material, from the 1880s to the 1930s, spans the eras before and after the construction of the Savo railway, Eastern Finland. The chapter situates this material in a temporal and geographical context, compiling it into an emotional heritage 'atlas' – necessarily partial but capable of evolving – of the travel landscape around the town of Kuopio.

This work is situated within a broadly materialist-realist ontology. Within such an approach, representations of places and landscapes, especially photographs, can be understood as mediums making a genuine and authentic connection with non-human material environments possible, through a capacity to evoke experience-based imagination through visual memories and encounters with similar environments. Thus, the idea of detached, disembodied visuality, also inherent in historically dominant models of representing the landscape, is challenged.

The exploration initially draws from the concept of proximity and the arguments of Finnish geographer J.G. Granö and German cultural historian Wolfgang Schivelbusch, both of whom, within different disciplinary contexts, employ the concept to signify the centrality of spatial nearness, closeness or immediacy to a subject's experience of the environment and as enabling the production of sensations of actuality, of truly 'being there'. In this discussion the notion of proximity is used to explore, firstly, the transformation of landscape experience that occurred in the wake of the mobility revolution caused by the construction of the railway in Savo province, eastern Finland, drawing in particular on the writing of Finnish novelist Juhani Aho, whose reminiscences about premodern travel show a world in which spatial immediacy was central to the apprehension of the environment. Secondly, the chapter discusses changes in the experience of space: the premodern traveller apprehended places through proximate sensations and through a necessarily active 'negotiation' with environmental conditions and various social situations, but this was no longer possible in the railway era.

In particular, Schivelbusch applies the concept of foreground to the changing experience of landscape brought about by the railway. Railway travel largely eradicated sensations borne of immediacy, effectively pictorializing the landscape: surroundings formerly experienced through all of the senses and active participation, were now increasingly encountered as 'external' visual impressions; for those who experienced premodern travel, landscape now involved existential distance with a corresponding reduction in the significance of the foreground. Yet, a widely accepted view maintains that landscape, as perceived within the popular imagination, was borne from movement and a sense of detachment from premodern, organic 'place', thus suggesting that railway effectively participated in the creation of landscape in this modern sense. Perception of the distant landscape from the train window is thus comparable to popular imagery, and the form of its aesthetic appreciation is influenced by models derived from the visual arts. Also in popular imagination, a canonical system of ideal landscape representations, with classicist roots, was dominant. This inclination towards scenic topographic variation and waterway views effectively diminished the aesthetic value of most of the 'in-between' landscape of modern travel. The images of the railway in the work of Finnish landscape photographers seem especially interesting against this background of pictorialization of landscape and the erosion of the foreground. The main argument developed in the latter part of the chapter is strongly inspired by Schivelbusch's claim that one reason for photography's historical success and miraculous sense of wonder was its ability to re-evoke the foreground eradicated by the industrial revolution.

Earliest, albeit aesthetically motivated, photographs of the Savo railway leaned towards the topographical documentation of technological structures. The photographic representations of the railway were not without contradiction and complexity, however. They reflect photographers' enthusiasm for their subjects, while also revealing the extent of the human-induced modification of pristine environments, uncovering structures normally invisible to the railway passenger, and drawing aesthetic and cognitive attention to the resources underpinning the railway passenger's experience (Barsokevitsch). Some images attempted, with growing difficulty, to achieve, symbolically, a balance between the inherent value of the tranquility of the backwoods and a celebration of the industrial progress of the nation represented in the building of the railway (Inha). Although photographic representations of the railway as a landscape element took a plurality of new forms, they were all influenced by canonical models of landscape representation. Probably the inclination of photographers towards the scenic in their representation of the railway as a spatial and material phenomenon reflects this convention; this type of pictorialism was prevalent in landscape representations more generally in the late 19th century.

Yet still, through their affective power, railway photographs suggest an adjustment and expansion of the canonical models of seeing and appreciating towards the inclusion of the modern everyday landscape. Each of these broadly pictorialist or picturesque photographic views reintroduced the foreground as a picturesque element of composition. Foreground composition constituted a familiar viewer's position, contributing to the visual affectivity of the images. And eventually, towards the end of 19th century, the railway itself become increasingly framed as a picturesque element, suggesting that the railway, too, could be a familiar, harmonious component of a modern cultural landscape. From around the turn of the 20th century, there was an increasing elevation of the railway itself to the foreground of the landscape, echoing the romantic trope of picturesque roadside views and evoking, visually, the proximity of the old premodern roadside.

In the imagery corpus of the Finnish railways a partial turn away from pictorialism can be identified in the interwar period. Especially in the 1930s there is a great expansion and thematic diversification of the imagery. In the work of industrial photographer Gustav Rafael Roos there is no longer any attempt to interpret the railway landscape through a pastoral lens, rather it emphasizes the modern machinery and technological equipment in the foreground, thus giving material, tangible and technological objects a very acute sense of presence through representation.

It is argued that the special significance of railway landscape photography was – following Schivelbusch – its capability to restore the material closeness of the environment in the field of vision, especially in the case of the foreground, which may evoke a strong sense of environmental closeness, involving an almost tactile and multisensory presence of objects. This is significant, because images thus possess a potential to challenge the limited scope of canonical models of seeing and appreciating the landscape, by affectively and performatively promoting an aesthetic sensibility in relation to the modern everyday landscape.

It may indeed be the case that certain historical views actually reflect a conscious 'therapeutic' attempt to constitute a revival of the spatial proximity photographers felt was lost in the era of industrial modernity. Historically, the performative potential of these images to challenge aesthetic conventions still remained largely unrealized, due, for example, to the limited public presence of these images. Yet, in the present, they still exhibit a distinctive affective power – independent of photographers' intentions – stemming from their material nature as a traces of environments that once were 'before the lens', but that are now lost as a consequence of transformational processes shaping the everyday landscape.

Premodern experience of proximity

The town of Iisalmi is located approximately 90 kilometres north of Kuopio, the capital of Savo Province, in the east of Finland. Both locations are connected by the extensive, interconnected system of navigable lake waterways, reaching out to most parts of the region. A network of steamship services had developed in the Kuopio area since the mid-19th century. However, roughly from November to May, the lakes are covered by thick ice, preventing ships from sailing. Before the railway from Kuopio to Iisalmi was opened in 1902, winter travel still relied extensively on horse-drawn sleigh.

In his novel *Kotipuoleni rautatie* (Aho 1929 [1917]), a prominent Finnish author Juhani Aho (1861-1921) reminisces about the wintry sleigh journeys from his home in Iisalmi to Kuopio. Juhani Aho – a priest's son, from Iisalmi parsonage – probably first made this journey in 1872, when he had begun at the secondary school in Kuopio. As the one-way sleigh journey between Kuopio and Iisalmi took about one and a half days, he spent the whole term mainly in Kuopio, travelling back to his childhood home only for Christmas and summer holidays. That the experience of proximity was central to the geographical space of the journey is clearly established in his account of a sleigh journey:

> The slow movement was optimal for impressing upon the mind all of the houses and the landscapes at the roadside; every bend, up or downhill, bridge, brook, lake, field, forest, pine stand, house and croft prompted memories and feelings from one's own life, producing sensations of joy, sorrow, pleasure or disgust, depending on the weather and conditions, or whether the journey was bound to home or school... Most memorable of the horse-feeding places was the Honkaniemi house in Lapinlahti, where the winter road went through the yard, coming from the rugged pine heath, past the windmill of the house, whose whistling sails almost always frightened the horses (Aho 1929 [1917]: 330, translated by the author).

Aho's description vividly evoking the details of the roadside close-by is comparable to Wolfgang Schivelbusch's (1980 [1977]: 65) discussion of the foreground as "the range in which most of the experience of preindustrial travel was located", a formulation bearing a striking resemblance to that of Finnish Geographer J.G. Granö, who writes that "proximity is a close, intimate world we always inhabit and the context in which we perceive our geographical object with all our senses" (Granö 1997[1929]: 18). According to the classic theory presented by Granö, objects are visually perceived more or less "life-size" and "in perspective" within this proximate field of vision (ibid.). Proximity is thus central to the subject's experience of the environment, producing sensations of actuality, of truly 'being there'. According to Granö a multisensory experience of proximity clearly surrounds us up to the distance of 20 meters (65 ft.). Schivelbusch (1980 [1977]: 59) makes a very similar claim by adding that within the foreground the "Newtonian" qualities of discrete objects (like size, shape and quantity) can be appropriately and clearly perceived.

Embeddedness

For Aho, the immediacy of the spatial experience can be found in close sensations of the body: he especially laments waking up early in the dark, bitterly cold winter mornings and departures "in the glow of the pallid morning moon". The sensations of winter coldness are, however, counterbalanced by pleasant warmth near the stoves of the roadside houses (Aho 1929 [1917]: 331-332). Aho pictures the pre-modern journey as a spatial event within which one is not an onlooker but definitely an active participant. The sensory experiences of proximity are intertwined with an existential condition of embeddedness in a regional socio-ecological system centred around travel. Roadside houses served as lunch shelters and feeding stops for horses, inhabited by friendly and close folks "who were like family members" (ibid.).

All his memories are far from being positive. For example, the overpass of the central Kallavesi straits, just north of Kuopio, was across potentially dangerous ice. Yet he still acknowledges the extent to which the successful completion of the journey required active negotiation with physical and social space and linked the individual passenger with regional socio-ecological space:

> [A]ll this [difficulties and uncertainties related to sleigh travel] was pertinent, so closely associated with the ways of living and being, that it is difficult to think of it as changed. And yet it is just a memory, a turned page in the history of a community's everyday life. It is a whole world that is now gone, with its well-organized customs and practices, and I would like to add, with its ideas as well. For such external upheavals change much of life's content too (Aho 1929 [1917]: 333).

Landscape

Also for Granö, the actual landscape is now characterized by separation and distance. He argues that "[t]his arena of our lives and activities is surrounded by the distant environment, or landscape, nothing more than a field of vision more or less tinged with blue by the air". (Granö 1997[1929]: 18). According to Granö, the landscape only begins beyond a fuzzy transitional zone separating it from the area of closer proximity, the inner boundary of which, in contrast to the more distant landscape, is hard to define, but as a general rule it is located at least at the distance of 100-200 meters from the observer (Granö 1997 [1929]: 52, 110-111).

It is clear that in this sense the landscape is not central to the premodern journey as described by Juhani Aho. His attention is directed to the distant landscape only occasionally. He, for example, mentions a special moment of pleasure when "we have arrived on top of a ridge, with a view to Nilsiä's [a neighbouring parish] bare-sloped hills gilded by the sunrise [...] and the road is downhill for several miles..." (Aho 1929[1917]: 332). Even such landscape observation is not a spatially 'detached' impression, as the premodern passenger was always embedded in proximity to his or her immediate vicinity. The foreground links him or her to the surrounding landscape through a sense of being 'there' at a certain location (Schivelbusch 1980[1977]: 65, 60-61). In similar vein, Timo Kalanti (2014: 43) writes of the experience of proximity as an "uncompromising massiveness of material presence", that always surrounded the premodern traveller and contributed to the heightened sense of location.

Railway and the loss of proximity

Premodern and recent travel experience are often strongly contrasted in the early descriptions of the railway journey. The very earliest of these frequently lament the alienating 'placelessness' of railway spaces – i.e. stations and railway carriages – themselves, as well as the unsympathetic, alienating sense of 'being transported' during the passage. Early Finnish examples of the trope include Zachris Topelius' *Mirabeau-täti* (Topelius 1910 [1863]) and Juhani Aho's *Rautatie* (Aho 1884). Aho looks back to his first journey on the Iisalmi-Kuopio railway in around 1902:

> I however must admit that the first ride on the Iisalmi railway gave me a strange, almost haunted impression.... [The station] does not have the slightest local colour, not a single old memory in those new rooms, everything just new. And the train compartment has the same universal atmosphere, the same sizzling warmth of the iron stove (Aho 1929 [1917]: 334).

It is well documented how many early passengers – unaccustomed to the new speed scale of the railway – could at first only see a blurred impression of a passing landscape (e.g. Solnit 2003: 9, 21). In contrast to many early descriptions of the train journey, Aho does not mention this problem, although the details he does give are clearly located further out in the landscape. As the railway in this section closely follows the old road, he is able to see the meaningful landmarks of the roadside; but they are out there, as if belonging to some other world:

> But out *there* [emphasis added] is the old road that the train crosses all the while. Its every bend is familiar, every tree, every fence. The Koivikko house flashed by right there, there is the Kallio house, over there the Peltosalmi crossroad... There the old innkeeper stands at the platform [at Pöljä stop] and watches this new going... (Ibid).

Panoramic vision

The railway rendered the landscape in a new way. The difficulty in perceiving the near foreground resulted from the combination of the train's speed and the fact that a passenger typically only has a view sideways to the direction of movement. In order to see anything, passengers needed to learn to focus on slower moving objects further out (Schivelbusch 1980 [1977]: 59). Schivelbusch emphasizes that as soon as the early passengers learned to give up trying to perceive the foreground details, but instead focused on general impressions or on more distant objects, a new way of seeing the landscape called panoramic vision evolved (ibid: 63-66). Schivelbusch argues that a panoramic vision "choreographs the landscape" and displays a fleeting, cubist assemblage of "objects and pieces of scenery that in their original spatiality belonged to separate realms" (ibid: 66).

Aho was already an experienced train traveller at the time of writing Kotipuoleni rautatie, the novel extensively quoted above (Aho 1929 [1917]). However, he deeply felt that the railway had caused a loss of the lived space of *his* roadside, personally meaningful through long-standing participation; he seemed reluctant to exchange existential embeddedness for a merely visual image of the landscape and his new position as a mere paying customer. Interestingly, he had already given a very aesthetic account of the panoramic vision as a young man in a much earlier novel, *Rautatiejunassa* first published in 1889:

> The ugliness of landscapes along our railways has become proverbial... But all this ugliness, dullness and melancholy does not feel like what you would expect, when the spectator sits in a second-class coach, enjoying a sweet-smelling cigar. As each location only momentarily stays under the gaze, when they know that they don't have to stay there, but may keep flying forward, ugly seems beautiful and dull makes a refreshing effect. Instead of melancholy, it is as if a cloak of secure well-being is being wrapped around one's shoulders. (Aho 1929[1889]: 358-359, translated by the author.)

The difference with Aho's description of his first journey on the Iisalmi railway is obvious: in *Rautatiejunassa* he is enjoying impressions of landscapes with which he had no previous lived connection. Indeed, a 'disinterested' attitude or some kind of distancing from routine and the everyday flow of events has often been stressed as the necessary condition for the paradigmatic aesthetic experience (Saito 2007: 244, Tuan 1993: 8-9). Arguably, the train passenger's condition of transported immobility – using the term proposed by Kalanti (2014: 40-41) – and a degree of isolation from the harsh conditions also affecting premodern road travel, may have provided favourable conditions for modes of reception and aesthetic enjoyment produced through the image-like impressions of panoramic vision.

Pictorialization of landscape

In the wake of industrialisation a mobility revolution pioneered by the railway occurred, leading to the democratization of travel. Following this it became commonplace for people to encounter regions as visual impressions. Modern spatial consciousness became increasingly formed through physical surfaces seen through the train window, and in the popular imagination these became effectively likened to and linked with pictorial representations of landscapes whose circulation was also booming (Häyrynen 2005: 59, 62-64, Wells 2013: 6). This process could be termed the modern transformation of land to landscape. Indeed, a certain existential distance, a sense of 'otherness', seems necessary for a landscape to be landscape (i.e. Sepänmaa 2000). Thus, movement, a departure from somewhere, is a necessary precondition for this distance and, therefore, for landscape. Thus, it appears that loosening of human bonds with the local soil and the mass-democratization of mobility facilitated by the railway, effectively promoted the creation of landscape in a modern sense. And yet the landscape of popular imagination was still impregnated with a nostalgic sense of loss and a misconceived desire to 'return' to premodern, organic 'place' (Wylie 2016).

The visualization of the world and the assimilation of landscape and imagery, however, also meant that popular ideas within which landscapes could be seen as worthy of aesthetic appreciation became increasingly informed by a more limited notion of the beautiful landscape. Yuriko Saito points towards the obvious problem that results:

> The general public tends to be more attracted to the unfamiliar and spectacular... we tend to admire those landscapes which can be made into a nice picture, but remain indifferent to other parts of nature which do not lend themselves to a nice pictorial composition due to a lack of sufficient complexity, variety, harmony or eye-catching features (Saito 2007: 61).

Model images for Western Culture's admiration of landscape derive from South European landscapes and their traditional representations. Thus, a preference for clearly defined and easily image-able landscape spaces, comprised of large-scale topographic variations of hills and valleys is evident (cf. Norberg-Schulz 1980 [1979]: 46-48). In Finnish landscape imagery, the 19th century European idea of the picturesque landscape, materialized in the form of the so-called "Topelian" landscape canon, first proposed by Zachris Topelius, publisher of an influential collection of lithographs, Finland framställdt I teckningar (1845-1852) (cf. Häyrynen 2005, Linkola 2013, Vallius 2013). According to art historian Antti Vallius (2013), in its most fundamental form this ideal landscape is represented as a view from a prominent hilltop, looking over a mosaic of lakes and forests. In a later phase, more signs of cultural influence became incorporated into this model of ideal landscape, although the 'pristine nature' that frames and supports the 'progress' of human culture remains elementary. The model has been very popular in Finland, even though a traveller encounters wide, open vistas of large-scale variation only very occasionally in such predominantly forested countries where a closed proximate view – in Granö's terms – of the forest interior prevails. In fact, in order to find views that would conform to the Topelian ideal, the 19th century artists had to intentionally climb onto hilltops to find carefully selected vantage points that would give them access to a wider view above the crowns of the trees.

Thus, effectively, the 19th century aesthetic-artistic landscape canon regarded most of the Finnish landscape as having little interest or aesthetic value, especially so for railway passengers, it could be argued. Due to geometrical demands and their designated purpose to connect larger settlements on a national scale, the Finnish railways were often aligned along previously little travelled watersheds that were often marginal areas for human settlement. These desolate forested hinterlands are characterized by relatively poor soils and peneplain topography, and therefore lack the large-scale variation and signs of historical human presence that are central to the Topelian model and other classical ideas of beautiful landscapes. Although for many railway passengers these backwoods may have inspired feelings of awe comparable to those Aho describes in *Rautatiejunassa* (Aho 1929[1889]), a preference towards scenic, spectacularly beautiful landscapes is nevertheless dominant within public imagery and probably constituted the taste of the majority of public.

A good example of this preference for scenic beauty and its inherent system of value is found in an account given by a prominent Finnish landscape photographer of the 19th century, I.K. Inha (1909: 85-86), writing on first arriving in Kuopio by train, probably in 1892. Inha first makes a note on the 'retarded' cultivation of the region, exemplified by a still thriving slash-and-burn cultivation practice, while also noting, albeit in a neutral tone, the long-term impact of such practices: an abundance of birch groves where naturally a spruce forest would prevail. Foremost, as a general verdict, he laments the lack of variation and a clear-cut structure to the landscape: "[N]ature near the railway is not so variable that it would give the traveller a proper idea of the natural beauty Savo is famous for. The beautiful landscapes of Savo are along the waterways that do not reach up to the railway except near Suonenjoki (Ibid, 85)". Inha, however, makes a positive note on the character of the relief that changes when approaching the shores around central lake Kallavesi basin near Kuopio. For him, the aesthetic highlight is obvious:

> Therefore, a traveller arrives in the Kuopio region a little unprepared; looking out of the window in the final part of the journey when the train passes the Vanuvuori hill, the experience is surprising and impressive. The train runs on a high embankment (see fig. 4), across a narrow lake, behind it a high coniferous hill rises unexpectedly above the broadleaf forest. Anyone who sees it will also pull the sleeve of his or her fellow passenger... From there on, the region becomes hillier, the forest more imposing, and occasionally the gulf of Kallavesi with its delicate shores, stretches towards the line, only to disappear in the next instant (Ibid 1909: 85-86, translated by the author).

In fact, the 'scenic' qualities of the landscapes surrounding Kuopio, with their watercourses and pronounced topographic variation were already well recognized in the Finnish landscape painting at the time of Inha's writing: an iconic painting by Ferdinand von Wright called View from Haminalahti (1853) – today belonging to the Finnish National Gallery and exhibited at the Ateneum Art Museum, Helsinki – represents a view from Haminavuori hill overlooking lake Kallavesi to the north, over a mosaic of forested, hilly islands and capes (see nr. 6 in fig. 2). The glimpses onto Kallavesi from the railway Inha mentions in the above quotation (see nr. 5 in fig. 2), actually overlap the space depicted in the painting.

The town of Kuopio is located on a peninsula of the large Kallavesi lake, itself part of an extensive system of interconnected watercourses covering much of Eastern Finland. The marked topographic variation of Kuopio's surroundings is evident, with several hills higher than 100 meters (330 ft.). A view from one of these wooded hills over the fragmented shapes of water, that fill the deepest recessions between them, forms a paradigmatic example the canonical ideal landscape.

Building of the Savo railway from Kouvola, on the Helsinki – St. Petersburg main line, to Kuopio was completed in 1889 (fig.1). In the last few miles, the relief posed many challenges for the railway builders and the engineering solutions that were needed to overcome them. Railway builders had to adhere to predetermined geometric parameters of the railway line: valleys and hollows had to be filled up by embankments and bridges, and the hills penetrated by cuttings or tunnels; or, as was often the case in 19th century Finland, circumvented through curving alignments (also visible on the map of Savo railway; see fig. 2.) This topographic variation, resulting in impressive structures as well as providing conventional scenic framing, likely explains why a definitive cluster of historical photographic imagery related to the Savo railway can be identified around Kuopio (See maps in figs. 2 and 3).

Figure 1: *Map of the southwestern quarter of Finland*

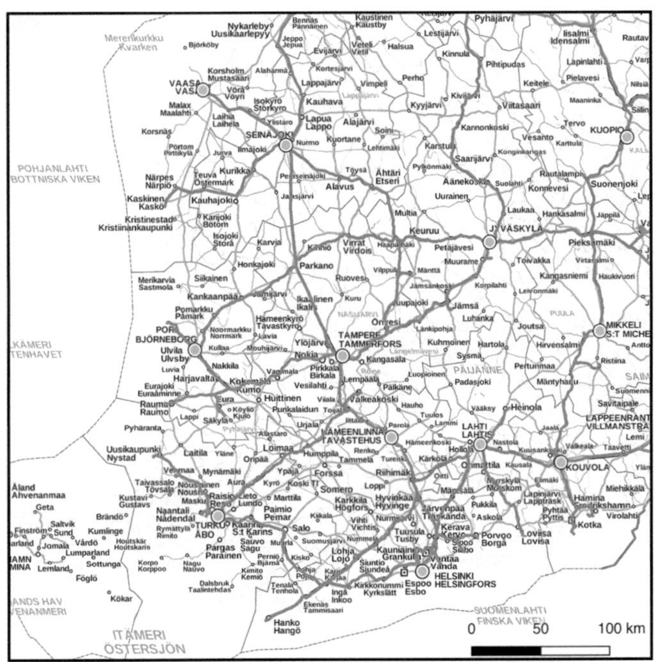

Figure 2: *The area south from Kuopio on a topographic map (1938)*

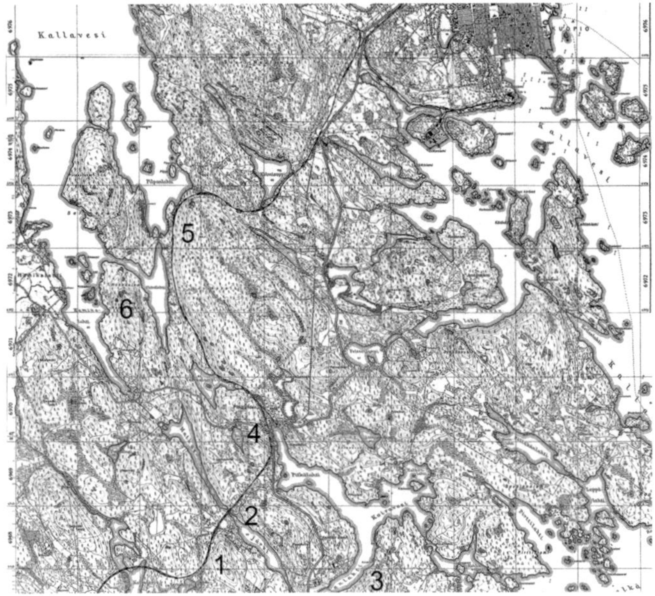

Figure 3: *Historical railway imagery slightly north from Kuopio*

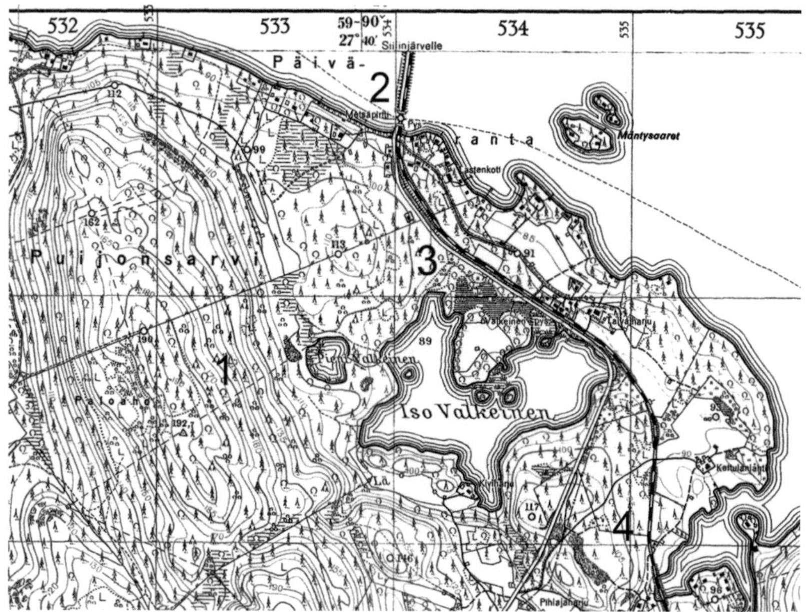

Figure 4: *Lake Matkus embankment* by Victor Barsokevitsch

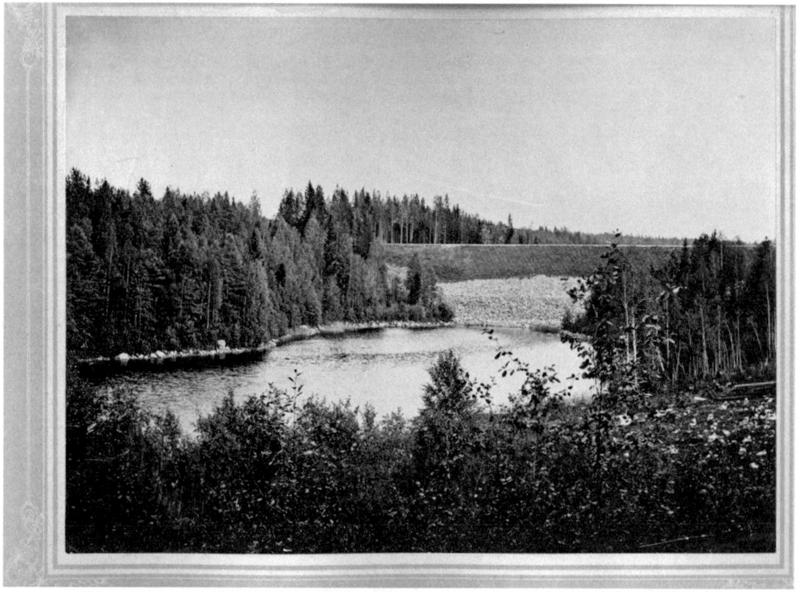

Victor Barsokevitsch was a prominent early Finnish photographer of Polish descent, born in Helsinki in 1863, who pursued an active career as a photographer in Kuopio from 1887. Alongside his principal occupation as a studio portraitist he also documented the landscapes in and around the town of Kuopio, especially traditional countryside landscapes affected by social and technological changes resulting from industrialization. On an early summer day, probably around 1890-1893, Barsokevitsch stood behind a large (most likely either 18x24 or 34x26 cm) plate camera on an abandoned fieldplot, overlooking a forest lake. In the background of the view his composition included towers and a massive railway embankment, structures effectively splitting the valley of lake Matkus in two halves while carrying the Savo railway across this recession in the landscape's relief (fig. 4). It is precisely this embankment that offered the scenic, fleeting view of Vanuvuori discussed by I.K. Inha (1909: 86). Barsokevitsch's view opens in almost the opposite direction, at an approximately 150° angle in relation to Inha's of Vanuvuori.

Barsokevitsch's work bears no indication of having being externally commissioned, nor does it have the aim of technological documentation. His early work on the Savo railway was probably, therefore, aesthetically motivated although topographic in its approach; aiming at an informative and 'truthful' representation of the aesthetic appearance of railway structures. Barsokevitsch composed the image of Matkus embankment (fig. 4) at a perpendicular angle towards the railway, resulting in a strong visual effect, revealing the scale of the industrial modification of a pristine environment. The massive, still barren, unvegetated railway embankment with a rigorously straight planar top, contrasts sharply with the surrounding non-human environment dominated by vegetation, water and a topography composed entirely of free fractal shapes. I am, however, inclined to believe Barsokevitsch's view of the railway was more enthusiastic than critical. The meticulous care and planning – based on knowledge of local topography – that is evident in Barsokevitsch's images is, in any case, clear testimony to the kind of enthusiasm the photographer had for his subject. It is also useful to remember that the original Topelian canon of landscape representation, that was born around the mid-19th century, embraced 'nature' as a virtually limitless resource base for cultural progress.

Barsokevitsch's photograph, apart from its general symbolic meanings, still has a clear cognitive implication through its making visible of a piece of infrastructure that would normally remain invisible for the railway passenger. Schivelbusch writes how the physical structure of the railway line rendered the landscape for the passengers in a new way, emphasizing how views from the high embankments gave an impression of 'flying' over the terrain (Schivelbusch 1980[1977]: 62). Inha's (1909: 86) view reflected such aesthetic pleasure, derived from being transported in dance-like effortlessness across the embankment, while enjoying the awe-inspiring vertical depth of the landscape. Thus, Barsokevitsch's image – and the topographical visual strategy exemplified by it – even has critical potential to draw aesthetic and cognitive attention to the resources underpinning the modern experience, but which increasingly remained invisible for the subject of that experience.

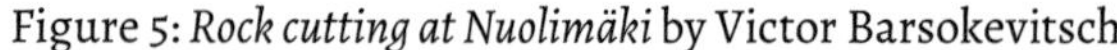

Figure 5: *Rock cutting at Nuolimäki* by Victor Barsokevitsch

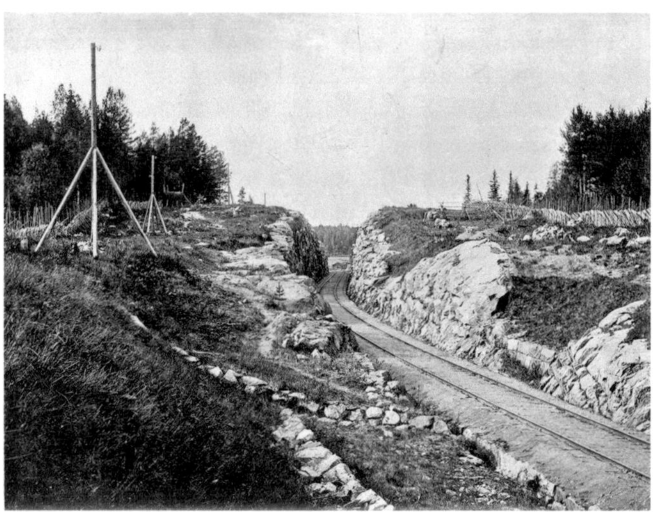

Figure 6: *View from Puijo hill onto Kallansillat* by Victor Barsokevitsch

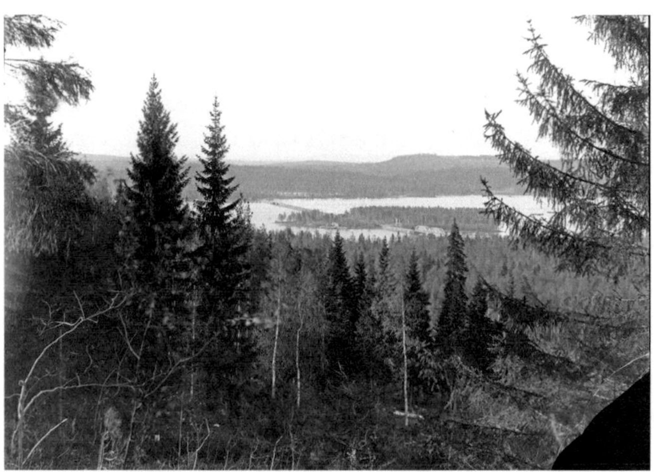

When the Savo railway was completed as far as Kuopio in 1889, planning of its continuation further north began immediately. Work on the Kuopio – Iisalmi stretch began in 1898 and was completed in 1902. By far the most expensive part of the Kuopio – Iisalmi railway project, which also involved enormous technical difficulty, was the overpass of Kallavesi straits just north of Kuopio. The chosen solution was a series of embankments using esker gravel across the 2.2 km wide and up to 18 meters deep strait (SVR 1916: 126-128). Three gaps were left and fitted with bridges to allow for the flow of water and passage of ships and boats.

For many Finnish artists and other cultural practitioners of the late 19th century, witnessing the fresh, violent traces of the railway being built in the landscape often evoked in their writing a direct and univocal critique of its cold, calculating technological rationality. The railway, as a symbol of industrializing 'culture', was sharply contrasted to the romantic 'pristine nature' through which the railway very insensitively and literally trod (cf. Suomalainen 1888[1885]; Inha 1909: 129). I.K. Inha's assessment of the Kallavesi overpass was that it "undoubtedly [had] an undesirable impact on the landscape's character" (Inha 1909: 123-124).

It seems, however, that Barsokevitsch was more optimistic about the railway, and might have aimed to create views suggesting that the railway could be a harmonious component of a modern cultural landscape. Barsokevitsch's image (fig. 6) is again a distant view of this massive, linear railway structure: the wide landscape of lake Kallavesi as seen from the slope of the Puijo hill, just north of Kuopio. It is evident that the topographic variation of the surroundings again meant that the location of a technically impressive structure aligned with the scenic landscape. Again, in order to complete the image, the photographer – probably not Barsokevitsch himself, but an uncredited assistant named Ms. Hilma Miettinen (Kankkunen 2019) – was required to carry a large 18x24 cm camera to a hard-to-reach vantage point on the forested Puijo hill, signifying a clear determination to capture this view despite the considerable efforts involved.

Through a classic Topelian model celebrating progress combined with a romantic, wilderness vision of the late 19th century, the image strongly suggests a 'conciliatory' aesthetic; a view of the railway indicating a shift from a more direct if not uncritical emphasis on the railway structure towards a softer view in which technology and 'nature' are 'reconciled'. This shift echoes the conventions of pictorialism, but possibly also environmentalist sentiments that were emerging in Finland in the late 19th century, a partial critical reaction to the destruction caused by industry and especially the impact of forestry (cf. Lintonen 2011: 111-123).

Proximity in photographs

The visual power of these photographs largely resides within their foreground compositions. As already discussed, following Granö (1997 [1929]) the emphasis on spatial proximity promotes an acute and multisensory landscape experience, an experience of being there. Similarly, the visual surfaces of the objects within the visual foreground of a landscape photograph – Granö's proximate view – may evoke a comparable, almost tactile sense of presence (cf. Tuan 1993: 43-44). According to Schivelbusch, the capacity of the image to re-evoke the foreground and thereby recall for its viewer the multisensory experience of spatial proximity was central to the miracle of photography in the 20th century:

> Thus, the intensive experience of the sensuous world, terminated by the industrial revolution, undergoes a resurrection in the new institution of photography. Since immediacy, close-ups and foreground have been lost in reality, they appear particularly attractive in the new medium (Schivelbusch 1980 [1977]: 65).

Surely, the idea that photography's affective power lies in the sense of nearness to the objects represented, is not new – Susan Sontag (1977: 183), for example, quotes a letter by Elizabeth Barrett, dating back to 1843, in which she already identifies this "sense of nearness" as a special affective quality of the photographic image. Mikael Pettersson (2011: 185-186) talks of the "proximity aspect" that has echoed in various writings through the history of photography. However, Schivelbusch importantly connects this power of the photographic foreground to evoke a sense of nearness with the discussion of actual modern spatial experience.

As visual proximity has the most acute presence, or weight, in the image, it has great importance for the overall composition of the landscape and the atmosphere of the image. Barsokevitsch's view of the Matkus embankment (fig. 4) virtually embeds the viewer into the premodern cultural landscape of the trackside, situating him or her next to a fresh slash-and-burn clearing on an abandoned fieldplot already overgrown with birch seedlings, constructing a familiar viewer's position within the premodern foreground. It is arguable that this sense of an embedded viewer's position in a 'natural' place, amidst the birch seedlings, renders the encounter between the human and non-human in this particular environment so affectively powerful, in all its contradictoriness. The foreground thus provides the context for the interpretation of the rest of the image; while the perspective distance necessary to accommodate a wide horizontal structure downplays the perception of the aesthetic impact caused by the railway structure.

The image of the Kallavesi overpass (fig. 6.), in turn, virtually embeds the viewer within proximity of the forest. The partially enclosed forest interior in Barsokevitsch's image has such a visual presence as to evoke a sense of the intimacy of 'being surrounded', of the comfort of shelter, feelings familiar to anyone with experience of a boreal spruce forest. To illustrate this point: from his sleigh journeys from Iisalmi down south to Kuopio, Juhani Aho remembers with delight how – having finally crossed the iced, windy expanses of Kallavesi straits – they reached the solid land and "the coniferous shelter" of the spruce forests at the foot of Puijo hill (Aho 1929 [1917]: 332). Something similar can be experienced through the prosthetic capability of the image and especially its foreground. In contrast, the distant landscape in Barsokevitsch's image, containing the railway and the expanse of water mirroring the sky, appears as merely a visual mirage, lacking a sense of presence and is insufficient in information capable of evoking tactile sensations.

It is very interesting to note that from around the turn of the 20th century, landscape photographs increasingly focus on the composition of foreground, in other words, on visual proximity. They increasingly elevate the railway itself and its proximity to its foreground, into the position of the old premodern roadside. Already Barsokevitsh' composition in his image of Nuolimäki cutting (fig. 5) emphasizes the small-scale details of the built railway environment; it gives a lot of weight to the recovering grass vegetation and curving patterns of the slope's stabilizing granite-laid walls in the foreground, as well as wooden roundpole fences – intended to keep the free-grazing cattle off of the railway – framing the view. I believe it is precisely the weight the composition gives to the foreground – with a lot of hand-built, small scale details – that actually creates a strangely picturesque, even pastoral, mood for the image. Indeed, Barsokevitsch's image of Nuolimäki cutting was published in a book celebrating the 50th anniversary of the Finnish State Railways, indicating that the railway organization also considered this view as contributing to its desired image (SVR 1916: 68).

I.K. Inha himself returned to the Kuopio railway with his camera most likely around 1894-1895, a few years after writing the travel description cited above. At that time, he was compiling a collection of photographs – Suomi kuvissa / Finland i Bilder / La Finlande pittoresque – that also included views of industrializing Finland (Inha 1896). In this collection, Inha decided to include a photograph of the minor railway station at Pitkälahti, located some 10 kilometres (6 miles) south of Kuopio (fig. 7). In his caption text, he emphasizes the idyllic character of the station milieu and also mentions the adjacent forest surrounding the railway line. Although his advocacy of the progress inherent in Topelian landscape symbolism is still evident, his caption also echoes the late 19th romantic ideas of romantic wilderness as well as environmentalist sentiments. The caption also reflects the difficulty he had in achieving a balance between the inherent value of the tranquility of the backwoods and the industrial progress of the nation represented in the building of the railway:

> Because of its idyllic nature, one could mistake that apartment for a villa built in the middle of the woods, if the cap and the flag of the station master did not indicate its function. It is the last station on the railway to Kuopio, opened in 1889. A high forest borders the station and the railway so that the passenger thinks he is in the gloomiest backwoods and not approaching the Savo capital. Our railways cross the heartlands and in vain the locomotive greets many stations. But these stations are seeds sown in the wilderness, through which cultivation will clear its way into the woods (Inha 1896, translated by the author).

Figure 7: *Pitkälahti Station* by I.K. Inha

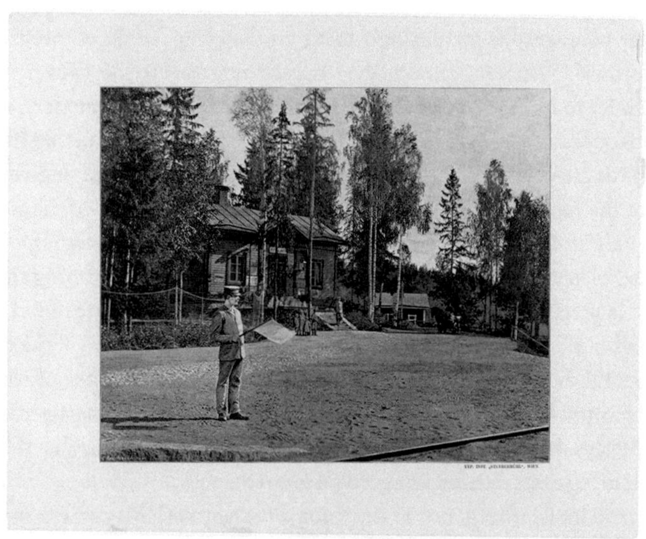

In choosing Pitkälahti station (fig. 7) as his subject, Inha had probably been struck not only by the appearance of the wooden station building but by the effect of the station park, created by preserving pre-existing trees around the station building; apparently a relatively rare solution applied in Pitkälahti and some other minor stations, contributing to a matured, wooded sense of place soon after the completion of the railway. Inha's choice of the word "villa" to describe the station building amidst the woods is indeed apt, for the Italian renaissance villa had been purposefully mimicked in the design of station buildings across Europe since 1840s. Although much of the original decoration was dropped towards the end of the century, picturesque impression was purposefully aimed at, probably in order to make the stations more approachable in the eyes of the travelling public (cf. Valanto 1982: 13). Inha probably did not want the track to lend too much industrial character to his view, either. The foreground in his composition is quite empty, with only a fragment of steel rail and a corner of granite platform edging visible in the close foreground. The station park, however, beginning at the distance of approximately 15-20 meters, delivers a great impression of proximity, in creating the mood of a rather small-scale, 'soft', woodland place.

During my research on the landscape imagery of the Finnish Railways I have identified the emergence of the railway itself as an increasingly picturesque landscape element around the turn of the 19th and 20th century. This visual trope, however, was already well-established: the railway was effectively incorporated into the tradition of picturesque roadside views (cf. Vallius 2013: 371-375). This shift in representational strategy seems to reflect increasing cultural familiarity with, and acceptance of, the railway; it seems clear that photographs in general worked towards that end. Victor Barsokevitcsh's image of Villa Granit-Ilmoniemi, Kettulanlahti, Kuopio (c. 1902, Fig. 8) is a good example. The photograph is a view from the countryside in the vicinity of Kuopio, featuring the Iisalmi railway, opened 1902, in its foreground, and the actual Villa Granit-Ilmoniemi, an urbanite countryside villa, in the background. The railway track bed is still brand new, lacking the softening impact of vegetation favoured by the picturesque. Still, it is a rather small-scale feature, built from sandy esker gravel, and seems not to cause any greater disturbance to the summery idyll of the landscape it passes through than the old country road. The soft evening light and glowing highlights (albeit an effect probably viewed undesirable at the time; cf. Lintonen 2011: 47) further contribute to the idyllic mood in this representation, suggesting that the railway is no longer a threat, rather it is now a humanized technology with a liberating promise of access to the increasingly leisurely rural landscape.

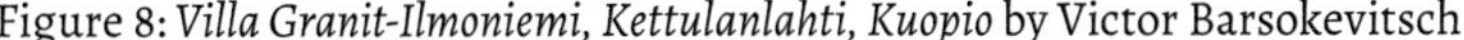
Figure 8: *Villa Granit-Ilmoniemi, Kettulanlahti, Kuopio* by Victor Barsokevitsch

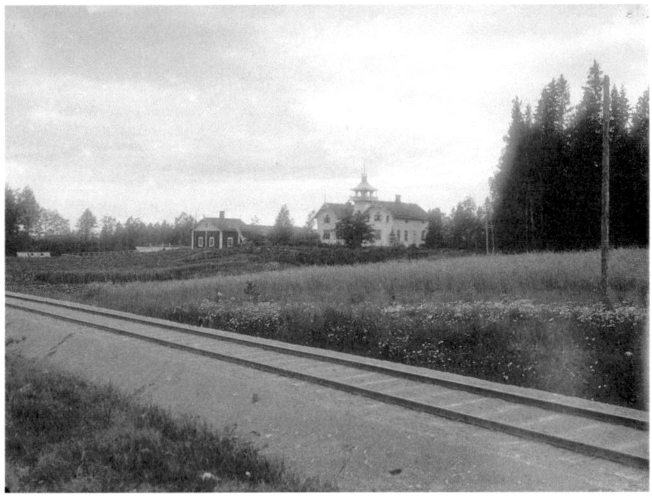

Although it has been shown that from the turn of the 20th century railway photography tended to elevate the railway to their foreground, it is notable that picturesque-influenced pictorialism put an increasing emphasis on the idyllic, organic, small-scale, traditionalist elements of the railway landscape, while seeking to avoid the coldness attributable to their industrial aspects.

In the imagery corpus of the Finnish railways a partial turn away from pictorialism can be identified in the interwar period. Especially in the 1930s a great expansion and thematic diversification of the imagery occurs with the introduction of the new trope of the technological close-up image, as well as landscape images produced for marketing purposes. The work of industrial photographer Gustav Rafael Roos (1895 – 1972) – who fulfilled several commissions for the Finnish railways in the interwar decades – is especially noticeable. Although this work was undoubtedly produced to serve the practical and technological interests of the State Railways, it still reflects a photographic vision that could be categorized as modernist in the spirit of Neue Sachlichkeit (Heikka 2014: 52-53).

Figure 9: *Kallavesi overpass, new road and swing bridge arrangements, Päiväranta, Kuopio* by Gustav Rafael Roos

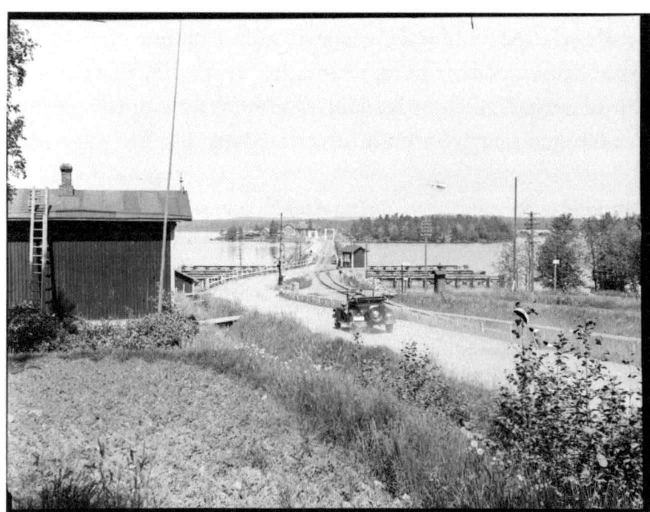

Figure 10: *Kallansillat swing bridge, opened for the lake steamer "S/S Maaninka" to pass through* by Gustav Rafael Roos

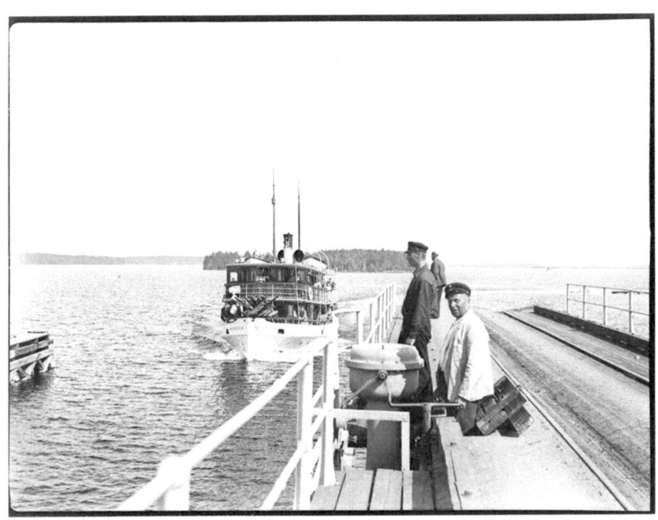

Figure 11: *A semaphore main signal preceding the Kallavesi swing bridge from the south* by Gustav Rafael Roos

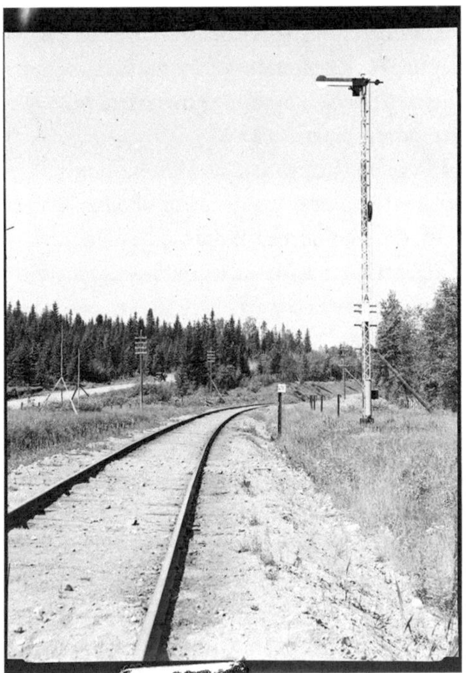

Roos' photographs no longer attempt to interpret the railway landscape through a pastoral lens, rather they emphasize the modern machinery and technological equipment in their foreground, thus giving them a very acute, almost tactile, sense of presence. In its attitude towards the landscape, Roos' photography is clearly topographic. His glass negatives contain neutral, rich tone-scale and often great sharpness though the depth-of field. He often uses flat daylight and he appears generally to have aimed at 'neutral', high-fidelity rendition of his objects. Yet, it is evident that Roos has composed his wider views with a delicate eye on the totality of landscape; in his photographs, the technological world appears familiar, natural and settled, suggesting that modernity, at that date, had already inscribed itself into daily life, albeit with a distinctive aesthetic ambience.

Conclusion

The railway was initially perceived by Aho and many 19th century authors as alienating and 'placeless', but images produced by Finnish landscape photographers, eventually, for their part, fostered cultural acceptance and familiarity with the railway. Early railway photography was produced under the influence of the scenic landscape canon – a mixture of Topelian, romantic wilderness and picturesque influences with their associated aesthetic value systems; and yet they still possess a performative potential to expand the scope of a popular landscape aesthetic through affective representations of the modern everyday landscapes. This is particularly evident in the case of railway infrastructure, lying as it does in the background of the modern experience.

The power of railway imagery to achieve this, however, stems from the (partly convention-related, partly optical) tendency of photographs to recover the foreground and to reduce the significance of the scenic distant view. This lends photographs a power of affect that is achieved through an evocation of the spatial proximity and sense of immediacy in the everyday landscapes, similar to the affective capacities of premodern travel before the era of industrial modernity. Indeed, the original underlying purpose of picturesque foreground compositions may have been to mitigate the effects of industrialisation by representing the railway as a harmonious component of the modern cultural landscape. Historically, the performative potential of these images to challenge aesthetic conventions of landscape appreciation were largely unrealized.

Yet, in the present, these photographs still exhibit a distinctive power to evoke a sense of closeness to past human environments. For a viewer embedded within the 21st century horizon, the sense of closeness to these environments – with their rich variety of detail, spatial arrangements at a human scale, building materials of largely recognizable 'natural' origin and evidence of skilled manual handicraft

– is very affective. Ultimately, this affective power stems from the material nature of photographs as traces of environments that once were 'before the lens'. We of course are aware of the actual absence of these environments, that they have been subject to profound material-ecological transformation, and that such processes continue to shape the landscape of the everyday.

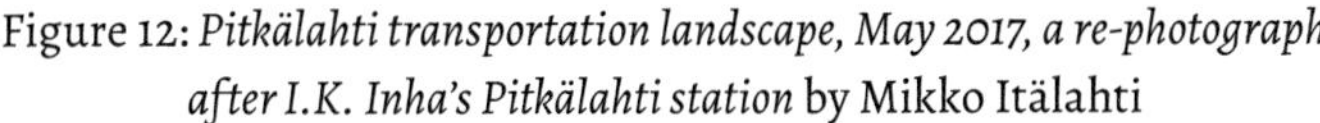

Figure 12: *Pitkälahti transportation landscape, May 2017, a re-photograph after I.K. Inha's Pitkälahti station* by Mikko Itälahti

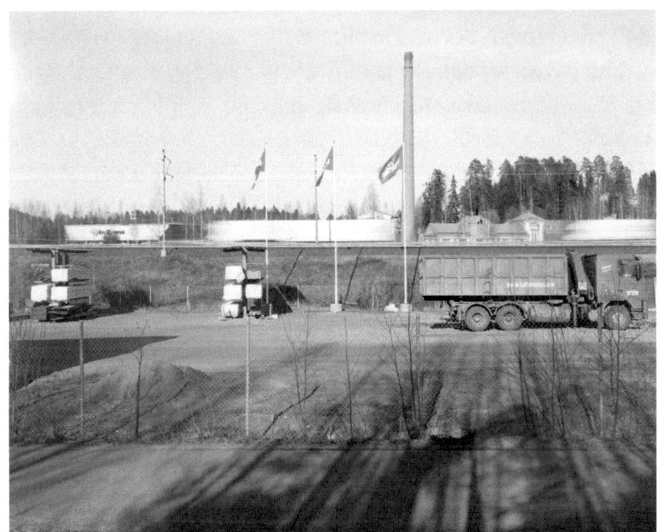

Acknowledgements

For the identification of Barsokevitsch's authorship in previously unidentified prints (figs. 4 and 5), I wish heartily to thank Jukka Kukkonen, a photo-historian specialized in Barsokevitsch, from the Finnish Museum of Photography, Helsinki.

References

Aho, Juhani (1884): Rautatie, Porvoo: WSOY.

Aho, Juhani (1929 [1889]): "Rautatiejunassa", In: Lastuja, Kolmas kokoelma, Porvoo: WSOY.

Aho, Juhani (1929 [1917]): "Kotipuoleni rautatie", In: Aho, Juhani: Lastuja IV-VII, Porvoo: WSOY.

Granö, Johannes Gabriel (1997[1929]): Pure geography. Baltimore: John Hopkins university press.
Heikka, Elina (2014): "Uudistava modernismi" In: Valokuvataiteen ydin: 1900-luvun suomalaiset valokuvat ja taidepuhe. Helsinki: Suomen valokuvataiteen museo & Maahenki, pp. 51-62.
Häyrynen, Maunu (2005): Kuvitettu maa: Suomen kansallisen maisemakuvaston rakentuminen, Helsinki: SKS.
Inha, Into Konrad (1896): Finland i bilder = Suomi kuvissa = La Finlande pittoresque, Helsinki: W. Hagelstam/U. Wasastjerna.
Inha, Into Konrad (1909): Suomen maisemia, Porvoo: WSOY.
Kalanti, Timo (2014): "Maailma ruumiissa" In: Arto Haapala/Ossi Naukkarinen (eds.), Mobiiliestetiikka: Kirjoituksia liikkeen ja liikkumisen kulttuurista, Helsinki: Erikoispaino.
Kukkonen, Jukka (2017). Interview in Helsinki, 20. December 2017.
Kankkunen, Pekka (2019). Intendent, Kuopio Cultural History Museum, Personal e-mail to the author, 7.1.2019.
Linkola, Hannu (2013): "As authentic as possible: Landscape photography in Finnish geography from the 1920s to the 1960s", University of Helsinki: Department of Geosciences and Geography A 22.
Lintonen, Kati (2011): "Valokuvallistettu luonto: I.K. Inhan tuotanto luonnon merkityksellistäjänä", Doctoral dissertation, University of Helsinki: Faculty of Arts.
Norberg-Schultz, Christian (1980 [1979]): Genius Loci: Towards a phenomenology of architecture, New York: Rizzoli.
Pettersson, Mikael (2011): "Depictive traces: On the phenomenology of photography". In: The journal of aesthetics and art criticism, 2/2011, pp. 185-196.
Saito, Yuriko (2007): Everyday aesthetics, Oxford: Oxford university press.
Schivelbusch, Wolfgang (1980 [1977]): The railway journey: Trains and travel in the 19th century, Oxford: Blackwell.
Sepänmaa, Yrjö (2000): "Face to Face with the Landscape" In: Kaia Lehari/Virve Sarapik (eds.): Place and Location. Tallinn: Proceedings, Estonian Academy of Arts.
Solnit, Rebecca (2003): River of shadows: Eadweard Muybridge and the technological wild west, New York: Penguin.
Sontag, Susan (1977): On photography, New York: Farrar, Straus and Giroux.
Suomalainen, Karl Gustaf Samuli (1888[1886]): "Maantie tampereelle (Hjalmar Munsterhjelm)" In: Suomi: Kuvia maasta ja kansasta etevimpäin kotimaisten taiteilijain maalausten mukaan [Finland – Pictures of Finland and its people], Helsinki: G.W. Edlund.
SVR (1916) Suomen Valtionrautatiet 1862-1912, II. Helsinki: Rautatiehallitus.

Topelius, Zachris (1910 [1863]): Mirabeau-täti, In: Topelius, Zachris: Talvi-iltain tarinoita 2, Porvoo: WSOY, Available at: http://doctrinepublishing.com/show book.php?file=56861-0000.txt.
Tuan, Yi-Fu (1993): Passing strange and wonderful, Washington: Island.
Vallius, Antti (2007): Kuvien maaseutu: Maaseutumaisemakuvaston luomat mielikuvat suomalaisesta maaseutukulttuurista, Jyväskylä: Jyväskylä Studies in Humanities 203.
Valanto, Seija (1982): Suomen rautatieasemat vuosina 1957-1920. Museoviraston rakennushistorian osaston julkaisu no. 11 Helsinki: Finnish heritage agency.
Wells, Liz (2011): Land matters: Landscape photography, culture and identity, London & New York: I.B. Tauris.
Wylie, John (2016): "A Landscape cannot be a homeland", In: Landscape research, 4/2016, pp. 408-416.

Mapping Norway. Knud Knudsen and the discovery of Norway in photography

Anne Wriedt

Introduction

In 1922 German-Norwegian travel journalist Ferdinand Scarlett reported: "For a long time, it remained unclear to the public what Knudsen had done for the promotion of Norway as a tourist country with his landscape photographs" (Scarlett 1927: 128), and not until the publication of the first Norway travel guide – "Tourist Country Norway" – featuring his photographs and discussing the reception of his work, was his reputation established. Arguably, no other photographer of the 19th century has captured the image of the Norwegian landscape like Knud Knudsen. Although traveller's accounts of their journeys through Norway already existed in texts and images before the advent of photography, they were mostly recorded by foreign scientists and artists. In the early 18th century, these memories were still most often illustrated by engravings and few in number. Some decades later, in the second half of the 19th century, this situation had changed. With the development of new photographic techniques and their arrival in Norway new possibilities for the reproduction of images became available. This coincided with a new mobility of photographers who could rely on the newly constructed railroads in Norway as a new means of transportation, granting easier access to the far flung regions of the country.

This essay considers the work of Knudsen during a period of transformation of Norway's landscape in the late 19th century, assessing the contribution of his landscape photography to the formation of Norway's national identity. During this era landscape photography redefined the nation by focusing on the biological and geomorphological characteristics of the country, while also representing the supposedly timeless and 'authentic' working life of the people. This moment in the formation of nationhood was also the beginning of a period of growing modernity, during which the development of tourism and newly commercializing forms of photography had a further impact on the changing landscape. Knudsen's work began in an earlier era, he then participated in the creation of Norway's new image through his landscape photography, and his work subsequently contributed to the landscape imagery of tourism, images which were developed within the new, commercial forms of mass circulation and which were also transformed in the context of new technical possibilities within the medium. This essay considers the evolution of Knudsen's work and his journey as a landscape photographer by taking into account these different moments: the development of his imaged in relation to previous artistic representations of the Norwegian landscape; changing logistical and technological issues in relation to his practice; and his work in the context of the commercialization of landscape and tourism photography.

The change of the landscape and the Invention of the North

In his essay on the discovery of the "Nordic Landscape" Ralph Tuchtenhagen explains how the North and thus also the Nordic landscape were redefined due to political shifts in the 19th century. While Russia formerly stood for the Nordic landscape, Scandinavia now became the new North – which began as the search for a new definition of landscape, which turned away from the ideas of the Arcadian landscape (Tuchtenhagen 2007: 130). Suddenly the focus was on the biological and geomorphological characteristics of nature – and thus on the characteristics of the landscape of each individual country. According to Tuchtenhagen, this retreat from the representation of the classical ancient landscape resulted in the creation of a "Nordic" and "national" landscape. In the second half of the 19th century, landscape painting and literature in the Scandinavian countries were primarily devoted to depictions of rural national life, a life supposedly 'authentic' and unadulterated by modernity, while there was also a commitment to the representation of the biological and geomorphological peculiarities of each country. The case of Norway is particularly significant because the shift in the balance of powers in the Baltic Sea region led to Norway being awarded to Sweden. Norway's territorial influence in northern Europe was considerably weakened, however, as Norway did not become an integral part of the Swedish Empire, but rather a kingdom linked by the Swedish king in personal union. In Norway – with its own constitution established in 1814 – the development from a Nordic to a national landscape can be traced particularly well. Against the backdrop of these political developments, Norway was more in search of a new identity than any other country in northern Europe.

In this effort to construct and communicate a new national identity, the influence of the young medium of photography can be cited as a decisive factor. In particular, Knud Knudsen – Norway's most important landscape photographer – made a significant contribution to the formation and communication of this national identity: through his pioneering of new techniques, formats and motifs; by helping in its representation abroad; and by popularizing these new ways of depicting Norway through his role in the commercialization of landscape and tourism photography. Knudsen's early photographs were taken before Norway was a tourist country and while still in the process of defining and building its national identity. Until the 1880s Knudsen's photographs show the rural working life of Norwegians – mainly from the region of the Hardangerfjord where he grew up – and landscapes from West Norway focusing on mountains, fjords and waterfalls. These pictures not only reflect the social and geomorphological reality of the country but also the self-conception of the nation.

The Nordic Landscape in Art – Knudsen and Dahl

The breathtaking view from Stalheim as a representation of the Norwegian landscape had not only become a popular tourist destination with the advent of tourism in the 1870s, but had also attracted artists since the 1820s.

Figure 1: *Stalheim Hotel and Naerødal Valley*

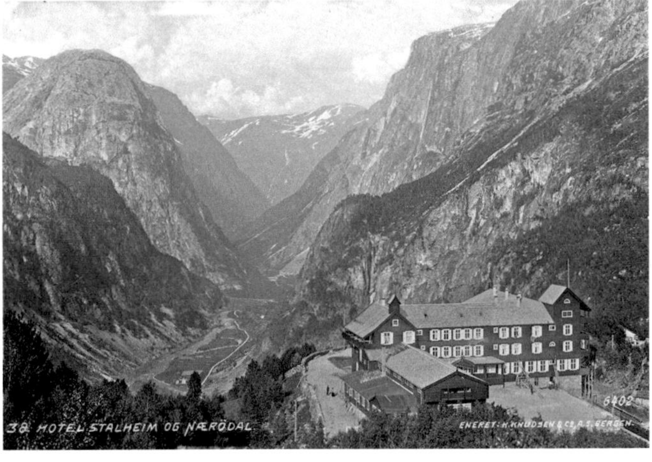

Knudsen's photography from 1888 (fig. 1) directly recalls one of the key works of Norwegian national romanticism, when he positioned himself in exactly the same place as famous landscape painter Johann Christian Dahl did 70 years earlier for his painting *From Stalheim*. Both artists depict a realistic Norwegian landscape in their pictures, that is topographically bound to an existing place – Stalheim and the Naerødal Valley. The Naerødal Valley had been the most important connection between Oslo and Bergen since the Middle Ages and was developed into the first postal route between the two cities in 1647. Stalheim's first hotel was built in 1885, replacing the postal station and making Stalheim one of the first tourist destinations in Norway. Dahlc's painting presents a cultural landscape that is already cultivated, populated and animated by people. Instead of bright sunshine, Dahl´s sky is darkened, reflecting the realistic weather conditions in Western Norway. The landscape depicted in the painting was not a product of his imagination but was created in 1826 from a sketch and his own experiences of nature. Even though Dahl came from Bergen and is considered to be the main representative of Norwegian national romanticism, he only visited Norway for study purposes. After being trained as a decorative painter in Bergen and studying at the Copenhagen Art Academy, he spent his entire life in Dresden. In April 1826 he travelled through his home country for half a year. This also led to the sketch of Stalheim, which later served as a model and *aide memoire* for his depiction of the Stalheim scene. But it was not until 20 years later that the painting for the sketch was produced during Dahl's creative phase, which focused on a realistic depiction and recognition of the landscape and was only possible from his own experience in nature. In his picture from the 1880s Knudsen visualizes how the modernization of the country has permeated the Norwegian landscape. He shows this by making the new path, which winds through the valley as a curved line, the central element of the composition.

Knudsen's landscape also reflects the modernization of Norway by documenting the touristic function of the landscape. While Dahl worked with colours, Knudsen's used light as a tool. Knudsen – like all landscape photographers in Scandinavia – only travelled in summer. The only manipulation Knudsen made in his early pictures was to use black paper to cover the sky on the wet collodion plates, so that no clouds became visible on the print. In Knudsen's photography, there are no references to a national-romantic ideal landscape, as he (like Dahl) was concerned with depicting a dramatic landscape. Here, the theme of the development of the landscape is integrated into the composition as an almost natural element.

From experiment to the tourist landscape

During Knudsen's career Norway had developed into a travel and tourism country, a change also conveyed through his photographs. While in the beginning the focus of his pictures lay on untouched nature, the forces of nature and travel itself, symbols of tourism or travel like hotels and roads later point to the human intervention in the landscape and nature. Knudsen's practice was shaped by the technological and logistical challenges of photographing the Norwegian landscape, these being the means of travel and the photographic process itself. The invention of the collodion process allowed for the taking of photographs on journeys. Before, the use of daguerreotype had only made it possible to take pictures of landscapes and city views in the immediate surroundings of the photographer and had thus kept him tied to his studio. With the advent of the collodion process in the 1850s, the photographic image was produced by printing from glass plates using a negative process. For the first time it was possible to photograph outside the studio and reproduce images in unlimited numbers. More importantly, the new method made it possible to travel with the camera. In his experimental phase from 1860-1880 Knudsen almost exclusively used stereoscopic photography, a small square format that was later replaced by a landscape format. Process and format played a role for his photography from the very beginning – even in the choice of motif and detail – and were highly dependent on the technical developments of the time. The experimental aspect of photography, the challenges of photographing while travelling, and, finally, the orientation towards the tourist market will be illustrated through three pictures, from the 1860s, 1880s and 1890s.

Figure 2: *Naerødal Valley from Stalheim*

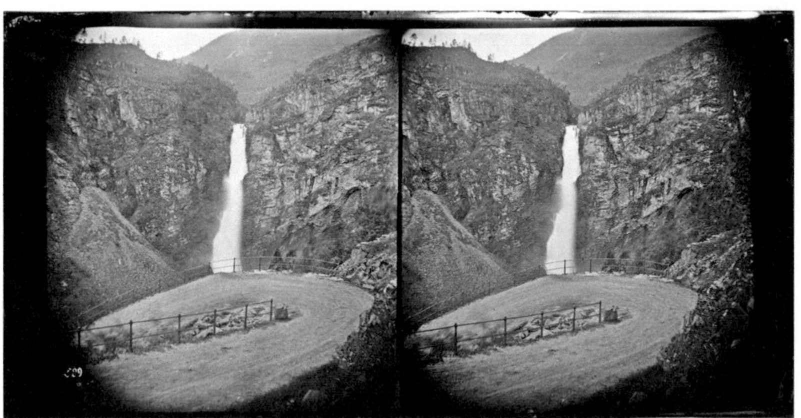

The stereoscopic image (fig. 2) taken in the Naerødal Valley, is of a place Knudsen travelled to many times in his early years, photographing it in different ways and experimenting with a variety of themes. This image shows a rather atypical view of the Naerødal Valley from Stalheim, which twenty years later had become one of Norway's central tourist destinations, but this place had an iconographic tradition predating the age of tourism. At first sight the observer is confronted with two identical images of a waterfall, its white flatness and blurriness in contrast to the sharp mountain landscape in grey and black tones. The waterfall is embedded in a jagged mountain slope, almost plunging towards the viewer. The impact zone of the river is not visible, as a fenced path carved into the rock has been built in front of it, leading in a serpentine shape past the waterfall into the valley. Since the photograph is taken from an elevated position, the observer is at some distance from the natural spectacle. Landscapes were particularly popular and successful in stereo format, as its effect was to convey the illusion of spatiality and realism to the contemporary observer. The contrast in the sharpness of the different image elements is due to the long exposure time, which made it impossible to capture the rapid flow of water with the camera. The focus on the white waterfall is emphasised by the fact that only a small part of the sky can be seen, as Knudsen focused strongly on the section of the rough mountain formation. The curvature of the path is further enhanced by the fact that the two lower corners of the negative are rounded in black, thus cutting off the image. The picture was taken between 1865 and 1870 on one of the photographer's early journeys.

The fascination in these early years with the logistical challenges of travelling and its associated elaborate photographic procedures, is also thematized in Knudsen's pictures, expressed by a seemingly random scene showing Knudsen's equipment (fig. 3), which he made the subject of the picture.

Figure 3: *Hornidalsrokken in Nordfjord*

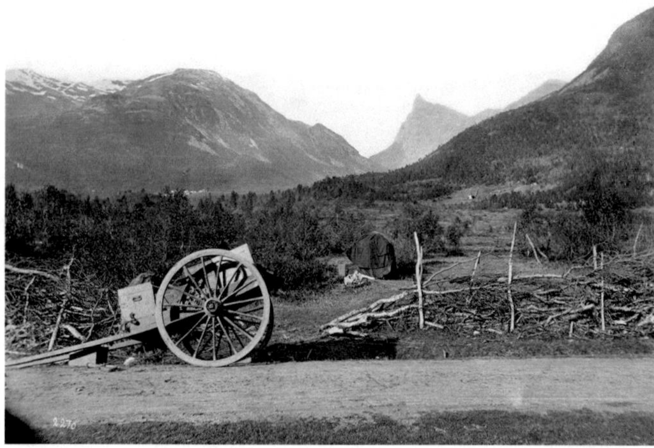

In this photograph from 1881/82 a handcart and a darkroom tent form the main object of the picture. While the handcart is loaded with four wooden boxes, the wood of the boxes is illuminated by the sun, and the black darkroom tent, in the centre of the picture, is difficult to see at first glance in the grassy landscape covered with bushes. Both objects are on the edge of the path and are framed in the upper part by the mountain landscape and in the lower part by the path. In this context the wooden boxes can be identified as glass boxes of collodion negatives and chemical boxes, the tent was used for the development process of the plates. When used on journeys, the collodion wet process required a portable darkroom. The complicated technical process necessary to produce an image, the struggles that came with the use of means of transport such as carts and boats, and the changing weather, were all complicating factors Knudsen confronted every day on his travels.

Against this backdrop, it may come as no surprise that Knudsen documented the arduous context of his work photographically. Thus, between 1870 and 1882, there are 22 pictures in which he staged the darkroom tent and its technical equipment as the main object of his photographs. These two objects not only stand for Knudsen's travel conditions and the technical requirements of his photographic work, they can also be regarded as symbols of modernity, technology and progress – developments in which the photographer himself was involved. And yet, this is the last image in which Knudsen ever photographed his equipment, because from 1882 onwards he no longer used wet collodion plates but worked with the dry method, which meant that a darkroom tent was no longer needed when travelling. The new gelatine dry plates came ready prepared from the factory and did not have to be developed immediately.

Within 10 years, the images of an experimental nature and those that focused on the photographer's journey had been replaced by photography focused on tourism. Around 1890 Knudsen took a photograph entitled "The Bondhus Glacier in Mauranger, Hardanger" (fig. 4) that depicts one of the most prominent fjords in Western Norway.

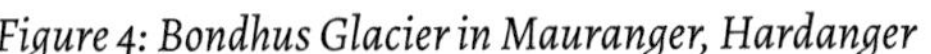

Figure 4: Bondhus Glacier in Mauranger, Hardanger

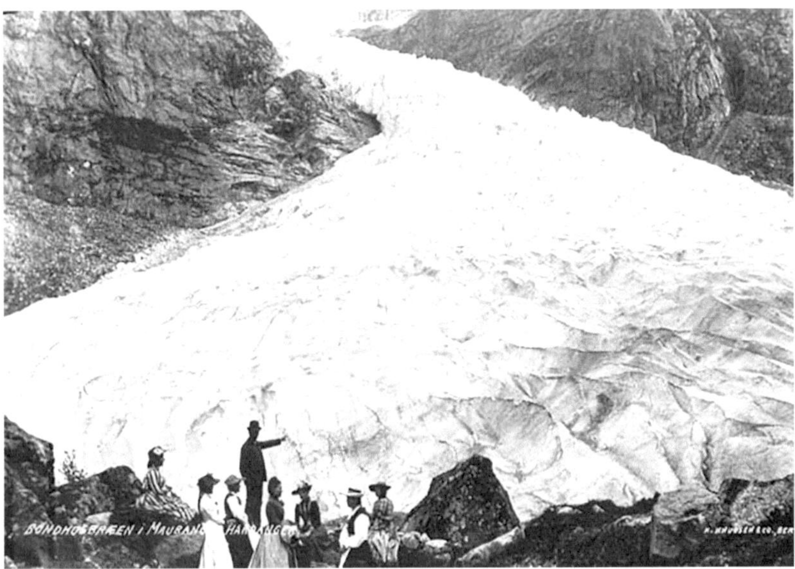

Knudsen's photograph is of a group of people at the foot of the glacier. The picture visualizes the fascination that emanated from a glacier as a natural phenomenon and made it an attraction for tourists. The picture is not only a documentation of touristic development, but also had the function of advertising specific places, which is still the case today. Knudsen's selection of themes seems to have become an integral part of tourist photographs, as a brochure from 1994 shows (fig. 5), using the same view of the glacier 100 years later, but presenting it in a new context.

Figure 5: *Kvinnherad brochure*

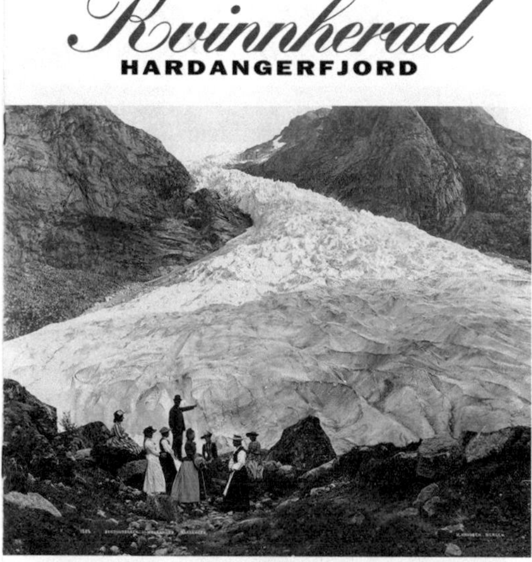

The new context and framing of Knudsen's photography indicates that the glacier remains a suitable medium for the Kvinnherad community to advertise the Hardangerfjord, using a photograph by Knudsen even a century after it was taken. Two effects are achieved through such a re-use and re-contextualising of the image: the nostalgic message of becoming part of a tradition as a traveller is conveyed to the reader and viewer; while it establishes the Hardangerfjord as symbolic of both its region and of the tourist experience of Norwegian fjords in general.

The advertisement, which is coloured in a blue tone and printed in the centre of a portrait-format A4 format, is framed by the headline "Kvinnherad Hardangerfjord" and the subtitle "The Bondhus Glacier in Mauranger, Hardanger, Norway". Furthermore, the brochure does not date the photography, which is why the date of origin of the photograph remains unclear to the reader. Knudsen is not mentioned in the text as the author of the photograph. The photo thus serves a purely illustrative purpose. Tourism as a fundamentally dynamic phenomenon suddenly seems timeless. While modern tourism follows trends and fashions like a caravan, the fascination with Norwegian nature remained the same at the time the brochure was published in 1994 as with the picture taken in 1890-1894. By using a historical photograph, the reader of the brochure is informed that the fjord and glacier were already tourist attractions 100 years earlier. On the other hand, the enduring presence of the glacier makes it a representation of nature's force that may have changed in form and shape during this period, but not in their symbolic essence. The construction of a landscape oriented towards tourism is superimposed on an already well-established, romantic perception of the Norwegian (and Western) landscape, this earlier way of seeing now subordinated to the presence of visitors. Knudsen adapted his pictures to this change. Symbols of tourism such as the hotel or even the presence of the tourist himself took on the function of visualising recreation, thus showing that the wild landscape has been conquered and penetrated by man and that nothing remains of the romantic wilderness and idyll.

Mechanisms of Commercialization

The consumers of landscape photographs, the original target group of the product, were foreign tourists. Norway's history in the years before the turn of the century was marked by strong economic growth that began in the 1880s. Industrialisation in the last half of the 19th century had laid the economic foundations for a social class with the capital and leisure to travel, in countries such as England and Norway (Meyer 1982: 20). In the course of this boom Norway changed from an isolated state on the edge of Europe to a modern industrial nation with a completely modernised infrastructure. Between 1850 and 1914, the development of the railway network was carried out at great expense by the state, but the most important traffic artery in Norway was still shipping along the long coastline. Infrastructural modernisation enabled new travel opportunities and tourists began to flow into the country. Rowboats and sailboats were replaced with modern steamboats, steamboat companies were established, new routes were introduced and there was a strong upswing in tourism and travel on the fjords (Brevig 2010: 98 ff.). In 1873 Oskar II, King of Norway and Sweden, travelled to the North Cape and his journey was reported in detail, which was an excellent advertisement for Norway as a tourist destination. Emperor Wilhelm's annual "Nordlandreisen", which took place for 26 consecutive years from 1888 to 1914, was also influential for Norwegian tourism. From 1886 to 1906, the number of foreign tourists doubled to over 30.000 (Erlandsen 2000: 163). The English formed the largest group, followed by

Germans, Dutch, Swedes and Danes. Slogans such as 'Norway – Destination par excellence', 'The Sanatorium of Europe' or 'Midnight Sunland' were used by the Association for Travel Life in Norway to promote Norway as a destination abroad.

This growing tourist market from the 1880s onwards was the context for the commercial development of Knudsen's photographic work. The Norwegian Trekking Association (DNT) had been founded in 1868, prior to these developments, and Knudsen, a member from 1871, had produced pictures for the organisation (Reiakvam 1997: 108). Other channels of distribution were Norwegian booksellers and publishers, but of great significance were exhibitions in which Knudsen´s landscape photographs reached an international audience. Knudsen presented his photographs almost annually at exhibitions in Scandinavia – first at the Art and Industry Exhibition in Stockholm in 1866 – later exhibiting in other European countries, in America and at 'world exhibitions'. In 1872 he took part in the Nordic Industrial and Art Exhibition in Copenhagen and in 1873 in the General Nordic Industrial Exhibition in Drammen in Norway. At the Centennial International Exhibition in Philadelphia in 1876 he was given an award for his landscape photographs from Lapland and received a further award at the World Exhibition in Paris in 1878. The fact that Knudsen's pictures were not only shown in Scandinavia but also internationally – in the Norwegian Pavilion at World Expositions in the 1870s, for example – illustrates the representative role of his pictures from a Norwegian perspective.

It was, however, Knudsen's strategic orientation that was decisive for the distribution and popularization of his pictures. In 1889 most of Knudsen´s landscape pictures were published in a sales catalogue which included a register of over 12.000 pictures in different sizes (Sollied 1967: 64). The catalogue lists all the photographs Knudsen took and sold between 1864 and 1896. Subdivided into various formats (stereo, 13×18, 16×22, 21×27), the pictures are arranged chronologically and titled, but not dated. An excerpt from the sales catalogue No. 1 shows that the numbered titles were combined into series under individual places or areas. The instructions for use in four languages indicate that the catalogue was intended for Norwegian, English, French and German tourists and that the publication was intended for the public. Beyond its commercial purpose, the catalogue can also be seen as an archiving system. Against this background, the catalogue was the starting point for the systematic archiving by the University Library in Bergen in the mid-1970s, on the basis of which the current archive is based. The intention of the catalogue and its structure can be explained by the fact that shortly before, Knudsen's studio was converted into a company named K. Knudsen & Company. This transformation from a studio into a company had the greatest impact on the commercialization of Knudsen´s photographs. From 1887 Knudsen's nephew Knut Digernæs took over the management of the business and from 1898 the entire company. The conversion of the studio into a company was associated with a huge expansion, because Digernæs had invented a special machine for the production of brochure cards and stereoscopic images, for which he had founded his own publishing house (Bonge 1980: 100).

The postcard

The postcard *Stalheim Hotel and Nærøydalen valley* (1906/07, Fig. 6) shows the familiar view of Nærødalen Valley. As a narrower detail of the picture has been chosen here, the focus is not on the Stalheimskleva, but on the hotel. The building is embedded in the landscape and serves as a symbol of Norwegian tourism. It has become part of the landscape, acts as a tourist icon and has subsequently become one of the most photographed postcard motifs in Norway (Nordhagen 1994: 43). Knudsen, however, was not the author of this view. The dating of 1906/07 names K. Knudsen & Company as authors of the picture. Even though the hotel shown here is not the same as in Knudsen's photograph, the view from the photo album replicated and probably served the company as a standard motif. However, Knudsen himself was no longer involved in the production of the postcards, as it only began after he had left the company K. Knudsen & Company in 1896.

During the course of postcard production, K. Knudsen & Company photographed Knudsen's old prints or created new pictures based on his image scheme, which shows that he had become a brand. Norway's largest and most successful postcard producer, along with K. Knudsen & Company, was photographer Anders B. Wilse. However, Wilse only issued a small number of his own postcards. He photographed in large quantities for other publishers, having acquired the negative collection of Swedish photographer Axel Lindahl – Knudsen's biggest competitor in the field of landscape photography – , which contained a large number of plates from the late 1870s that were used by him for the production of numerous postcards until the 20th century. While photo albums were tourist products designed to preserve memories, the photographic postcard like the one from Stalheim discussed above was also an ideal medium to promote tourism commercially by allowing travellers to share their memories with others.

In Norway, postcards replaced photographic brochures from the mid-1890s onwards. The postcard, which was mainly distributed by publishers and booksellers, developed into a mass product and was distributed worldwide beginning around 1900. As a modern means of communication, it satisfied the desire to transmit short messages as well as the personal transmission of experiences, which brought the exotic close to others. In this way, the recipient could not only be given a visual impression of what had been experienced, but the photograph could also serve as proof that the place depicted on the card had actually been visited. In addition, there is the timeless and aesthetic character of photography, which is particularly evident in photographic postcards. Both examples make it clear that the medium of postcards represents the climax of the commercialization of landscape photography.

The two most successful landscape photographers in Norway – Knudsen and Lindahl – were the main suppliers of images and motifs, as was the case with the brochures in the past, but they gave up their authorship in the course of product development. It is not they themselves who are responsible for postcard production, but companies or publishers who have turned them and their photographs into brands. These actors were responsible for selection, reproduction and distribution. The travel agency Thomas Benett & Sønner in Christiania reveal why Knudsen's landscape motifs from Western Norway were ideally suited as postcard motifs. They stated that among the best-selling postcards were almost exclusively motifs from the route along Nærøfjorden and through Nærødal (Erlandsen 2000: 148). In total, the 50 most popular motifs represent elements of the Central and Western Norwegian landscape such as fjords, waterfalls and valleys. The list also includes motifs from stave churches and hotels, but not from Northern Norway, Sørlandet or Oslofjord.

Conclusion

This essay has argued that Knud Knudsen was one of the most important pioneers of Scandinavian photography and shaped the pictorial imagination of northern European landscapes, especially that of Norway. Beginning in the 1860s he travelled his homeland for nearly 40 years and photographed its landscapes and people. At the end of the 19th century, he had not only made himself a name but built a brand as Norway's first commercial travel and landscape photographer. He had taken thousands of images, which were sold to publishers beyond the country's borders and that were sent as postcards by travellers visiting Norway to countries all over the world. In addition, his pictures became Norway's visual representative at world exhibitions in Europe and America. Knudsen's, pictures are among the most famous photographs of the 19th century in Norway today.

Most significant, perhaps, is Knudsen's pivotal role in the development of commercial landscape photography, a process intimately connected to Norway's industrialisation in the second half of the 19th century, its development of modern infrastructure in terms of both the railway network and steamboat lines servicing the coastline and fjords, and the growth of tourism. Knudsen's early photography represented the rural working life of Norwegians as well as the mountains, fjords and waterfalls of West Norway. He was also fascinated in these early years with the logistical challenges of travelling and with photographic technique. Many of his images were of the bulky apparatus required by the collodion process but these can also be regarded as symbols of modernity, technology and progress. In his photograph of Stalheim from the 1880s Knudsen similarly embraced modernity. In this image of the first tourist destinations in Norway he visualized how modernization had permeated the Norwegian landscape, including the presence within it of the new hotel. Knudsen's role in representing the Norwegian landscape to an international audience had been established as early as 1866, in exhibitions throughout Scandinavia and further afield, but it was his relationship to tourism that had the greatest significance, in particular through a strategic orientation involving the mass production and worldwide distribution of the postcard, the end of a long process of reinventing the Norwegian landscape through photography.

References

Austad, Ingvild/Leif Hauge (2008): "The 'Fjordscape' of Inner Sogn, Western Norway", In: Michael Jones & Kenneth R. Olwig: Nordic Landscapes. Region and Belonging on the Northern Edge of Europe, Minneapolis/London.

Barthes, Roland (1989): Die helle Kammer. Bemerkung zur Photographie, Frankfurt am Main.

Bonge, Susanne (1980): Eldre norske fotografer. Fotografer og amatørfotografer i Norge frem til 1920, Bergen.

Brevig, Hans Olaf (2010): "Wege ins Reiseland Norwegen. Die Infrastrukturentwicklung um 1900", In: Sonja Kinzler & Doris Tillmann (Hg.) Nordlandreise. Die Geschichte einer touristischen Entdeckung, Kiel.

Casey, Edward (2006): Ortsbeschreibungen. Landschaftsmalerei und Kartographie, München.

Crang, Mike (2006): Circulation and Emplacement: "The Hollowed-out Performance of Tourism", In: Claudio Minca & Tim Oakes: Travels in Paradox: Remapping Tourism, Lanham, p. 47-64.

Digranes, Åsne/Solveig Greve/Oddlaug Reiakvam (1988): Det Norske Bildet. Knud Knudsens fotografier 1864-1900, Bergen.

Erlandsen, Roger (2000): Pas nu paa! Nu tar jeg fra Huldet! Om fotografiets første hundre år i Norge – 1839-1940, Oslo.

Friedman, Martin/Henning Bender (1982): The Frozen Image: Scandinavian Photography, New York.

Hellmann, Karen/Brett Abbott (2013): Landscape in Photographs, Los Angeles.

Lippard, Lucy (2005): "Park-Plätze", In: Brigitte Franzen & Stefanie Krebs: Landschaftstheorie. Texte der Cultural Landscape Studies, Köln, p. 110-138

Lundberg, Anders (2008): "Changes in the Land and the Regional Identity of Western Norway: The Case of Sandhåland, Karmøy", In: Michael Jones & Kenneth R.

Olwig (Hg.): Nordic Landscapes. Region and Belonging on the Northern Edge of Europe, Minneapolis/London, p. 344-371

Morgenstern, Neil (1993), Fotograf Knud Knudsen. Bilder fra hans tidlige ar-en nylig oppdaget samling, Oslo

Morgenstern, Neil [unpublished manuscript]: The Foto Knudsen Collection, Bergen

Meyer, Robert (1982): "The Primal Landscapes of Knud Knudsen", In: Martin Friedman und Henning Bender: The Frozen Image: Scandinavian Photography. New York, p. 22-27.

Nordhagen, Per Jonas (1994): From National icons to tourist photography. Grand themes in the depiction of Norwegian scenery, In: Roger Erlandsen & Vegard S. Halvorsen: ìDarkness and light ì, Oslo.

Reiakvam, Oddlaug (1997): Bilderrøyndom. Røyndomsbilde. Fotografi som kulturelle tidsuttrykk, Oslo.

Scarlett, F. (1921): Turistlandet Norge. Turisttrafikkens begyndelse og udvikling til verdenskrigens udbrud samt 30 aars erindringer som turistagent i Norge, Kristiania

Sollied, Ragna (1967): Eldre Bergenske Fotografer, Bergen, Eget Forlag.

Sontag, Susan (2011): Über Fotografie, Frankfurt am Main

Tuchtenhagen, Ralph (2007): "Nordische Landschaft" und wie sie entdeckt wurde, In: Andreas Fülberth, Albert Meier & Victor Andrés Ferretti (Hrsg.): Nördlichkeit – Romantik – Erhabenheit. Apperzeptionen der Nord/Süd-Differenz (1750-2000). Imaginatio Borealis. Bilder des Nordens Bd. 15, Frankfurt am Main.

Aurora Borealis Recordings: Wilderness Spectacle in "Real Time"

Lena Quelvennec

Introduction

Landscape, traditionally, is concerned with the land: how 'natureculture' relationships have shaped it and how human beings have looked at it.[1] However, for this chapter, I'm going to follow Tim Ingold's advice and for once not only look at the land but at the sky (2011). Indeed, the sky, as the light source of many landscapes, tends to be an integral part of them while being distinguished as separate. The sky is the connection between the material and the immaterial. Not only a "surface" on which landscapes are revealed, the sky surrounds the viewer and includes them in the experience of the environment. This text will conceive of the experience of northern landscape as something to "move through" instead of to "move across" (Ingold, 2006: 17).

Among all existing types of celestial phenomena, aurora (northern or southern lights) is a natural light display which exclusively happens in both polar regions of the earth.[2] Solar winds, which are charged particles emitted from the sun, enter the planet's atmosphere and become ionized by colliding with the atoms present there. These particles then lose their energy and produce light as a result. Their forms and colours vary greatly depending on which particles enter at which speed. This accounts for their constantly moving shape. The outcome is known to look spectacular and mysterious. Therefore, traces of people trying to explain and capture the phenomenon through mythologies or science can be found since Antiquity and beyond, particularly in the northern hemisphere (Jóhannesson/Lund, 2017: 186).

1 The term 'natureculture' is developed by Donna Haraway (2016). It expresses the idea that culture and nature should not be systematically separated since they both intersect biophysically and socially. On the same level, nature and technology should be considered as co-constitutive of the social as humans.

2 Aurora happens on other planets, though. It is not only a terrestrial characteristic.

The northern lights are emblematic of the Nordic landscape and have become one of its main tourist attractions. They transform the northern landscape into a mystified and romanticised experience in which one can participate and hopefully bring home a souvenir. In the past ten years, the number of recordings of the phenomenon have actually exploded. Aurora borealis recordings are the reproduction of the natural phenomenon on storage devices such as canvas and film. They can be preserved as evidence, maintained in an archive, or kept as a trophy to then be presented to a new audience. The attempt to record northern lights is not a new practice but it has become more common with the development of new technologies, as can be observed on forums and websites such as Space Weather, but also on less specialised platforms like YouTube.[3]

In other words, with the development of nature tourism in Nordic European countries, with the technological development of the video camera, and with the new diffusion possibilities of the internet, the northern landscape appears closer than ever. This text intends to study how the perception of remoteness, inherent to the idea of Wilderness, may or may not have been affected by this second life on the web.

To focus my research on this touristic performance, I will look at the YouTube video titled *Northern Lights in Iceland, in REAL TIME!!!* directed by Alessio Perboni and posted on February 2013.[4] Indeed, the video's background and structure are symptomatic of this recording practice: a man travels to Iceland to record the Northern lights and brings back raw footage that he then edits and shares on YouTube. Keeping in mind the specificities of this platform – the capability of feedback from viewers – I will also take the comments of the video into account.

Furthermore, I intend to investigate two questions raised in Jonathan Crary's book, *Techniques of the Observer* (1990). I will demonstrate how Perboni's video appears as the product of a visual history – the observer's gaze performing the tourist's gaze – leading to the first question that will be asked: is there a continuity between the visuality of this video and previous visual materials representing aurora borealis? The video will be compared with examples from painting, photography and film. I will examine how the observers of aurora borealis are influenced by three interconnected narratives revealed by the analysis of the video comments: the 19th Century narrative of the wilderness exploration, the pleasure of the aesthetic spectacle, and the narrative of technological progress.

3 Space Weather. BISA/EU, (1998-2018) Internet Archive Wayback machine. Website: <https://web.archive.org/web/20100804164127/http://spaceweather.com//> (accessed June 18, 2018)

4 Video, 1:53', 76637 views, 264 likes, 9 dislikes, made by Alessio Perboni on January 13, 2013, posted on YouTube by Alessio Perboni on February 13, 2013. Online video: <https://www.youtube.com/watch?v=dGQ7EZs5xu8> (accessed June 18, 2018)

The second question addresses practices formed in the context of new modes of social, economic and technological production, specifically YouTube, an online distribution platform offering to others the ability to comment. Viewers of the YouTube video perceive the world through a particular technology, within which there is an emphasis on 'real time' experience in the form of immediacy and the opportunity for feedback, but also connected to the technical production of moving images and the perception of movement and speed. Thus, there is produced an interesting connection in this form of cultural reception between the original experience and its being shared with an audience.

An observer is "one who sees within a prescribed set of possibilities, one who is embedded in a system of conventions and limitations" (Crary, 1990: 6). Crary's observer may be more related to the scientist and the artist, as these positions in the 19th Century were often occupied by small groups of people, mostly white bourgeois males. These same people were also the first tourists, having the opportunity to travel, first in relation to their work, later just for the purpose of cultural adventure. The contemporary tourist's motivations remain quite influenced by these figures even if they have been developed into many different practices (Urry/Larsen, 2011, chap. 1: 4). In respect to the history of the aurora borealis, travel to the northern wilderness had been reserved for a few explorers and scientists. Extremely perilous, these expeditions were extensively documented with the goal of bringing back images of these distant places.

James Moir (2011) also connects the observer and the tourist in his text, *Seeing the Site: Tourism as a Perceptual Experience*. He elaborates on how "scientific practice involves observation and the visual construction of 'facts'", which implies "constituting and labelling a phenomenon which is then placed prior to this process as an already-existing feature of the world" (Moir, 2011: 167). This process can also be found in the tourist industry, in the tourist's performances on the site, or in the latter's transcription into images. Urry and Larsen (2011, chap. 5: 14) offer the terms "corporeal travel" – the physical movement to visit a place – and "imaginative travel" – the experience of travelling somewhere through representations (texts, photographs, videos, etc.). Both influence each other and produce different kinds of "tourist gazes" that are useful theoretical tools in the context of Perboni's video. This relationship to the "observation and visual construction of 'facts'" also reflects on the notion of 'authenticity' in tourism. Concerned with meeting the extraordinary, the tourist often desires to bring back proofs of these encounters. In tourism studies, 'authenticity' is a contested word and, if it is admitted that it is one of the drivers of tourism, it is now described as a "staged authenticity" (MacCannell, 1973: 595-596; Urry/Larsen, 2011, chap. 1: 8). In this text, I will show how the authentic aspects of the aurora borealis recording are changing in relation to technology.

The tourist has become one of the key figures of postmodernism. Some, like Zygmunt Bauman (1996), have even erected 'him' as one of the representatives of contemporary times. However, this author has also been criticised for forgetting that his tourist figure has a body and this body often heavily influences how the tourist is able to move into this world. For example, if this tourist figure were to be female or black, her movement would have become a lot more complicated, maybe even impossible (Jokinen/Veijola, 1994: 29). Therefore, the tourist experience is fully embodied, while often according a particular attention to a visually dominated practice (Urry/Larsen, 2011: 189-216). The tourist performed the act of gazing at the world in the quest for what is out of the ordinary (Rojek, 1997: 52). Finally, an observer or a tourist needs tools to help in the formation of their gaze. For example, although photography was almost born at the same time as tourism (Urry/Larsen, 2011, chap. 7: 8), not all parts of the world were easily captured on photographs. The production of northern lights images – and even more so moving images – was also a technological challenge. They required heavy modifications and interventions creating a very particular visual culture that will be explored here. Even if the tourism industry surrounding the northern lights has been studied from different perspectives (Edensor, 2010; Lund, 2016; Jóhannesson/Lund, 2017), the recording of the phenomenon is still not really researched, neither as an act nor as a form of technological reproduction. Questioning how Nordic landscape and the northern lights are experienced and represented, this chapter will try to understand what happens to the tourist gaze and experience while recording.

Northern lights, in real time!

Perboni's video was chosen partly due to YouTube's browser and research algorithms: it was the fourth video to appear when typing "aurora borealis real time" in October 2017, when I first started my research on this topic. As of June 2018, it was ranked twenty-second, which illustrates the consistency of the practice. There are always more videos produced and referring to these key words. At the time, I didn't select the three previous videos because: the first one was promoting a tourist trip; the second was for relaxation; I could have chosen the third video but its extensive length and its popularity, resulting in numerous comments, would have made it more challenging to analyse for this study without gaining in relevance. Indeed, the following analysis aims for a qualitative approach. I will apply a semiotic analysis of the aesthetics of the video, a historical comparison of the visuality of the video with other representations of the northern lights, as well as a content analysis of the video's comments. These methods combined situate the video in its current position in time. The sole focus here is on Perboni's video as a sample to show an approach which could be applied for future visual analyses of the northern lights.

Northern Lights in Iceland, in REAL TIME!!! lasts 1 minute and 53 seconds. It starts with a black screen with text that reads: "we travelled across Iceland, chasing Northern Lights", and "That is what we saw," then followed by five short shots of driving on icy roads, starting during the day and finishing at dawn.

Figure 1: *Still frame: 00:00:26.* Perboni, Alessio

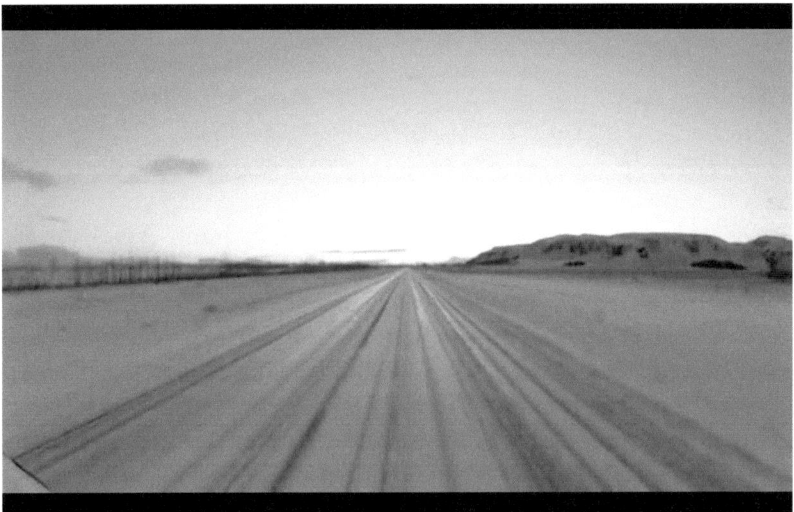

The text already states the importance of the 'chase' and reports on what was 'seen'. Depicting the Icelandic landscape in daylight, these shots are a means to illustrate the distance covered reinforced by the speed up effect of the editing. The camera was placed in the centre of the car's windshield and creates central perspective images of the road crossing the Icelandic land, thus rendering a white, empty, and grandiose landscape. The horizon line equally separates the sky from the ground. Rebecca Solnit (2007: 143-144) reminds her readers that when focusing only on the sky, the viewers may lose their sense of place; it is disorienting. In this respect, this first part of the video plays a role in both proving the remoteness of the landscape and delimiting the space where the main event will take place.

The second part of the video depicts four short samples of the 'real time' aurora borealis. The image is shimmering with noise – dark pixels that cannot really make up their mind to become black when there is not enough light for the camera sensor – but the celestial phenomenon is clearly visible, without apparent filters or aestheticizing effects.

Figure 2: *Still Frame: 00:01:36.* Perboni, Alessio

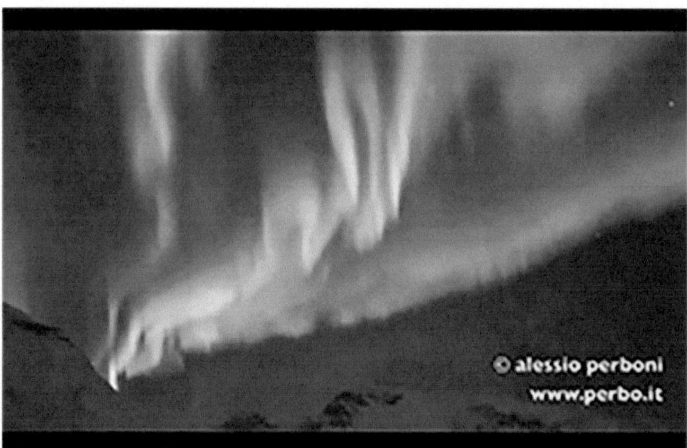

The image is shaking too, reinforcing the documentary quality of the video and assuring that the live and 'authentic' dimension of the event is not being faked, even if the editing could be considered as diminishing the authenticity. The video ends with a black screen with the written text, "real time footage, alessio perboni, www.perbo.it". There are no diegetic sounds to be heard, instead the author has added the Tron: Legacy (2010) soundtrack.

After considering how the video is edited with jump cuts and an additional soundtrack, a question immediately comes to mind: where is the 'real time'? The answer appears in the comments. Indeed, the video comments, 69 in total, are an integral part of its display. I applied a light form of content analysis to each comment, focusing mainly on their intended meanings to identify similarities. In this analysis, I found three recurrent topics: Tourism / Exploration, Beauty / Spectacle, Video capture technique / Real time. These categories tend to overlap, as people sometimes address many points in the same comment. These themes will guide my interpretation regarding the meanings that this recording practice may have today for their observers and for their viewers, and why the term 'real time' is being used.

Tourism/Exploration

The category Tourism / Exploration has the largest number of comments. They are testimonies of previous holidays in the North, often in Iceland, the same location as the video. They cover also questions about people planning to go and asking advice about where and when to see the aurora borealis. The video author himself answered many of them, happy to share his experience.

Figure 3: Comment 1, "Perboni's answers"

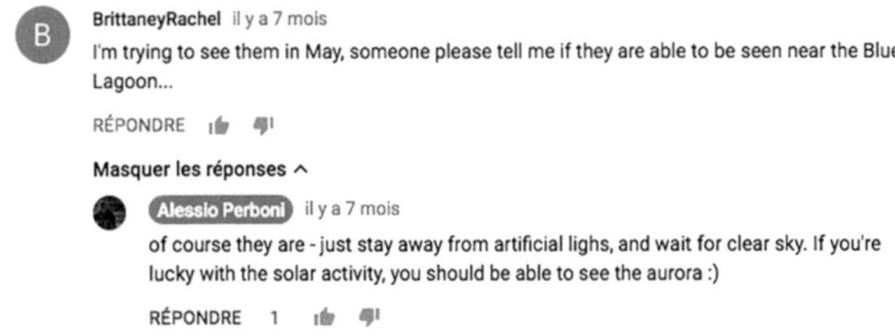

These comments reflect how the northern lights are definitely perceived as a tourist attraction, an integral part of the Nordic landscape experience. Indeed, northern countries such as Iceland have promoted the northern lights as a tourist product since the 2000s (Lund: 2016: 50). This could seem quite recent in the history of tourism, but it should not be forgotten that the conditions of travel in the Far North are still quite extreme. It is still difficult for travel to be pleasurable without good equipment and preparations. Additionally, the phenomenon is not easy to capture. Comments argue that it is necessary to avoid "artificial light", and to be "lucky with the solar activity" (fig. 3).[5] The encounter can never be guaranteed. Comments asks for patience, commitment and some sense of adventure to be able to brave the darkness and the cold and to maybe have the chance of catching something. You have also to be careful to not get lost in the wilderness, as one of the comments advised, "stay with the group."

Figure 4: *Comment 2, "Stay with the group"*

The wilderness is not nature emptied of all human presence. William Cronon explains in The Trouble with Wilderness:

5 YouTube comments are complex to reference so a screenshot has been made of them as figures. When quoting the comments, the figure number will be indicated at the end of the sentence. The full reference of the figure can be found in the list of images at the end of the chapter.

> Far from being the one place on earth that stands apart from humanity, it is quite profoundly a human creation – indeed, the creation of very particular human cultures at very particular moments in human history (1995: 7).

Both the history of the North and its identification as wilderness were constructed concurrently in the accounts of 19th century Western explorers. Indeed, even if the first European Arctic expeditions can be dated from the early 15th century (Mirsky, 1997), the notion of wilderness as something to be studied and explored for resources – and later fun – appeared with the development of modern sciences during the industrial era. Iceland, for example, which is still sometimes promoted as "Europe's last Wilderness" shows an interesting connection between when it was settled and the development of the concept of wilderness (Oslund, 2005: 314; Sæþórsdóttir et al., 2011: 250). Before the 19th century, wild areas were mostly considered by Europeans as frightening and uncivilized; this vision completely ignores the indigenous histories of these same places by describing them as 'virgin' (Cronon, 1995: 15; Sæþórsdóttir et al., 2011: 253). This justified large expeditions organized to 'discover' new territories, to map and claim lands which progressively started to be narrated as adventure. During these explorations, the northern lights were encountered, for instance, during the Arctic expedition of Dr. Isaac Hayes memorialized in Frederic Edwin Church's painting, Aurora Borealis (1865).

Figure 5: Aurora Borealis (1865), by Frederic Edwin Church

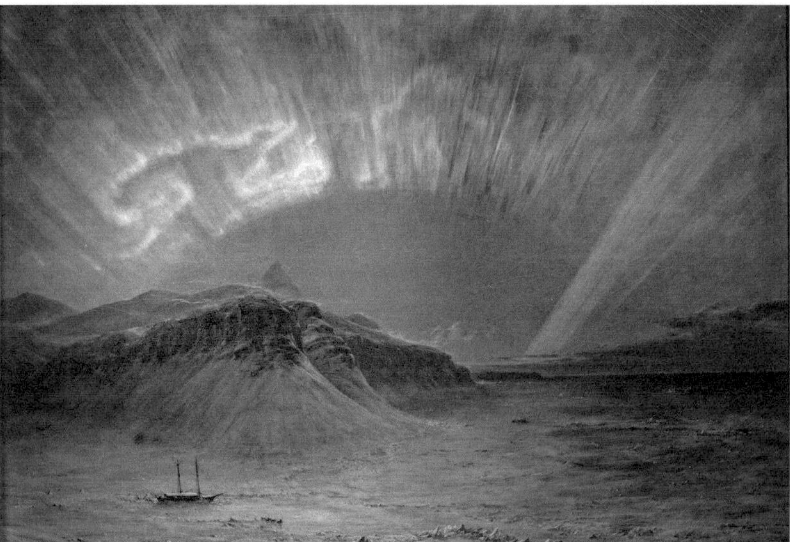

This painting shows a Nordic landscape illuminated by the northern lights. It is a sublime image, depicting the terrible and beautiful nature of the North in an almost divine and supernatural light. The explorers, on their small ship, look insignificant and isolated in the middle of a borderless and frozen landscape. Still, they are there, an incarnation of solitary romantic heroes. This 1865 painting may seem far from Perboni's video. First, it could be pointed out that Hayes' expedition was not in Iceland but near Ellesmere Island, between Canada and Greenland (Encyclopaedia Britannica, 2018). However, this does not preclude the comparison since, as it will be explained later, wilderness is not really located in a specific place but rather in the observer's gaze (Cronon, 1995: 17; Sæþórsdóttir et al., 2011: 253).

In Church's painting, wilderness is perceived both through its aesthetic and scientific value (Rosenbaum, 2015: 26). Nature is perceived as distinct from humanity, hostile and rich in unpredictability. It is qualified as remote since any encounter with pure nature necessitates travel to the edge of the civilized world. In this sense, it also promotes national pride for an American explorer, who has mastered a piece of wild nature by documenting it. This domestication process is also applied in the painting itself which depicts nature in the threatening but actually safe framing of the sublime.[6] This leads to the second difference with Perboni's video; Church has carefully constructed the composition of his painting. The high perspective in a far distance produces a mysterious and impressive atmosphere, while situating the viewer in a floating area often used to foster the impression of a clear visualization of the scene. Church wanted to render an objective view, providing the observer with a scientific and romantic gaze for his topic.

In the video, however, the images look a lot more chaotic. The shots are cut very short, as if the strength of Perboni's video does not reside in the composition of his images. If it also aims for an 'authentic' representation, the point of view chosen is radically different. Indeed, the tourist gaze wants to render its subjectivity accessible while showing this natural event. In this sense, the images situate the viewer close to Perboni's body. From his eye level the video, by its chaotic movement, shows the intensity of the encounter with the aurora, trying to capture both the natural phenomenon and the observer's experience at the same time.

Nevertheless, Church's narrative of the wilderness is still present in Perboni's experience of the northern lights. Today, the heroic gesture of the encounter with wild nature incarnated by the Arctic expeditions has become an integral part of

6 Sublime in the context of landscape painting is defined as follow: "Of a feature of nature or art: that fills the mind with a sense of overwhelming grandeur or irresistible power; that inspires awe, great reverence, or other high emotion, by reason of its beauty, vastness, or grandeur." (OED, 2018) It is characterised by a delightful horror, since it depicts the terrible while in the safe position of a distant observer.

the nature-tourism industry. As Jóhannesson and Lund describe in *Aurora Borealis: Choreographies of Darkness and Light* (2017: 187), the northern lights guided tour plays the card of the adventure, of the hunt, promoting the effort such an expedition should involve, recalling the hardships of 19th century exploration, always accentuating the 'authentic', and taking into account the potential tourist that the northern lights need to earn. Nature-tourism, while sometimes encompassing ecological concerns, often still promotes values from the 19th century. At this time, a group of white and bourgeois men started to feel the need to escape the alienating effect of a system from which they benefited: industrialization (Cronon, 1995: 14; Jokinen/Veijola, 1997: 39), and the whole history of outdoor tourism is still tainted by their search for the 'authentic' experience of a 'virgin' nature. This narrative maintains the idea of a nature separated from humanity, which needs to be dominated and preserved (Lund, 2013: 169). In Perboni's video, this appears through the choice of words, "chasing" and "saw", in the introductory text, and then the first shots, showing the road and the kilometres covered in the middle of nowhere. It is important that the viewer does not believe that the northern lights can be seen with this quality in the middle of Reykjavik.

One series of comments, though, shows that the reality of the northern lights guided tour is a little more complicated nowadays, stressing the "buses full of tourists".

Figure 6: *Comment 3, "Buses full of tourists"*

PianoMan Smith il y a 3 semaines

Dammit all. I spent 18 months in iceland.....back in the 1950's, and never saw anything as great as this light show. Evidently the SUN is a lot more active somehow and is helping to create all these natural wonders. I wouldn't mind being back there right now.

RÉPONDRE

Masquer les réponses ^

Alessio Perboni il y a 2 semaines

PianoMan Smith We've been very lucky! But Iceland is very touristic right now... my first time there has been in 2011, and it was amazing - almost no one around. Now it's crowded with buses full of tourists... they're everywhere. You've seen something that no one can see anymore! And that's more valuable than northern lights, to me :)

RÉPONDRE

PianoMan Smith il y a 2 semaines

I was lucky enough to spend time in Iceland but not lucky enough to see the Northern Lights in all their splendor. I assume in those were the years when the SUN must have had an ebb in activity. I wish i had been there recently. I have read that 1.6 MILLION tourists visited Iceland in 2016. That's a lot.

RÉPONDRE

Lund (2016: 59) elaborates on how the tourism industry has set up all the necessary infrastructures to facilitate access to the wild North, and as is also indicated by Iceland's official tourism website, millions of people travel there each year.[7] For those seeking 'authenticity', however, the whole experience is diminished by the presence of other humans; as the comments underscore, the exclusivity of the experience is where the most value resides. This exemplifies what Crawshaw and Urry call the "romantic tourist gaze" where "the emphasis is upon solitude, privacy and a personal, semi-spiritual relationship with the object of the gaze" (1997: 176), thereby reproducing the same nostalgia the first 19th century privileged tourists felt when looking for a beautiful, lost heaven.

Beauty/Spectacle

The category Beauty/Spectacle contains 17 comments, more or less affirming a positive experience based on how the video looks. Cronon states: "As more and more tourists sought out the wilderness as a spectacle to be looked at and enjoyed for its great beauty, the sublime in effect became domesticated." (1995: 12) Nature is perceived as a spectacle and the auroras are literally natural light shows. One comment describes how the landscape is given a magical and emotional atmosphere, adding to its natural beauty.

Figure 7: *Comment 4, "Add to its beauty"*

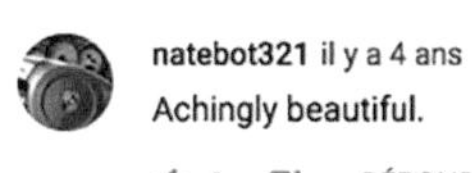

1 RÉPONDRE

Masquer les réponses ^

kappelmeister123 il y a 1 an

natebot321 I was just there..in Iceland..I travel quite a bit..I have been to every continent except Antarctica..that's a trip I am planning.. Iceland is very very very magical...the northern lights add to its beauty..but I even went inside a glacier!

RÉPONDRE

If wilderness has become a spectacle, it could also be asked how this notion, implying remoteness and the absence of other human beings, can still be imaginable in the 21st Century. Living in an era that some are ready to call the Anthropocene, the idea of a place outside of human reach can be perceived as paradoxical. In this sense, wilderness may not be found in any specific location anymore, rather it

7 "Number of foreign visitors", Icelandic Tourist Board. (https://www.ferdamalastofa.is/en/recearch-and-statistics/numbers-of-foreign-visitors) (accessed June 20, 2018).

has become a way of framing. It can be argued that certain types of tourists have become quite talented at taming nature: they avoid conventional forms of mass tourism – such as the ubiquitous tourist bus – travelling as individuals or in small groups, in the hope of erasing any human traces that could contradict their imaginative expectation of the spectacle of Nature.

Being able to offer an experience out of the ordinary is an important criterion for tourism. This is related to its history and how Western society has defined the notions of leisure and work (Urry/Larsen, 2011, chap.1: 4). As certain comments discuss, holidays should contrast with normal, everyday life.

Figure 8: *Comment 5, "Just perspective"*

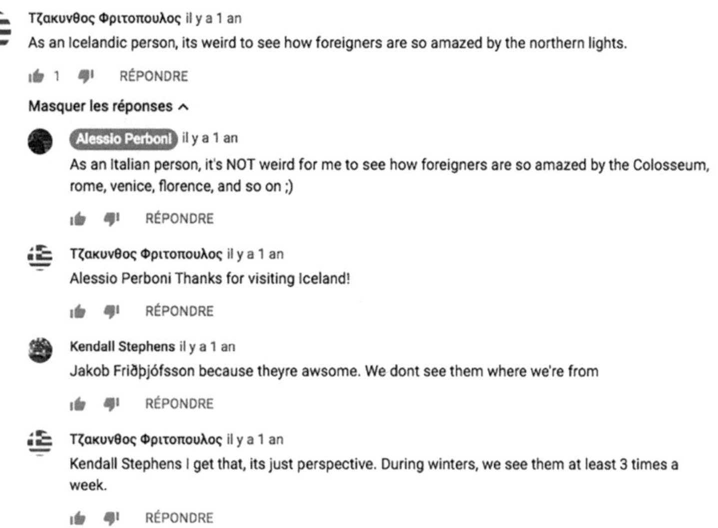

The northern lights with their unpredictability and their very specific locations still possess a wild dimension perfectly matching some tourists' expectations, even if the framing to capture them has become commodified. This capacity for framing is sustained by an assemblage of factors such as how the tourism industries of the concerned countries have reinforced their winter economies, promoting them and making them accessible (Lund, 2016: 49). Furthermore, all guided tours promoting the northern lights also guarantee assistance so that travellers can rest assured they will catch the aurora with their camera. Being able to share the experience on the Internet is important because it possesses a social meaning; the captured image functions as a trophy, a proof of one's presence, but also a token of social exchange. Some viewers express their gratitude.

Figure 9: *Comment 6* "Beautiful"

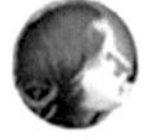

Zahyra94 il y a 3 ans
So beautiful... thank you for putting this up. Sei grandioso :)
RÉPONDRE 1

This reveals the two sides of tourist recording practices mentioned before: corporeal travel where the observer sees the real event, captures it and shares it, and imaginative travel where the viewer enjoys the recording. Both sides need each other to keep this recording practice meaningful. In his text about the social construction of the tourist sight, Rojek points out that this could indicate a "collage tourism" (1997: 62) where the consumption of images replaces travel; but it also produces anticipation (Crawshaw/Urry, 1997: 179). Many comments in all of the content categories express people's wish to see the northern lights themselves, or that they plan to see them in the future. For the time being, these viewers watch recordings instead, participating in the construction of the visual representations of the phenomenon – its framing – and perpetuating this digital experience. Many of these representations already exist on the internet; my search on YouTube for "aurora borealis real time" resulted in 283000 hits (June 20, 2018). This is significant for two reasons. First, the aurora borealis have been a difficult phenomenon to capture in the past and there is still a real accomplishment in managing to record them. This could explain why people are still so eager to represent the 'authentic' experience even in the current time of simulations and self-reflexivity (Baudrillard, 1981; Rojek 1997: 69-70). Second, among the observers in this constant flux of images, some seem to have developed specific criteria affirming what an 'authentic' aurora video should include.

Video capture technique/Real time

The content category Video capture technique / Real time contains 19 comment discussing mostly three interconnected points: which camera equipment is used to get this recording; the difficulty in recording the phenomenon; and the joy of seeing the 'real time' effect underlined in the title of the video. In the case of Perboni's video and comments, recording the northern lights and collecting images is not enough, the experience must be truly shared through the production of a visual realism. This visual realism is reminiscent of Barthes's L'Effet de Réel (1968) where the author deconstructed the relationship between what could seem insignificant details in realist novels and historiography and the construction of a 'realistic' description. Barthes's "reality effect" is the product of a technological development at an historical moment when there was a desire to authenticate the 'real'. When the technologies change, the conventions articulating realistic representations change too. Some comments are a confirmation of Barthes' insights because the shaking movement of the camera described previously and the chaotic image it produced, were definitely the effects desired by the viewers.

Figure 10: *Comment 7*, "shaking camera"

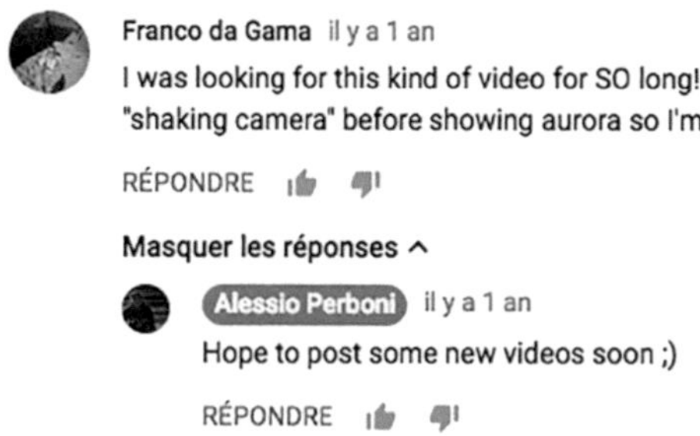

The desire for realism, or a "reality effect" evident in these comments on Perboni's video can be put in the context of earlier efforts to capture the northern light event visually. The northern lights occur in a very cold environment, visible only in the dark. The ability to record the phenomenon has only recently been made possible for many, because of cheaper recording equipment and air travel. Previously, this practice was reserved for explorers and scientists, with a large budget and complex instruments and techniques. In Church's painting, for example, a lot of attention is given to scientific details but Church didn't encounter the aurora himself, rather, he used sketches provided by Dr. Isaac Hayes. This landscape is a reconstructed image, and this has often proven to be the case in many representations of the northern lights. Even 20 years ago, the production of Aurora recordings required complex technical apparatus.

In the 1990s, a movie discussed this issue. *Picture of Lights* (1994), by Peter Mettler, is a documentary about an expedition to Churchill, Manitoba to film the northern lights. The pretext for the movie is the intention to record the aurora for "real", as the human eyes see it, but at the time this was accessible only to a rich eccentric man (again the figure of the bourgeois tourist appears). His camera, built especially to support extremely cold temperatures, was large and extremely complicated to carry around.

Figure 11: *The special camera*

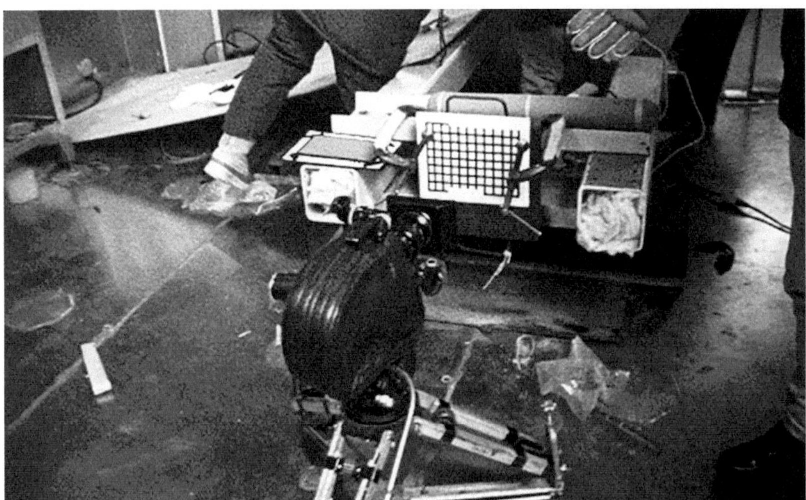

During the filming of *Picture of Lights*, technical and meteorological problems occurred, and it was only possible to record a few images of the aurora. Significantly, the director then decided to have the film evolve into a philosophical discussion about the northern lights' meaning for the local populations. In other words, if this movie is a beautiful example of technological failure, it managed to remain relevant to its topic.

Figure 12: *"Aurora Borealis"* from Picture of Light

In most cases, though, people were unable to access this kind of equipment. Time lapse, although first used for scientific purpose to record the northern lights, possesses its own aesthetic value and has become the most commonly used technique.[8] It consists of taking a series of pictures with a very long exposure time and then editing them into a video. This technique results in a speeding effect of the phenomenon and an intensification of its colours. The resulting moving images are impossible to produce without a lengthy editing process. In many comments, time lapse seems not to be considered acceptable anymore. It looks fake because it does not accurately reflect human vision.

Figure 13: *Comment 8*, "real time"

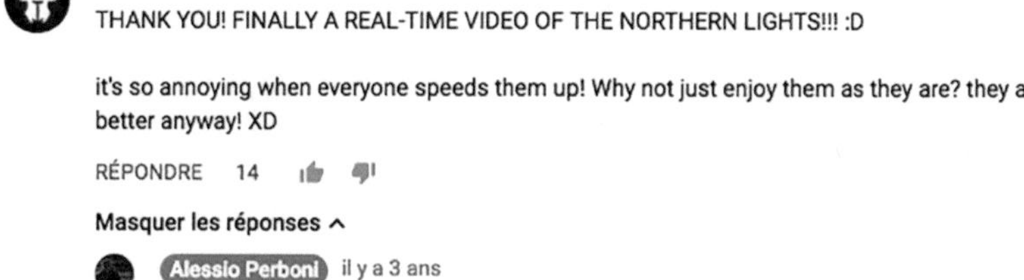

All these perfectly clean images of the northern lights, full of oversaturated colours, almost like disco lights, may not correspond to what current observers look for while travelling through space or behind their screen. The 'authentic' aurora must appear difficult to capture, as the four sequences of Perboni's video illustrate with the camera struggling to record them. The video is dark, short, pixelated. It gives a sense of speed, of how fast the northern lights actually move. In this respect, the technological narrative and the natural narrative seems to coalesce into a 'real time' aesthetic.

8 In the 1980s, for example, David Malin, a scientist and photographer, produced famous images by adapting astronomical photography filters to get multiple exposures and by recombining the images in the laboratory. His images were created by and for scientists, for collecting data and understanding the phenomenon. He fixed them in time or speeded them up as for time lapse. (cf. davidmalin.com).

Conclusion

As Paul Virilio discusses in *Vision Machine* (1994), 'real time' is generally used to describe the simultaneous effect of the direct, the live. Something happens somewhere and recording the event produces direct access to it, an effect of simultaneity. However, the notion of 'real time' used in this video title and by its commentators is the idea of a recording that simulates the speed perceived by human vision. Perboni's video, with its short footage clips edited together, can only be understood as 'real time' in the technological history of the aurora recording.

The 'real time' effect, both for tourist observers and tourist viewers, is an important gage of authenticity. 'Authenticity' is understood as conforming to the observer's experience, but it is more than that; it gives authority to the person creating the representation. Rojek (1997: 56) explains why authenticity should not be considered as the main purpose of the tourist experience, underscoring how tourists today are often aware of the staged aspect of authenticity. He called "post-tourism" this awareness that come from the individuals' intensive practice of "dragging and indexing" representations of specific sites (guidebook, movies, photographs, blog, etc.) (ibid.: 62). However, 'authentic' criteria do not completely disappear. In the case of aurora recordings, there is still a quest for the most 'authentic' representation, the one reproducing the real time or rather the 'real' perceived speed and generating its own "reality effect."

It has been suggested in the course of this essay that an important part of the contemporary tourist experience occurs through the creation of images, which are often more immediate and accessible than reality. This constructed realism is a social exchange within which both the observer and the viewer's gazes can be connected. Viewers do not see the northern lights directly but their ability to react with comments to shared digital images and receive responses to their reactions creates an experience comparable to the 'real time' and corporeality of the actual event. This contemporary experience can be considered in relation to the two questions raised at the beginning, both of which arise from Crary's *Techniques of the Observer*: an examination of how sharing and interaction are key aspects of new forms of visual production and distribution through online platforms, considering the impact of this on the experience of the aurora borealis; and assessing the extent to which there is continuity between the visuality of Perboni's video and earlier representations of the aurora borealis.

In relation to the first question, changes in the qualities of the gaze are the product of recent technological, economic, and social transformations: the development of tourism in Nordic regions leading to more corporeal travel; and the development of technology allowing imaginative travel with an interactive aspect. The tourist gaze, it has been argued, involves look at the world through a body. The valued qualities of a touristic image are in its capacity to connect with corporeal activity. Understood in relation to the enhanced corporeality of the tourist gaze changes can be identified in the framing of the northern lights, making its reception as mere spectacle inadequate, emphasising instead the performance of an embodied gaze which, through the possibilities inherent in the new technologies of social media, can be shared and experienced in 'real time'. When watching the act of gazing in Perboni's video the viewer can get close to this performance, because it is perceived to occur in 'real time', which is more than a purely visual experience of the aesthetic properties of the aurora; aspects of corporeal travel are transmitted into the virtual and imaginative travel, so the distance between the tourist observer and the tourist viewer becomes smaller.

In relation to the second question, a continuity does exist, the motivation behind the act of recording has, nevertheless, been transformed, specifically in relation to the gaze of the observer. This is not to argue that the visual and aesthetic aspects of newer representations of the aurora borealis are absent. In fact, the appearance of the northern lights is heavily transformed in recent representations, reinforcing their aesthetical qualities. Thus, alongside of the corporeality of the gaze there is also their representation as a pure visual experience. Furthermore, elements of historically more distant motivations for seeking out and representing the aurora borealis continue in the narratives behind this new performed gaze. If it is difficult for tourists to explore, map, explain and control the extraordinary in the way of 19th century travellers, the desire for the beauty of wilderness and the adventurous achievement of travelling in remote areas still influences the perception of the Nordic landscape, while the nature-based tourist's gaze is also still tied to a white male perspective, which is also strongly present in the nation branding of Iceland (Loftsdóttir, 2015: 246). What this suggests is that even though the 'real time' effect of new technology has allowed the viewer to get closer, imaginatively, to the observer's experience, notions of an authentic nature distinct and separate from humanity prevail, represented still through the figure of the explorer and the narrative of wilderness (Cronon, 1995). Thus, new technologies have provided the observer with more efficient tools, and these modes of representation have introduced a sharing aspect, collapsing the temporal and spatial distance between observer and viewer, but older conceptions of landscape, with their emphasis on authenticity, wilderness and remoteness have continued into the 21st century.

References

Barthes, Roland (1968): "L'Effet de Réel", In Communication, 11, Recherches Sémiologiques le Vraisemblable, Paris: Persée, pp. 84-89.

Baudrillard, Jean (1981): Simulacre et Simulation, Paris: Gallilé.

Bauman, Zygmunt (1996): "From Pilgrim to Tourist – or a Short History of Identity". In Stuart Hall/Paul de Gray (eds.), Question of Cultural Identity, Los Angeles, Calif.: Sage, pp. 18-36.

Crary, Jonathan (1990): Techniques of the Observer, London: MIT Press.

Crawshaw, Carol/Urry, John. "Tourism and the Photographic Eyes", pp. 176-195.

Cronon, William (1995): 'The Trouble with Wilderness, or Getting Back to the Wrong Nature'. In Uncommon Ground: Rethinking the Human Place in Nature, New York: W. W. Norton & Co, pp. 8-28.

Edensor, Timothy J. (2010): "Aurora Landscapes: Affective Atmospheres of Light and Dark". In Benediktsson Karl/Lund Katrín Anna (eds.), Conversations with Landscape. Farnham: Ashgate. pp. 227-240.

Haraway, Donna (2016): Manifestly Haraway, Minneapolis: University of Minnesota Press.

Ingold, Tim (2006): "Rethinking the Animate, Re-Animating Thought". In Ethnos, Vol. 71:1, March, pp. 9-20.

Ingold, Tim (2011): "Landscape or Weather-World?" In Being Alive, Essays on Movement, Knowledge, and Description, London: Routledge, pp. 126-135.

Jóhannesson, Gunnar Thór/Lund, Katrín Anna (2017): "Aurora Borealis: Choreographies of darkness and light". In Annals of Tourism Research 63, pp. 183-190.

Jokinen, Eeva/Soile, Veijola. "The Disoriented Tourist, The Figuration of the Tourist in Contemporary Culture Critique", pp. 23-51.

Loftsdóttir, Kristín (2015): "The Exotic North: Gender, Nation Branding and Post-colonialism in Iceland". In NORA – Nordic Journal of Feminist and Gender Research, Vol. 23, N°4, London: Routledge, pp. 246-260.

Lund, Katrín Anna (2013): "Experiencing Nature in Nature-Based Tourism". In Tourism Studies 13-2, pp. 156-171.

Lund, Katrín Anna (2016): "Chasing the Lights, Darkness, Tourism and the Northern Lights". In Simone Abram/ Katrín Anna Lund (eds.), Green Ice, Tourism Ecologies in the European High North, London: Palgrave Macmillan, pp. 49-71.

MacCannell, Dean (1973): "Staged Authenticity: Arrangement of Social Space in Tourist Settings". In American Journal of Sociology, Vol. 79, No. 3, University of Chicago Press, pp. 589-603.

Mirsky, Jeannette (1997): To the Arctic!: The Story of Northern Exploration from Earliest Times, University of Chicago Press.

Moir, James (2011): "Seeing the Sites: Tourism as Perceptual Experience". In Peter M. Burns/Cathy Palmer/Jo-Anne Lester (eds.), Tourism and Visual Culture, Volume 1, Eastbourne: University of Brighton, pp. 165-169.

Oslund, Karen (2005): "The North Begins Inside: Imagining Iceland as Wilderland and Homeland". In GHI Bulletin 36, pp. 91-99. In Chris Rojek/John Urry (Eds.) (1997): Touring Cultures, London: Routledge.

Rojek, Chris. "Indexing, Dragging and The Social Construction of Tourist Sights", pp. 52-73.
Solnit, Rebecca (2007): Storming the Gate of Paradise, Landscapes for Politics, Berkeley: University of California Press.
Sæþórsdóttir, Anna Dóra/Hall Micheal C./Saarinen Jarkko (2011): "Making Wilderness: Tourism and the History of the Wilderness Idea in Iceland". In Polar Geography 34-4, pp. 249-273.
Urry, John/Larsen Jonas (2011): The Tourist Gaze 3.0, London: Sage Publications.
Virilio, Paul (1994): The Vision Machine, Indiana University Press.

Multimedia

"David Malin Images", DavidMalin (http://www.davidmalin.com/index.html) (accessed October 2018)
"Isaac Israel Hayes" Encyclopaedia Britannica, February 26, 2018. (https://www.britannica.com/biography/Isaac-Israel-Hayes) (accessed November 19, 2018)
"Number of foreign visitors", Icelandic Tourist Board, May 21, 2018. (https://www.ferdamalastofa.is/en/recearch-and-statistics/numbers-of-foreign-visitors) (accessed June 20, 2018).
Perboni, Alessio, Northern Lights in Iceland, in REAL TIME!!!, YouTube, February 13, 2013. (https://www.youtube.com/watch?v=dGQ7EZs5xu8) (accessed November 19, 2018).
Picture of Light (1994): dir. Peter Mettler, Canada/Switzerland, Andera Zuest/Grimthorpe Film.
Space Weather. BISA/EU, (1998-2018), Internet Archive Wayback machine (https://web.archive.org/web/20100804164127/http://spaceweather.com//) (accessed June 18, 2018).
"Sublime, adj. and n.". OED Online. July 2018. Oxford University Press. (http://www.oed.com.ludwig.lub.lu.se/view/Entry/192766?rskey=pnI6BI&result=1&isAdvanced=false) (accessed November 19, 2018).
Tron: Legacy (2010): dir. Joseph Kosinski, USA: Walt Disney Pictures.

Ghosting the Castle: the case of (re)landscaping in a Northern place

Nicky Bird

A northern place

Figure 1: *Photograph by John Ross Polson,* late 1960s

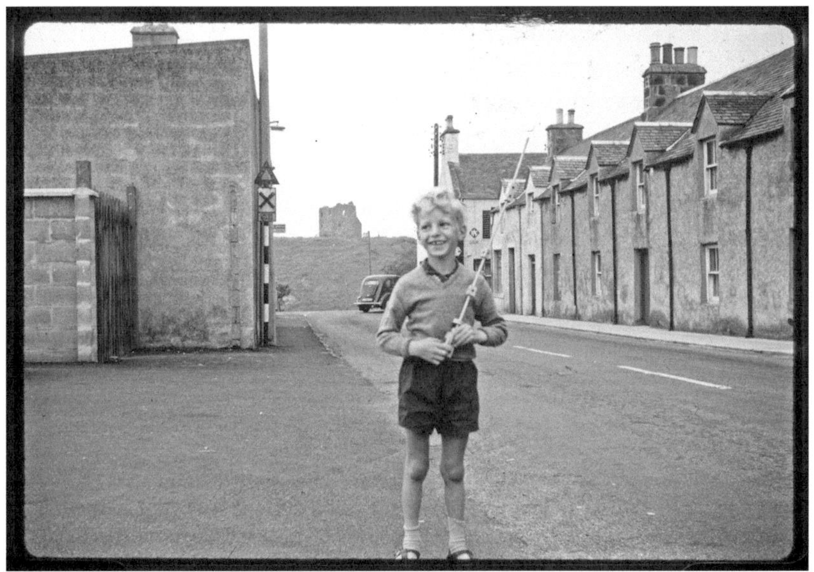

> North is a direction, a relative placement, it is defined by climatic conditions, by cultural richness, economical remoteness and described in myths and legends (Timespan, 2017).

The above photograph, a 35mm Kodachrome taken by John Ross Polson in 1965, was made in Helmsdale, a fishing village on the North-East coast of Scotland. The boy, Alasdair Polson, stands on a path alongside the A9. The photographer is his uncle. The camera points southwards, and the A9 forms a strong diagonal line behind the boy leading to the middle distance. Beyond that, land rises in the form of a cliff on which stands a silhouetted building: the ruins of Helmsdale Castle.

Early in 2017, I stand in a similar spot to John Ross Polson. Looking at a copy of his photograph, I compare it to the present-day scene in front of me. The Belgrave Arms is in plain view. Some of the houses that obscured the hotel in 1965 have long since been removed. I also point my camera southwards. The A9 road now curves ahead in the middle distance, and rises gently behind the Belgrave Arms. The land line is dramatically lower in height, the castle ruins gone.

Ghosting the Castle (Bird: 2017) was commissioned by and produced in collaboration with Timespan, a heritage museum with an art gallery and an archive, located in Helmsdale. The focus of this project was on the layered histories and issues related to Helmsdale's medieval castle and the A9 bridge which replaced it in the early 1970s. Archival photographs played significant roles in local people's narratives, shared with me while I was working on location.

Timespan was aware of my work investigating the contemporary relevance of found artefacts and hidden histories of specific sites. My working methods involve community engagement to produce the final artworks. These have incorporated new photography with oral histories and collaborations with people who have significant connections to the original site and its photographic archive. Timespan's commission was therefore to make connections between art and archive, and to create new works in collaboration with local community members. The project combined a series of residency visits to Helmsdale, viewing materials in local and national archives, guided walks through Helmsdale with community members, project-in-progress talks leading to an archive-exhibition workshop and other closing events in September 2017. From this process, Ghosting the Castle realised a number of art and archive outcomes, which will be discussed later.

Throughout this time, there were ongoing informal discussions with staff, the archive volunteers and the Timespan Heritage Group. The Heritage Group was predominantly women, a mix of 'Helmies' who had various histories of growing up in the village, others originally from elsewhere who had spent childhood summer holidays in Helmsdale visiting family, and others who had retired to the village with no previous connections.

During an exploratory visit to Timespan in October 2016 the subject of Helmsdale Castle and its demolition to make way for the modern A9 bridge came up in conversations almost immediately. I was struck how these conversations included those who had personal memories of the castle as well as others who had no direct memory of it at all. Photographs, therefore, in this context, triggered divergent community memories, viewpoints and speculations. In this chapter, I want to consider how photography in its widest sense, prompted memories and knowledge of the site, as well as raising critical questions. Through this particular site and depictions of change, I will reflect on how a diverse range of 'landscape' photographs, belonging to the recent past, came to make uncanny connections with present-day concerns about heritage, conservation, erosion and community sustainability.

Situated in the area of Sutherland, in the Highlands of Scotland, this small village has a population of just over 850 people, the majority of whom live mostly in a grid of streets at the foot of Creag Bun-Ullidh or eastside above the harbour. The distinguished engineer Thomas Telford built a road bridge across the river in 1811. Up until the modern bridge was opened in 1972, the Telford Bridge was an essential part of the London-Edinburgh-Thurso road, and I will come back to the significance of this. Today it remains in use for lighter traffic and pedestrians.

Helmsdale was planned in 1814 as a fishing village to resettle and provide an alternative livelihood for farming tenant families, forcibly evicted by their aristocratic landowners during Scotland's Highland Clearances. Helmsdale's own 'cultural richness' is therefore indelibly intertwined with this history and the consequent history of its herring industry, once one of the largest in Europe. Anna Vermehren, Timespan's then director, evocatively writes, "You can find memory and longing in the landscape, and history buried in the ground; the history of people living in this area for over six thousand years." (Vermehren 2016: 5).

The 273 miles long A9 runs from central Scotland to Scrabster, a harbour gateway to another North that includes the Orkney Islands, Shetland Islands and Iceland. Travelling north to catch a ferry means travelling through Helmsdale, with the village's approach signified by The Emigrants Statue, a monument to the Clearances standing over 2 metres high in Couper Park, which itself rises 7 metres above the main road. The drive over the bridge and River Helmsdale is short, and passing the spot where Alasdair and John Ross Polson once stood, the A9 soon begins an ascent that runs through the east side of village. This is also now the main route for heavy goods vehicles.

Helmsdale's passing trade is largely seasonal. The summer is the busiest period in the year, when bikers, cars and coaches turn off at Dunrobin Street and into the village, where Timespan is a welcome stop-off point for food and drink as well as for visiting its museum. It is also a gathering place for its community members, and describes itself as "a meeting place between our past, our present and our future." (Timespan 2017).

As the opening statement to this chapter suggests, Timespan has done much to unpack what 'north' means. The choice of the term "economical remoteness" is equally nuanced, and needs to be teased out with care and sensitivity. A useful starting point, but by no means the whole story, is the colour-coded mapping based on the Scottish Index of Multiple Deprivation (SIMD). In 2012, Fragile Area Mapping of Scotland, where red indicates the most fragile and green the least, show Helmsdale and the surrounding area as a deep pink. In 2016, SIMD mapping shows Helmsdale in an amber category, with geographical access being in the highest red. According to these governmental statistical tools, Helmsdale is a village that faces particular challenges. These might be summarized by the Highlands and Islands Enterprise's definition of fragile areas, which are, "characterized by weakening of communities through population loss, low incomes, limited employment opportunities, poor infrastructure and remoteness." (2007). 'Sustainability' has since become the more commonly used term, along with understandings that SIMD in rural areas needs to be understood differently from urban experiences of deprivation (Thomson 2016: 10). 'Helmies' would have their own things to say about the strengthens and challenges associated with sustainability, so Timespan's own use of "economical remoteness" is very precise. It resonates with its community members and at the same time, it contests other assumptions about 'remoteness.'

This is embodied in Timespan's archive, its users, and the photographs that make up its collection: many community members have a strong sense of lineage with Helmsdale's past and its uniqueness. These identity linkages are materially and digitally present in Timespan's archive, which holds, "11,000 digital copies of photographs held by its community members" (Timespan 2018). The photographs and their digital counterparts, have specific connections with living subjects literally within a few streets away. Genealogy and tracing ancestors are key activities for Timespan's volunteers as well as visitors, many of whom have descended from a Scottish diaspora covering Australia, Canada, New Zealand and the USA. Remoteness is often equated with 'lack' of connectedness. Timespan has remarked, "this is not our focus, nor is it our experience." (Timespan 2014) . It has also deliberated on the importance of the networked archive, housed in the North, and a key question: "does a thematic of 'North' encourage a different way of looking – about where we are – that still sits on the edge of sorts but is untethered from the centre?"[1] Having set the scene of a very specific northern place and its related archive for Ghosting the Castle, I will now turn to some of its photographic images.

A location marker

In Timespan's archive, the ruins of Helmsdale Castle are represented by a variety of analogue and digital media including prints and postcards as well as photographs. According to Timespan's information, it was built in 1466 as the hunting seat for the powerful Sutherland family. In landscape images, the castle ruins are a key landmark, composed as part of a 'picturesque' scene overlooking Helms-

1 This emerged from a dialogue between Timespan's Archive Development Manager Jo Clements and Curator Frances Davis with The Glasgow School of Art's Reading Landscape Group at Timespan as part of Practising Landscape, a research journey in November 2015. Jo Clements and Frances Davis were both instrumental to Ghosting the Castle.

dale's fishing harbour and beyond to the North Sea. When captions appear alongside an image of the castle ruins, these often remind the viewer that the castle was the scene of a 16th century poisoning. Today, 20th century photographs of the castle, such as the one above by Graeme Dodd, can be found reproduced on outdoor interpretation boards in Couper Park, with similar but more expanded captions: a triple murder committed by Isobel Sinclair, who poisoned the 11th Earl of Sutherland and his wife, so her own son would inherit the title, only to also poison him by mistake. This well-told layer of history has also acquired a mythic quality, purportedly the inspiration for Shakespeare's Hamlet.[2] Feminine villainy, Scottish Clan nobility and Shakespearean tragedy have become the 'default' reading of landscape photographs featuring the ruined castle. While bringing specific, yet historically distant, gender and class dimensions to the photograph, this illustrates Roland Barthes' description of how "the text loads the image, burdening it with a culture, a moral, an imagination" (Barthes 1997: 26). The problem with loading the photograph in this way is that it also obscures other photographic meanings. A closer look at Dodd's rather beautiful photograph, in Timespan's archive, leads to an entirely different reading.

Figure 2: *Photograph by Graeme Dodd*, 1962

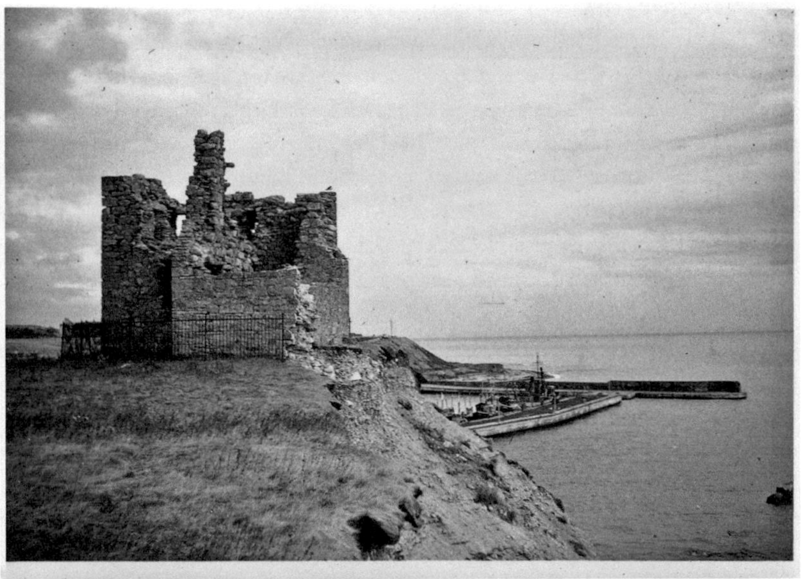

Handling the photograph, in its original window mount, brings to the fore its materiality: it has still retained its colour range; there are no signs of the fade to

2 This narrative is also included in Timespan's museum interpretation panel, viewed June 2017.

red usually suffered by commercially produced colour prints of the 1960s. In common with many other photographs in the archive, the castle ruins appear to be the main object of the photograph. Helmsdale's fishing harbour is in the middle distance, the cliff in the foreground. To help move beyond a conventional description of a landscape photograph, the photographer Thomas Joshua Cooper's preferred terms "of the near field and the far field" (Cooper 2017: 45) brings the viewer closer to Dodd's experience. At the bottom, in the centre of the photograph and in the photographer's 'near field' is a telling detail: the precarious, overhanging cliff edge. The photographer stands on this edge, directing the camera northeast. His presence, and the horizon level in the photograph, recalls the camera viewfinder and the photographer's eye on the scene before him. Imagine then being in Dodd's shoes, looking through the viewfinder and using its gridlines as compositional tools; in particular, run your eye along the horizon that meets the headline and runs to the base of the castle ruins; notice a seagull perched on a wall, and picture how one of the viewfinder's vertical gridlines runs parallel with this wall. Note that the wall sits perilously close to the cliff edge. Then look across to a crumbling wall. Dodd is making a photograph of a local monument that is falling into the sea. It is about land, erosion and impending loss.

Consequently, this photograph is far from 'picturesque,' and not simply because this notion has its cultural, historical roots in idealizations of the English landscape as David Bate (2009), John Taylor (1994) and Liz Wells (2011) have discussed. Wells suggests, "In terms of pleasures of the imagination, the picturesque as a constructed visual mode within broader concepts of beauty feeds a sense of order and harmony which, by extension, contributes to a reassuring sense of security. Nothing untoward is likely to happen here" (Wells 2011: 47). Something definitely untoward and unstoppable is happening in this photograph of the castle ruins. There is a sense of memento, perhaps unsurprising given Dodd's local connection and likely knowledge of the castle and cliff's disintegration over the preceding years. Over 50 years later, there is an uncanny resonance between Dodd's photograph and Brian Dillon's observation on the critical effect of photographing ruins, "[...] the technology is as likely to be turned without nostalgia (but perhaps with regret) on new destruction, or on recent collapse, as on ancient relics and fragments. To photograph ruins also means turning one's gaze on the present, and towards the future." (Dillon 2014). Within a decade of Graeme Dodd making his photograph, the castle ruins and its headland will be gone.

Moving from a private reading of this photograph to turn attention to its place in Timespan's archive, photographers such as Graeme Dodd are part of a familial network embodied in the museum's 20th century archive of 'family' photographs where named and actively remembered individuals also pose for their picture in front of the castle ruins. What should be evident by now is that these are in an archive of photographs, where the photographic eye includes the familial alongside the artistic. These are not neatly divided, but connected.

This leads to a consideration of the role of a photographic artist, an outsider, in mediating the memories and knowledge of others. This is firstly, in relation to photographic materials, and secondly, in understanding the location, in order to eventually realize in this case, collaborative photo-based artworks that respond meaningfully to place and people. This is, after all, a form of memory work. Annette Kuhn identifies that "the task of the practitioner in memory work is not merely to analyse but also to understand – that is to try and enter the memory-world of the text, the account, the performance [...]. Negotiation and intersubjectivity, then, are key features of memory work." (Kuhn 2008: 284). Martha Langford also argues how through paying attention to orality this leads to "shifting the focus of inquiry from *identification* (the detective-work) to *process* (looking and talking)." Original emphasis, (Langford 2006: 227). While Kuhn will go on to elaborate through an examination of one individual photograph, and Langford will make a close analysis for a photographic album located in a museum, each helps to articulate the complexity of the artist's position when entering the memory world of other people's photographs and the importance of paying attention to the process. Therefore, along with Langford's looking and talking, I would add walking and art making as part of this process. However, in the case of where a location marker has been erased and its site re-landscaped, detective work involving different forms of insider knowledge remains crucial. I will return to all these elements later.

Figure 3: *Photograph by John Ross Polson*, 1970

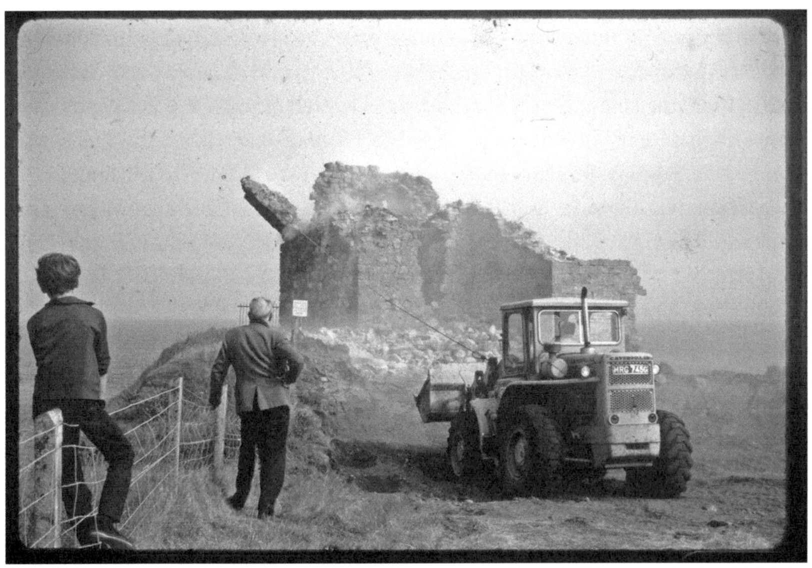

John Ross Polson's striking Kodachrome photograph of the castle's demolition was made on 3 August 1970 on the headland of Couper Park. He is only a few metres away from the ruins and catches the moment when the remains of a north-facing wall towards the village, are being brought down by a chain attached to a yellow bulldozer. The ruins are in a light shroud of dust: the castle, aesthetically speaking, is already fading away. Two bystanders stand watching the scene, their backs to the photographer: a young man straddles the wired fence; an older man with hand on hip, holds onto the same fence. Beyond the photograph's frame, across the River Helmsdale on Shore Street, another local man is recording the event on cine-film. From this vantage point, he also films other community members watching the demolition. Partly the effect of hand-held camera movement, the cine film shows a demolition that seems brief and chaotic; the photograph turns it into something iconic.

I heard about both film and photograph before I saw either on my first research visit. Their existence came up in the conversation about the castle ruins between staff, volunteers and members of Timespan Heritage Group, with the opinion that I would have to see these. These were clearly memorable visual artefacts to both those who could remember the castle ruins as well as those who had no memory of them at all. Therefore, it was evident that film and photograph were forms of cross generational memory-texts, enabling a number of participants, from community members to temporary visitors such as myself, to enter the memory-world of photographs of the castle ruins.

Polson's photograph was pivotal, partly for practical reasons but also because it is a compelling image. Polson's image was already circulating in Timespan, from computer screen to digital print-out. Since the original was a Kodachrome colour slide, the colour quality had not deteriorated greatly. It was easy to recognise why this image had lived in the minds of those that saw it. I will now turn to how this photograph operated as a memory-text, and how its mnemonic role gave expression to wider issues and questions concerned with community sustainability, heritage and preservation. This included not only other photographic materials in Timespan's archive, but extended to community members' individual albums, and key elements in the surrounding landscape.

For some individuals, especially those in the Heritage Group, the photograph was shocking evidence of heritage destruction. For others, the photograph was a source of humour with its nonchalant bystanders and implied absence of health and safety. While this may sum up different responses to the photograph, a shared view among those who remembered the ruins and its headland was that change was inevitable. This was due to on one side, years of dramatic and unstoppable coastal erosion, and on the other, serious structural damage to the Telford Bridge, the village's only other bridge at the time.

Old postcards and photographs, from the 1930s to the early 1960s, evidence a shrinking headland to the point the ruins became dangerous and fenced off. Reminiscences included how the ruins were spaces of childhood play, with wry observations on how other photographs such as Graeme Dodd's, made the castle look much better than it did in real life. Landscape photographs were therefore not treated uncritically as 'memory joggers', and these kinds of comments reveal how the aesthetics of the photograph both aids, but can be at odds with, someone's memory.

For some, the castle ruins were merely as a heap of rubble, the remains of a hunting lodge, and which in itself was of no particular historical value other than a murder site: there was no other option other than demolition. For others, the possibility that the ruins could have had heritage value, raised a number of 'what if' questions related to heritage and preservation: could the castle ruins have been saved? If not, as a local monument and site of interest, why was no record done before its destruction? General knowledge of the uses of photography within present-day archaeological and planning practices, shaped the critical edge to these 'what if' questions raised by some community members. A passion for heritage, and a commitment to its value, also underpinned the critical questions the photograph seemed to prompt. Visual imagery of the castle ruins seemed to signpost a lost heritage site, its medieval origins long since layered over with other 20th century meanings, often linked to familial attachments and childhood memories. This fits with a complex notion of heritage, so well described by Raphael Samuel:

> It necessarily gives a privileged place to local knowledge. Territorial attachments, both real and imagined, are stock-in-trade. Whether concerned with living legend, hereditary tradition or historical context, it opens itself up to the spirit and romance of place. In terms of human geography, it brings a new awareness of the historicity of both landscape and townscape, treating as contingent what used to be the grand permanences of climate, vegetation and soil, and linking the evidence of human activity to that of flora and fauna (Samuel 2012 [1994]: 277).

Helmsdale has long been used to impermanences from climatic ones to industries that have come and gone. The Polson photograph prompted a vivid oral account of how heavy goods vehicles, transporting enormous industrial parts to Dounreay Power station (now itself decommissioned), became stuck on the Telford Bridge. Flickr provides visual support for the anecdotes triggered by the Polson photograph. A 1958 photograph shows a lorry loaded with a cargo of industrial pipes, and at purportedly over 18 metres long, unable to turn off the bridge (Mason: 2007). By the late 1960s, the extent of damage led to weight restrictions and temporary structural support to stabilise the bridge and their concrete bases can be seen in the river bed today.

Old and new bridges are nowhere to be seen in the above Polson photograph. However, the mnemonic role of his photograph and others, brings in a location's key identity markers, even when these are on the brink of erasure, or lie outside the photographic frame. Consequently, what hovers around the Polson photograph is the geographical and economic significance of an ailing bridge at a time when it was a central link in the old A9. Local reminiscences bring tangible examples of "economical remoteness," and the choices that have to be made when facing challenges of geographical access. This would include observations on how later the modern A9 bridge would fundamentally change the rhythm of village life, including its economic life.[3] Starting with photographs in Timespan's archive, we can begin to see how a process of (re)landscaping a small coastal peninsular, teases out the ways heritage, conservation, erosion and community sustainability all intersect. I will now turn to how narratives told locally, would reverberate with other photographs located in two of Scotland's Edinburgh based national archives.

(Re)landscaping a northern place

Figure 4: *Oblique aerial view of bridge under construction and the site of Helmsdale Castle*, June 1971

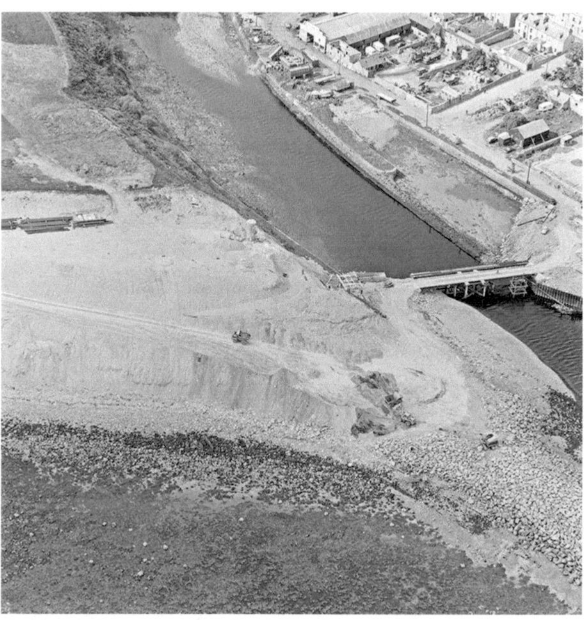

3 These included the closure of village shops and how the renewable energy industry could bring employment opportunities to the area.

The aerial photograph above is taken less than a year after John Polson's photograph. It evidences the extent of the re-landscaping of the small peninsular on which the castle ruins once stood. The steep cliff is now gone, with the area looking more like a quarry as trucks and bulldozers work into the land. A new breakwater, made from two tons of rock armour, is under construction. A temporary access bridge crosses the River Helmsdale as part of preparations for the engineering works to come with installing the new bridge.

This is among a small series of aerial coastal views made by John Dewar in June 1971. They document a stage in the 'Route A9 Helmsdale Diversion' and building of the modern A9 Bridge, that would be completed in 1972. I am looking at these photographs in the Historic Environment Scotland archive in Edinburgh. Another aerial photograph, taken on 3 June 1955 by an unidentified photographer, is also part of the collection. Although taken further afield, so Helmsdale, its harbour and the surrounding hills are in full view, it shows the same coastline as the Dewar photograph above, with the castle ruins on the cliff edge. The ruins are more substantial compared with Dodd's colour photograph that was taken seven years later. Looking at the visual differences between the coastlines of 1955 and 1971, I am reminded of an evocative vignette told by the son of a fisherman: how, on a cold, frosty, sunny winter's day, fishermen would hear parts of the cliff and castle crumbling into the sea. I am also reminded of a handwritten note among letters between the local district council and the Scottish Home Department. Made after a site visit to the castle ruins in May 1955, the note concludes "We must resign ourselves to its loss."[4]

Equally evocative, and even strangely haunting to me, is the John Dewar photograph. I note the neutrality of its aesthetics and the photograph's status as a documentary record, and am aware of the influences of New Topographics in my reading. I am also aware of 21st century critical reappraisals of 'vernacular' photography (Pollen 2016, Pasternak 2018) and Geoffrey Batchen's argument that, "The critical historian's task is not to uncover a secret or lost meaning but to articulate the intelligibility of these objects for our time." (Batchen 2001: 79). I think of the environmental aerial works of degraded landscapes and coastal change by Patricia Macdonald and Angus Macdonald, and their explorations in particular contexts, such as the Hebrides, where "The environment of the edge has always challenged ingenuity and tenacity..." (Lawson and Macdonald 2010: 35). With its square format, the tonal range between sea and land, the site of the castle as part of a strong diagonal composition, the John Dewar photograph is of a landscape in the process of being re-made, which has, in retrospect, acquired other envi-

4 In File number DD27/4233, "Helmsdale Castle, Kildonan, Sutherland, 1940-1976, Erosion by Sea," National Records of Scotland: within three months of it becoming a scheduled monument in 1940, the precarious state of the castle ruins was an already an issue.

ronmental and cultural meanings. It is a photograph that is part document, part memory-world text, the site where an erased, de-scheduled monument and long term sustainability intersect.

In a (re)landscaped northern place

Figure 5: Photograph by Nicky Bird. *Untitled work in progress*, April 2017

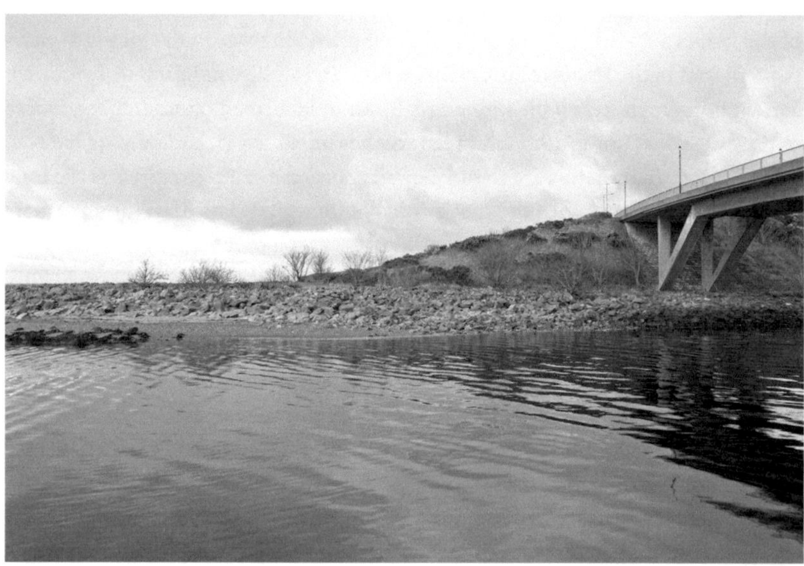

Today the Canmore Grid reference ND 0272 1515 marks the spot for Helmsdale Castle, among the yellow gorse bushes, half down on the small breakwater peninsular. Across the bridge, a concrete stone marks the castle's existence in Couper Park car park. Neither grid reference nor stone can give a sense of the castle's scale or completely dispel present-day uncertainty of where the castle once was, even for those who have clear memories of it. The re-landscaping appears to disorient memory, even block it.

In Spring 2017, a son of the fisherman, who spent his working life on civil engineering projects in various parts of the world, takes me on a walk. From Timespan, we walk away from the Telford Bridge, along Shore Street that runs alongside the river, under the A9 Bridge to the car park in the harbour. We loop back onto Stafford Street, and across the bridge. The top of the breakwater rises up on one side, Couper Park and the Emigrant's Statute is on the other. He points to clues in the landscape, where the land has been cut and lowered so I can begin to visualize the

1960s land line where the castle ruins, 7 metres high, stood on top of 7 metres of land, now removed.

I make this photograph in the early morning, with a digital SLR on a tripod. There is little traffic on the bridge at this time, and the light is soft. Apart from the tops of the yellow gauze bushes, the colour is muted. The photograph is made not only drawing on the detective work, knowledge, experience and memories of others, but also with reference to another photograph made by John Ross Polson. He stood in a similar place in the late 1960s, photographing the cliff and castle ruins on a sunny day from Shore Street. His photograph also guides my framing of the scene in front of me. Later I create a work-in-progress composite photograph, where Polson's detail of castle and cliff is incorporated via a layer in Photoshop. The detail is made semi-transparent, and scaled in relation to the clues pointed out to me during the walk. The composite is a step towards visualizing something missing from a landscape, still within living memory, that can communicate to others not directly connected to either memory or place. Later in the Spring, when I show the composite both at a public talk event in Timespan and to a group of young people on location, there is an audible in-take of breath. Yet the melancholic atmosphere, and the creation of a landscape that is haunted in some way, felt at odds with the sociability and generosity of people who were sharing stories and different viewpoints. The composite also revealed nothing of the connections that were being made with a range of public and private photographic materials throughout the project's process.

I was also aware that the photograph had perhaps the all too familiar photographic motif, the trope of absence, which brings in critical voices. Informed by the aesthetic strategies of photographers working with the reoccurring themes related to land such as John Kippin, Liz Wells asks "How can critical questions be posed differently?" (Wells 2011: 178). She casts a critical eye on what she describes as the "industrial sublime" – of abandoned mines, derelict factories and so on – in photography, where the aesthetics "arguably detracts from social implications" (ibid: 178). In David Campany's critique of photographic depictions of aftermath scenes, which he calls "late photography," (2003) Campany draws on Allan Sekula (1980) summarizing his warning "of the political pitfalls of decontextualizing a document in order to make it enigmatic, or melancholic, or merely beautiful" (ibid: 131-2). My work-in-progress photograph was of neither an abandoned or aftermath site, but an altered site. It says something about my own, artistic sense that there is an uncanny dimension to this site and how to visualize this: but what of the social implications, the collective, cultural meanings attached to this particular re-landscaped place? After all the social engagement side of my practice was a key component of being commissioned by Timespan in the first place. So, while not entirely without value, Ghosting the Castle needed other visual strategies, in addition to re-making the work-in-progress composite.

The panorama[5] that followed was one outcome of the 'oral and walking framework' that had evolved over the summer of 2017. This framework included to-ing and fro-ing between Edinburgh and Helmsdale, local and national archives, personal and collective memories, local history and heritage. The diverse range of photographic materials both in, and now being brought back to Helmsdale, continue to navigate 'what if' questions and other speculations. So, in addition to the whys of no archaeological surveys, no photographic records mentioned earlier in this chapter, there were others: what if the ruins have been taken down and relocated, or the stones used for a more fitting commemoration than a concrete stone? The differing viewpoints, even sceptical ones, point to the nuanced relationship between heritage and sustainability.

Through looking, talking and walking with photographs of land, a form of heritage was emerging: this was not in the conventional sense, given that the built materiality of the castle, was long gone. Raphael Samuel remarks, "Heritage, in short, so far from being a stationary state, is continually shedding its old character and metamorphosing into something else" (Samuel 2012 [1994]: 303). Although written in the 1990s, his words remain pertinent, given both the fluidity of, on the one side, the digital circulation of analogue photographs, and on the other, the rise of digital developments within heritage visualization, including computer animation and 3D scanning. During my time at Timespan, the possibilities of re-imaging the castle in these ways were on Timespan's radar.[6] The critical questions surrounding the resulting "digital heritage objects" (Jeffrey et al, 2018: 49-50) are relevant here. Through his work in heritage visualization and with communities, Jeffrey has been concerned with the critical effect of proximity and distance in digital visualizations of an original object: how aesthetics can distance and sanitize the past, and also how co-authorship becomes obscured. The relationship between the original and digital matters as, "Breaking the chain of proximity [...] is not about proximity to an object, building or site in itself, but rather a sense of proximity to the people associated with them" (Jeffrey 2017: 51). Jeffrey, among others including UNESCO, are also alert to emerging forms of community-based "intangible cultural heritage," which according to UNESCO, "can only be heritage when it is recognized as such by the communities, groups or individuals that create, maintain and transmit it – without their recognition, nobody else can decide for them that a given expression or practice is their heritage." (2018)

5 This included the whole bridge, breakwater, harbour edge and the Polson detail, with scale adjustments made responding to the retired civil engineer's comments. And a sunny day.

6 For example, in her talk "Helmsdale Castle: An exercise in 'what if'?" Architectural Technician Kate Morrison used 3D modelling to reconstruct the castle's past structure. She also visualized what would the castle look like if it was given the 'Grand Design' treatment. Timespan, 19 May 2017.

For UNESCO the matter of claiming and communicating intangible cultural heritage is clearly a matter for the community, where local knowledge, family histories, working life histories, as well as shades of folklore, can all play their part. If a small re-landscaped peninsular on the North-East Coast of Scotland is the site of intangible heritage, UNESCO's statement leads back to two issues: the role of a commissioned artist, an outsider within this context, and an aesthetic strategy beyond an overlay photograph of 'now' and 'then.'

Conclusion

Figure 6: *Ghosting the Castle A Map between Archive and Memory*, by Nicky Bird, 2017

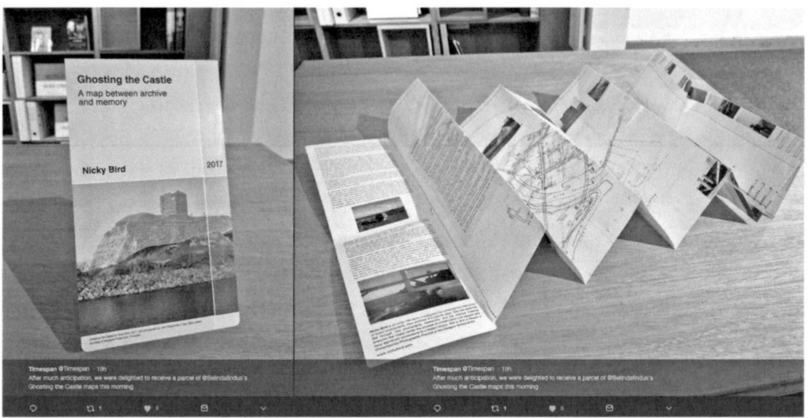

The oral, talking, walking and making framework, indebted to the work of Annette Kuhn and Martha Langford, has intersected with other critical voices, such as Batchen, Wells, and Samuel. In Kuhn's argument, negotiation and intersubjectivity are central parts of memory work, (Kuhn ibid: 284), and I would argue, these are resonant terms in the role of the commissioned artist, in relation to articulating intangible heritage of others. So, while the artist is ultimately responsible for the resulting artworks that claim to respond to an aspect of intangible heritage, community members will determine for themselves on whether to participate or collaborate on an art project. If the process and resulting works are deemed meaningful, it will be community members who in the long run, will maintain and use these works. With creation and transmission in mind, I conclude with Ghosting the Castle: A Map between Archive and Memory, 2017.

The above smartphone photograph shows an art map, based on the OS Landranger format in the Timespan archive. On the cover is a detail from the panorama described earlier. The map is partially unfolded on a large viewing table, revealing the original 1967 civil engineering plan by Babtie Shaw and Morton. This plan was also overlaid on an undated map of Helmsdale. It is the only archival artefact where the castle ruins, old bridge and new bridge co-exist, a detail the reader can see in the third fold of the map. The art map adds another overlay of photographic images which reflects public archives along with individual sources. The reader may also see the numbers five and two in the third fold. Five numbered vantage points on the art map corresponded with reproduced photographs, all from Timespan's archive. These marked the spot where each image could be viewed through a vintage Kodak viewfinder on location, as part of Ghosting the Castle's closing guided walk event in September 2017. (Bird: 2017). As an art map to be actively used on location, between archive and memory, it gives expression to the process of re-landscaping a Northern place. It also alludes to the way that both personal and social histories are caught up in this process.

The 1967 plan was among papers in the National Records of Scotland in Edinburgh, that included the 1968 order from the Secretary of State authorizing the Helmsdale Diversion, budgets, tendors from proposed contractors, and letters related to the displacement and compensation of two of Dunrobin Street's shopkeepers. The plan was a compelling artefact showing four colour-coded road options, in addition to the present-day A9 route. It therefore mapped a landscape of the past, present, and future. In a strange way, the plan was its own 'meeting place', connecting with Timespan's description of itself. Bringing a copy of the plan from Edinburgh back to Helmsdale, the response to it confirmed its communicative potential. Community members engaged with each proposed route, discussing what the impacts and implications would have been on the village and the surrounding landscape. One route would have cut straight through the middle of Couper Park and over the river, meaning Timespan would now be on a busy main road; another route that skirted around the cemetery and looped over the hill was laughed at for its improbability.

Throughout my discussion of Ghosting the Castle I have shown how a photographic process and archival photographs can navigate ways in which we may frame a landscape and detect the meaning of its missing pieces. Through this particular case of (re)landscaping in a Northern place, present-day concerns, mediated through photography, were revealed: specifically, questions related to heritage uncovered the presence of intangible cultural heritage. This, in turn, has been created by very real environmental pressures such as erosion and transport infrastructure. All this was expressed through looking, walking, and listening to a small distinct community that has pride in its history as well as long term sustainability on its mind.

References

Barthes, Roland (1977): Image, Music, Text, London: Fontana Paperbacks.

Batchen, Geoffrey (2001): Each Wild Idea, Massachusetts: MIT Press.

Bate, David (2009): Photography: The Key Concepts, Oxford: Berg.

Bird, Nicky (2017): Ghosting the Castle, https://nickybird.com/projects/ghosting-the-castle/ (19.11.17).

Campany, David (2003): "Safety in Numbness: Some Remarks on Problems of 'Late Photography.'" In: David Green (ed.), Where is the Photograph? Brighton: Photoforum. pp. 123-134.

Canmore, (2018): Helmsdale, Helmsdale Bridge, https://canmore.org.uk/site/7477/helmsdale-helmsdale-bridge (19/11/18).

Cooper, Thomas Joshua (2017): Gauging the Distance – The Reach for Extremity and Emptiness, University of Glasgow Degree of PhD by Published Work, University of Glasgow: The Glasgow School of Art.

Dillon, Brian (2014): "The detritus of the future and pleasure of the past." In: Tate Etc. 30, Spring 2014 https://www.tate.org.uk/context-comment/articles/detritus-future-and-pleasure-past (22/10/18).

Highlands and Islands Enterprise Fragile Areas Review (2007) [2010]: In: "Socio-Economic Briefing on Rural Scotland: Identifying Fragile Rural Areas," Scottish Government https://www2.gov.scot/Publications/2010/07/30101940/4 (19/11/18).

Jeffrey, Stuart (2018): "Digital heritage objects, authorship, ownership and engagement." In: Paola Di Giuseppantonio Di Franco, Fabrizio Galeazzi and Valentina Vassallo (eds.), Authenticity and Cultural Heritage in the Age of 3D Digital Reproductions, Cambridge: McDonald Institute for Archaeological Research. pp. 49-54.

Kuhn, Annette (2007): "Photography and cultural memory: a methodological exploration." In: Visual Studies 22:3, Taylor & Francis Online DOI: 10.1080/14725860701657175 (19/11/18) pp. 282-292.

Langford, Martha (2006): "Speaking the Album: the Oral-Photographic Framework." In: Annette Kuhn and Kirsten McAllister (eds.), Locating Memory: Photographic Acts, Oxford and New York: Berghahn Books. pp. 223-246.

Lawson, James and Macdonald, Patricia (2010): "Patricia Macdonald, Edge: Hebrides." In: Portfolio 52, 2010, Edinburgh: Portfolio. pp. 32-39.

Mason, David (2007): https://www.flickr.com/photos/helmsdale_org/446918264/in/photostream/ (19/11/17).

Pasternak, Gil (2018): "Popular Photographic Studies." In: Ben Burbridge and Annebella Pollen (eds.), Photography Reframed: New Visions in Contemporary Photographic Culture, London and New York: I.B.Tauris. pp. 39-47.

Pollen, Annebella (2016): Mass Photography: Collective Histories of Everyday Life, London and New York: I.B.Tauris.
The Glasgow School of Art Reading Landscape Group (2015): "Practising Landscape," http://radar.gsa.ac.uk/4018/ (19/11/19)
Samuel, Raphael (2012) [1994]: Theatres of Memory, London: Verso.
Scottish Index of Multiple Deprivation (2016) [2012]: http://simd.scot/2016/#/simd2016/BTTTTTT/14/-3.6690/58.1083/ (19/11/17).
Scottish Government (2013): "A Successful, Sustainable Place." In: National Planning Framework 3 https://www.gov.scot/Publications/2013/04/2377/5 (19/11/17).
Sekula, Allan (1980): "Dismantling Modernism, Reinventing Documentary (Notes on the Politics of Representation)." In: Terry Dennett and Jo Spence (eds.), Photography/Politics: One, London: Photography Workshop.
Taylor, John (1994): A Dream of England: Landscape, Photography, and the Tourist's Imagination, Manchester: Manchester University Press.
Timespan (2017): "North." In: Archive (2013-18), https://timespan.org.uk/programme/archive-2013-2018/ (19.11.18).
Timespan (2014): "2014: Remoteness." In: Archive (2013-18), https://timespan.org.uk/programme/archive-2013-2018/ (19.11.18).
Timespan (2018): Archive, https://timespan.org.uk/museum/archive/ (19/11/18).
Thomson, Jennifer (2016): "Rural Deprivation Evidence Summary, Scottish Index of Multiple Deprivation," https://www2.gov.scot/Resource/0051/00514495.pdf pp.1-12 (19/11/18).
UNESCO (2018): "What is Intangible Cultural Heritage?" https://ich.unesco.org/en/what-is-intangible-heritage-00003 (19/11/18)
Vermehren, Anna (2016): True North: From Documentation to Re-writing History, Helmsdale: Timespan.
Wells, Liz (2011): Land Matters, London and New York: I.B.Tauris.

Primary archive

Historic Environment Scotland.
National Records of Scotland: DD27/4233 "Helmsdale Castle, Kildonan, Sutherland, 1940-1976, Erosion by sea."
National Records of Scotland: DD4/4016 "Trunk Road Orders made under Section 1 of the Trunk Roads Act 1946, 1948-1968. A9 Helmsdale Diversion, Sutherland."
National Records of Scotland: DD4/4672 "Trunk Road Works 1951-1976 A9: Helmsdale Diversion."
Timespan, Helmsdale.

Other sources

Community Members, Helmsdale.
Jo Clements, Archive Development Manager, Timespan.
Frances Davis, Curator, Timespan.
Timespan Heritage Group, Helmsdale.

Matrix of Movement: Post-industrial Wetlands of the North West

Tracy Hill

> The surface, at a distance, looks black and dirty, and is indeed frightful to think of; for it will bear neither horse nor man, unless in an exceeding dry season, and then so as not to be travelled over with safety... What nature meant by such a useless production, is hard to imagine; but the land is entirely waste" (Defoe 1724:10).

Apparently featureless ancient wetland landscapes have long been represented as places of darkness, disease and death within Western culture. Despite increasing recognition for the need to readjust our perceptions of these spaces and to acknowledge their environmental importance as living landscapes there is, as yet, little imagery to promote this new way of seeing. As a visual artist my practice challenges historic perceptions of Northern landscapes such as those expressed by Daniel Defoe when he described Chat Moss (Channoffe) as "land entirely waste" (1724:10).

My recent research projects *Matrix of Movement* (2016-19) and *Haecceity* (2018), investigate how developing technologies and personal encounters when walking for leisure can challenge and shift perceptions, revealing the tensions between ideas of a picturesque landscape and the values a community may associate with a place. Digital imagery and data are collected during my journeys on foot across wetlands, informing printed works on paper and drawing installations. These artworks bring together the worlds of fine art, environmental sciences, conservation and industrial and commercial surveying technologies, demonstrating a new trans-disciplinary way of seeing these unique post-industrial landscapes.

My art projects question an unconditional acceptance of information presented to us in modern maps and through digital navigational aids as the only truth. Robert Macfarlane (2007:10) writes that "It can take time and effort to forget the prejudice induced by a powerful map," and warns us that "maps organise information about landscape in a profoundly influential way. They carry out a triage of its aspects, selecting and ranking those aspects in an order of importance, and so they create forceful biases in the ways a landscape is perceived and treated." My art works challenge the restrictions imposed by the bias of the map by suggesting an alternative perspective, encouraging an intuitive understanding and a willingness to experience economically redundant landscapes through exploration and discovery.

Figure 1: *Cadishead Moss*, 2015, Irlam

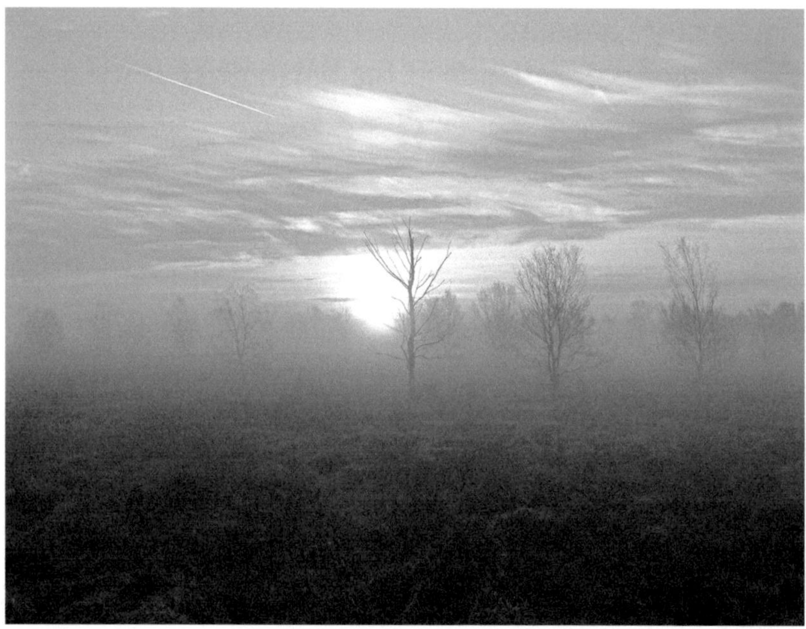

My art practice appropriates these technologies but in a way involving the visual mapping of the embodied experience of walking within the landscape. In an era of digital mapping and data control, my work offers a view of unmapped movements. I explore our changing relationship to wetlands using digital mapping technology as a basis for prints and drawings, but by doing so challenge the usual function of these mapping and navigational aids in supporting the modern obsession with locating, ordering and control, leading to an abstracted experience and dislocation from place. These technologies allow me to offer a view beyond my own visual capability, which combined with the traditions of a hand-created mark results in a re-imagined vision linking the technical and the aesthetic, bringing a unique vision of journeys taken on foot through a post-industrial Northern landscape. My art works are situated in the intersection between our digital and aesthetic worlds: a hybrid space where technological control meets emotion and memory of the human experience. The work reflects on dislocation while proposing that knowledge and experience of place when defined through personal attachment and an emotional engagement can mitigate its effects, leading to knowledge and understanding, the uncovering of hidden narratives, and new discoveries of the world around us.

The art projects have developed through an engagement with the writing of several critical thinkers. Anthropologist Tim Ingold argues that walking is a way of feeling, being and knowing. He goes on to suggest that wayfinding is a movement in time akin to playing music or storytelling, that our world is one of experiences, which are suspended in movement, and that through our own movements we contribute to its formations and connections "along paths of action and perception" (Ingold, 2000:242). Deleuze and Guattari in their seminal publication *Thousand Plateaus* (1980) suggest that thought and human relationships are inter-connected and in order to achieve understanding of a whole place one must connect with the many different multi-sensory elements within it. Similarly, Humanist geographer Yi-Fu Tuan suggests a relationship between movement and place and that within the pauses of our movement a true connection to place occurs:

> What begins as undifferentiated space becomes place as we get to know it better. The ideas 'space' and 'place' require each other for definition. From the security and stability of place we are aware of the openness, freedom, and threat of space, and vice versa. Furthermore, if we think of space as that which allows movement, then place is pause; each pause in movement makes it possible for location to be transformed into place (Tuan 1977:6).

Tim Cresswell (2015) also discusses the character of place as necessarily involving connection. He outlines the view of political geographer John Agnew who identifies three fundamental elements constituting place as a "meaningful location" (Agnew 1987): the notion of "location" as the simple understanding of where; "locale" as a material setting for social relations; and "sense of place" as the subjective and emotional attachment people have to place. Cresswell further suggests that in order to understand place you must make a clear distinction from "other familiar concepts such as space and landscape" (Cresswell 2015: p.14), and that the concept of place is not just a thing in the world but is in fact "a way of understanding the world" (p. 18).

The ideas of these geographers, archeologists, philosophers and artists offer new ways of thinking about and understanding landscape and place, ideas that inform my own attempts to make sense of post-industrial spaces through walking, to better understand our position within our local surroundings, and to preserve our knowledge and understanding of place by making a connection with it. By engaging with these approaches to place and landscape my project aims to communicate the precarious existence of wetland environments, making visible the human connection, which is necessary to ensure its future protection.

Since 2014 I have been regularly walking the remaining wetlands of Greater Manchester and this discussion is largely based on research undertaken in the UK, but *Matrix of Movement* was in fact based in two locations: the Mersey Estuary in the north-west of England, and the Hunter Valley, New South Wales, Australia. These two rivers are connected through their similar historical significance in the 19th century, their role in fostering trade, human and material movement and fueling the industrial revolution on both continents. The cities of Liverpool, UK and Newcastle, Australia are inextricably linked with the rivers and wetlands running through them. Both locations revealed the importance of memory and personal connection to place and offered very different experiences. The Mersey River is a location I have known for many years and it was possible to make lengthy visits there over a two year period. In contrast, access to the Hunter River was limited to the duration of a three-week residency and I was reliant on the knowledge and memories of others to extend my own limited experience, requiring a new approach. Knowledge and personal experience of the Hunter landscape was minimal and new works were more evocative of immediate sensory experiences, conversations held and, importantly, the memories of the indigenous people with whom I was walking. These similarities and differences provide an important context for what follows; they are indicative of the global significance of peatlands, shared histories of their exploitation, and the need to think about the connectedness of place in precisely the way advocated by Cresswell and others.

According to Natural England and Defra, intact peatland is one of the scarcest and most threatened wetland habitats in the UK, its total area being lost by 94 per cent since the beginning of the 19th century. The UK's peatlands store around 5.5 billion tonnes of carbon, and, if in good condition, can sequester carbon dioxide from the atmosphere into the accumulating peat, helping to mitigate climate change. Globally, peatland stores approximately double the amount of carbon that is stored in all the world's forests: an estimated 550 billion tonnes. This means peatlands are a vital and irreplaceable resource for regulating the climate.

Historically the strategic importance of the peatlands and estuarine wetlands in the North West UK was widely recognized by local communities who understood that for anyone wishing to travel north or south, the knowledge of a safe route afforded them great power. Added to the formidable obstacle of the River Mersey itself, the peatland and wetland areas acted as gigantic barriers, protecting and safeguarding the communities that lived amongst them. Complex, precarious, transient and unpredictable, these semi-aquatic spaces have adapted to accommodate the changing economic and urban world which surrounds them, but have never completely surrendered to the desire for human occupation or control. The peatlands and estuary wetlands of Greater Manchester have, throughout history, been considered some of the most remote and frightening areas of the British countryside yet they link and connect communities; they mark borders and define modern transport links. Most importantly, though, they provide a geological and archeological heritage which links back to a time when life was lived in tune with the seasonal flux of a semi-aquatic landscape.

Improvements in drainage and particularly deep drainage, which came with the use of steam during the industrial revolution, meant that coal deposits previously unavailable to miners could be accessed. As a result, collieries were established at Astley Moss and particularly Ince, with a massive impact on the mosslands. Subsidence and contamination from colliery spoil resulted in large areas of mossland disappearing. What remains today is a collection of fragmented, smaller wetland sites surrounded by the urban sprawl of Greater Manchester and Liverpool. Remnants of this once vast spatiotemporal landscape provide us with a land which is unique; simultaneously preserving both geological and archeological histories, whilst revealing and evolving as a living landscape. It is an environment full of contradictions, a glimpse into a unique and ancient Northern landscape which, once plundered of peat, has alternately been abandoned and left desolate or drained and reclaimed for agricultural use, leaving the land contaminated, peatlands extinct and fields susceptible to flooding and collapse.

Figure 2: *The Boundary*, 2015, from the series Sensorium

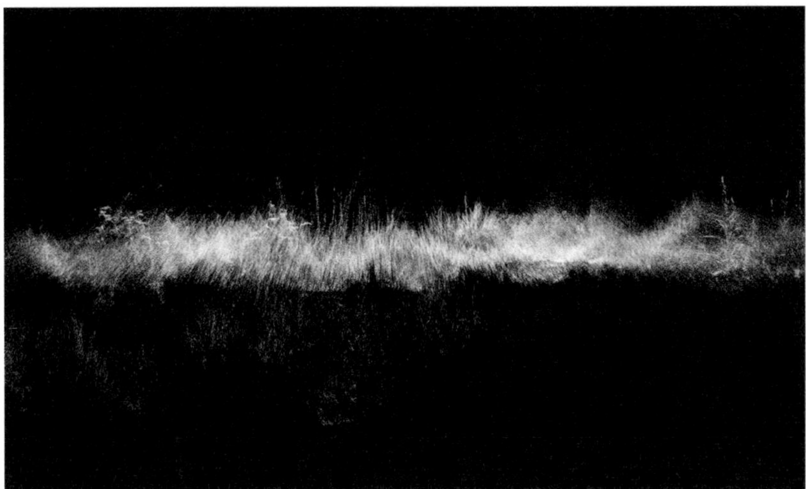

Matrix of Movement and *Haecceity* propose a necessary shift in cultural approaches to wetland environments, through examining the traditions of wayfaring and navigation. These projects strive to reinforce a shift in thinking and consider, if through inaction and ignorance, we are complicit in the loss of these vital landscapes. For communities in these places the rivers and wetlands hold memories of a life in tune with seasonal patterns of wet and dry, inviting stories of imagination, mystery, refuge and escape. Sadly, however, it is my perception from conversations with visitors to my exhibitions and community members linked to regional Wildlife Trust groups, that these wetland spaces continue to be seen by many as worthless, These places – regarded as expendable, empty wasteland or *terra nullius*, as belonging to no one – have been left vulnerable to commercial, industrial and military exploitation.

The relentless need for housing has led to increased intervention on the remaining wetlands of Greater Manchester. Urban development requires control to be exerted upon the geological structure. The need to provide infrastructure to enable development results in devastating environmental changes for these historic wetland sites, causing underground aquifer levels to drop faster than can be replenished naturally, leading to uncontrolled drainage and land shrinkage followed by an invasion of species and destruction of biodiversity. Evidence of this can be seen widely across the remaining mosslands of greater Manchester but particularly in the south of Wigan on Chat Moss, where increased agricultural use and urban development have caused land levels to sink lower than the lanes and tracks created within the mossland. Reinforced with hardcore and a hard surface, these lanes are more resilient to the drainage than the adjacent land but are still subject to constant subsidence and slippage.

This challenge to biological diversity has led to feelings of disconnection being expressed by local residents, because drained wetland cannot sustain useful production or protection from high tides and flooding, as its ability to absorb water is compromised or removed. My drawing installations and printed works communicate the precarious existence of these environments, offering a sensory response to walking in these liminal landscapes, suggesting forgotten ways of seeing the land. Now a fragmented legacy of social and political progress, these landscapes hold the key to many of our uncomfortable environmental truths.

My methods for collecting and processing data have been developed over the past few years. Multiple visits to locations are necessary before decisions about scanning or planned work is made. Developed and sold as precision instruments, Lidar scanners claim to be the perfect solution to documenting and measuring in 3D. Such scanners are now commonly used for investigating forensic sites, architectural structures and accident sites where it is necessary to accurately record and measure in minute detail. The actual equipment often does not look very different from a regular camera, commonly mounted on a tripod with mirrors, infrared distance sensors and an optical digital camera, these machines stream vast files of data as the scanning takes place. Marketing and promotional literature for this technology aptly suggest that the capturing process is akin to sensing space. Ethereal qualities such as tonal values and colour are scientifically replaced by the technology of precision mapping, surpassing what our human perception can achieve, or so these companies would have us believe.

The more visits made to the wetlands the more I began to appreciate the layers of understanding necessary to lay down my own relationship to this unique landscape. At first I read the land through my feet during wetland visits, and this altered my perception and way of walking. The act of testing the stability of the ground beneath our feet is basic and instinctive but an understanding of how the ground responds is not; it demands an awareness of our own bodies that most of us no longer commonly need. In both these projects my fine art practice engages with increasingly complex and divisive issues such as land ownership, commercial exploitation and hidden cultural heritage; all factors which prevent connection to place.

Figure 3: *Black Waters*, 2017, from the series Matrix of Movement

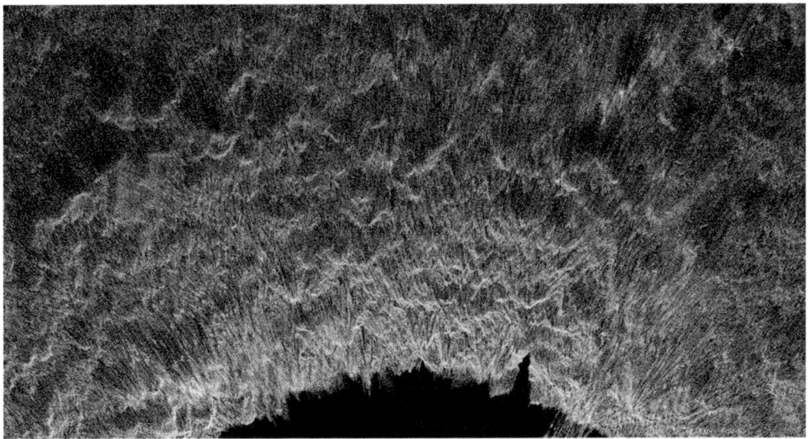

The identification and selection of locations for my projects are always done in consultation with local trusts and agencies. Wetland locations are challenging environments in which to make creative work, needing sensitivity to environmental factors as well as an understanding of the physical geography of the land.

Western culture has historically characterised wetlands as places of darkness, disease and death, perpetuating a misguided belief that wetland landscapes are connected to horror and the uncanny, linking them with madness and disease, scientifically positioning them as a threat to health and sanity. In Postmodern Wetlands, Rod Giblett observes the historic response of Western society as being "simple and decisive: dredge, drain or fill and so reclaim." (1996:3), but also suggesting that a re-examination of wetlands as expendable spaces is beginning to take place. In each case my chosen locations have played an important roll historically in the development of the local community as well as being significantly altered over the last 60 years in the name of modernity and progression. Having been stripped for peat and coal deposits, drained and reclaimed in the name of agricultural and industrial progress, new understanding brings with it a reconsideration that wetlands are places which are vital for life on earth. Wetlands are living landscapes and sinks of dangerous greenhouse gases; their destruction causes significant CO2 emission and ultimately environmental harm, which threaten life on a global scale.

The locations of the projects offer a snapshot of wetlands indicative of their regions. All of these post-industrial sites are now protected and managed in an attempt to reestablish a living system of wetland, which can offer value to their communities and address the wider environmental impact of industrialisation. The shared social and economic politics of these sites is hugely complicated but an increased global understanding of the environmental cost of human misuse of wetland sites has provided a platform for artists and scientists to form meaningful partnerships, offering new visions and new ways of connecting with place.

Figure 4: *Temporal Wandering*, 2016, from the series Matrix of Movement

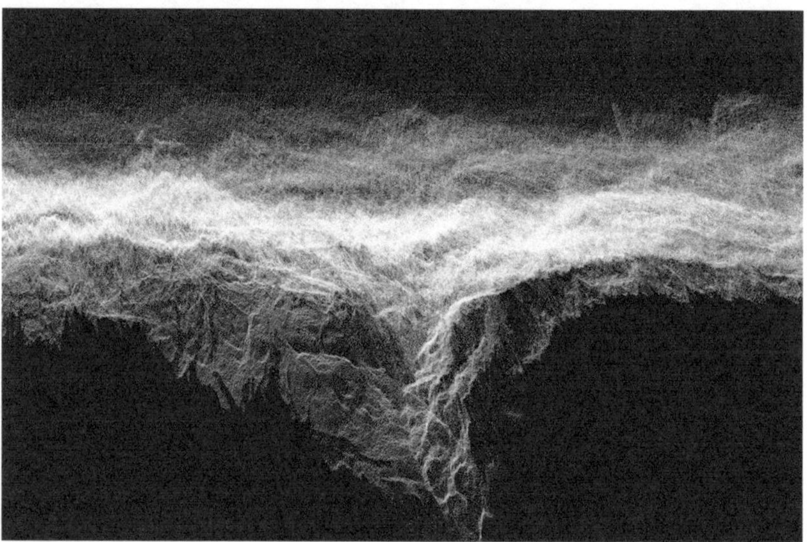

The significantly lengthy and complex process of taking the scan data off the computer and then recreating it as a traditionally printed etching or large-scale charcoal drawing is key to the success of the work. *Matrix of Movement* and *Haecceity* specifically explore a tactile awareness of landscape experienced when walking. Multisensory stories and memories are intertwined with practical geographical knowledge of constantly shifting and vanishing pathways. Images from these projects create an opportunity to explore the visualization of the point where one thing becomes another; the edge between our physical world and how it feels to be part of it. Once the Lidar data has been collected I then deliberately de-construct, manipulate and reconfigure the visual information. This is quite different to the manufacturers intended use and in their commercial and scientific terms my process of editing and reconstruction renders the data useless. The resulting images take the form of either large immersive wall drawings in charcoal or limestone or intaglio prints on paper. They are my reimagined vision; one that resonates with subtle, rhythmic and immersive experiences. My works are not a description of what lies before us but offer the possibility to explore what we feel, a re-imagining which goes beyond the static moment, creating a dialogue between memory and visual perception.

My Imagery resonates with its digital origins, providing a counterpoint to Western mapping traditions where the aim is to measure, to catagorise and to control. In the Western system of classification wetlands are an anomaly in which identification of the landscape is based on the distinction between land and water. Such representational traditions of mapping do not lend themselves to the transitory nature of wetlands, instead what is needed is a system of temporal mapping. Aesthetic decisions made during the production of my drawings and hand-printed works record my memory and the experience of walking, through the physical interaction of touch. These are temporal works, which strive to depict a spatial history; a history which is shown in relation to the present and to what went before. Particularly intriguing is the possibility to offer new knowledge; created when new approaches within the visual arts explore the potential of combining traditional techniques and developing digital technologies in order to communicate trans-disciplinary ideas.

Figure 5: *Genius Loci, 2017,* from the series Matrix of Movement

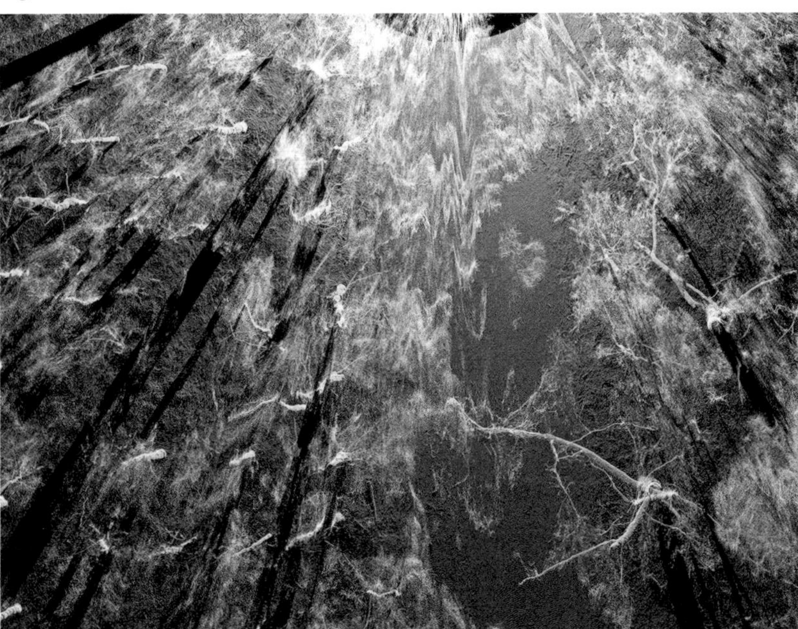

Intaglio plates are created using etching processes and photopolymer films. These films have been an important development for artists using print in the last 20 years; developed originally for the circuit board industry, they have the ability to record and transfer huge amounts of information. For artists, this technology is also able to translate images directly, creating intaglio surfaces, which respond to the traditional act of hand inking and printing without the need to use chemical etching. My prints created through this process are often large scale, with individual plates measuring nearly a meter long by half a meter wide. The images themselves are highly tonal and rich in ink, requiring a constant balancing between saturation and achieving a sense of light and movement, making them extremely labour intensive to produce.

Many of my images appear to be floating above an invisible horizon; a decision made to connect with the uncertainty I feel when walking across the semi-aquatic ground. The understanding of touch when walking is crucial in order to connect to seasonal geological and hydrological changes experienced under foot. The very vegetation that makes these areas unique is what also makes it so dangerous to those without local knowledge. Sphagnum moss grows in floating islands on the edges of hidden pools of acidic water. Growing in dense clumps these large colonies give the illusion of solid ground but will willingly collapse when stepped on. While different species of vegetation help to indicate a change that is hidden from view, cotton grasses and reeds suggest standing water while heathers and hazel suggest higher drier ground.

By altering perspectives in the work I hope to draw attention to seasonal and transitory elements of the landscape, all of which are natural signifiers, helping us navigate in wetland environments when normal lines of vision are removed. Abstracted images further demand that the viewer searches for clues in the shapes and forms presented in the prints or drawings, making personal experience and memory vital for reading and making sense of the work. Within a gallery space my images create an imaginary horizon line, the intense black surface creating a dynamic visual description of form, which may be familiar but never prescriptive. My images represent an intuitive and temporal rendering, visualising the sensory perception required and memory associations triggered during walking.

> Place, landscape is not reducible to co-ordinates on a map or a digital data set. It is a complex hybrid of myth and memory, an amalgam of all we have ever known, can never find out, and of long abandoned ways of living. Landscape is an aggregation of shadows, reflections, tremors and textures; it contains traces of our ancestors, lost narratives and unimaginable futures (Stevenson, 2018:2).

Figure 6: *Standing Ash*, 2017, from the series Matrix of Movement

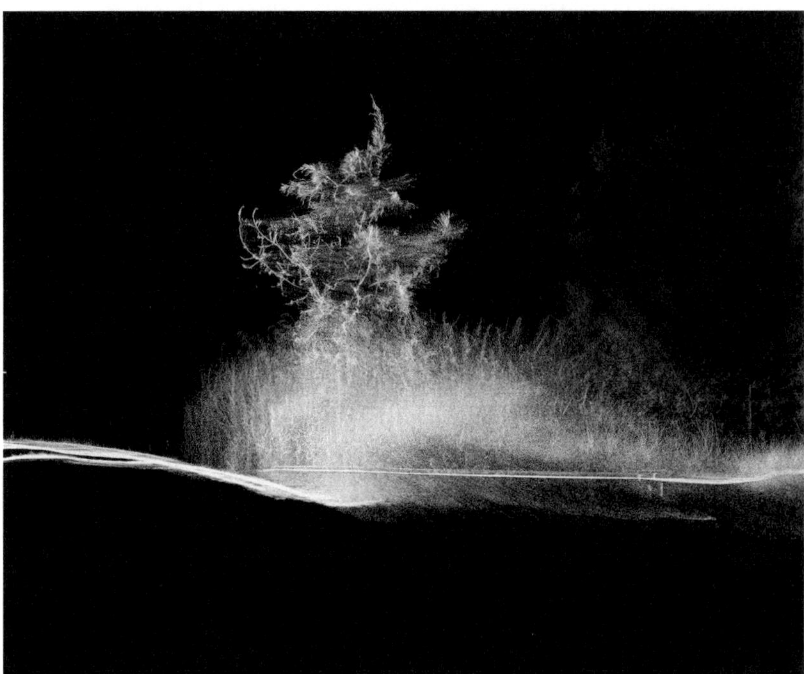

In 2018 I was commissioned to be artist in residence as part of the Warrington Contemporary Arts Festival, enabling me to further explore these ideas. The 6-month residency period provided me with the opportunity to revisit wetland sites in and around Salford and Warrington, collecting new scan data with which I worked in the Museum. Warrington's 150-year-old Museum is situated in the historic centre of the town and located on one of the two thoroughfares crossing The Mersey River. *Haecceity* was an exhibition of site specific work, the culmination of research and data collection resulting in the installation of two large wall drawings and 4 interactive screenprinted panels.

The term Haecceity was first proposed by John Duns Scotus (1266 – 1308), it is a non-qualitative property: that property or quality of a thing by virtue of which it is unique or describable as 'this (one)'. It is an elusive principle and one that many have sought to capture. Deleuze and Guattari reflect: "A season, a winter, a summer, an hour, a date have a perfect individuality lacking nothing [...] They are haecceities [...] capacities to affect and be affected" (Deleuze and Guattari, 1980:288). Here, Haecceity is used to describe the change between states. Seasons and time are constantly reoccurring measures and events within our lives, but are states which differ from what went before in a constant process of change. Likewise the places I seek to portray in my drawings are the beginning of seeing and experiencing a memory or reimagined space. The immersive gallery drawings provide a space for the audience to bring their own interpretations and local knowledge. For each individual the experience of the drawing then becomes a unique experience and one which is in a constant process of change.

The wall drawings were created over a period of three weeks; applied directly onto the gallery walls, they became part of an evolving performance, portraying landscapes which were revealed as sites of action and a threshold between the audience and the slowly unfolding narrative on the walls. During the residency period in the museum my conversations with visitors revealed how wetland locations around Warrington continue to suffer from the entrenched, misguided identity expressed by Daniel Defoe in 1726. A view was expressed that a landscape is somehow seen as representative of its community, with wild, un-kempt wetland understood as symbolic of an unruly, undervalued or disparaged community. In contrast more worthy and respectable communities are thought of in association with the picturesque. The drawings, for some, evoked childhood memories and a reluctant acceptance that the wetlands had been places of adventure and beauty. For others, my drawings created tension, bringing unwelcome memories that, in some instances, actually led to an acknowledgement and acceptance of the past. A number of visitors experienced a shift in their way of thinking and expressed a willingness to revisit the wetlands and explore again those places which had been long forgotten over time.

Reflecting on what Tim Ingold refers to as the "permeable interface" (2001:121), my drawings explored the point at the surface where land and weather combine, immersing us in a multisensory response that informs new knowledge and ancient memory. These were not fixed drawings; created with limestone they were constantly moving and at risk of falling from the wall. Responding to Ingold's idea of place, the drawings needed to be understood as a visualization of my embodied experience during the walks. Places, I believe, are constructed of human activity and engagement and, as such, are being constantly reconstructed and reimagined on a very personal level. It was this reconstruction and reimagining to which I wished to give agency through the drawing installations.

I refer to these drawings as a form of cognitive surveillance: a personal survey of a memory or inner map. The material vulnerability of the wall drawings is a clear metaphor for the threatened, fragile environments the drawings strive to represent. The view was very obviously temporary and its pending disappearance created an anxiety for some visitors who needed to believe that what was before them could be controlled and preserved. Their lack of control caused an inability to engage fully as some individuals then became reluctant to invest time in something they perceived to be impermanent and therefore of little value or use to them. For others, the transience of the drawings was embraced, carried away as a memory or an encounter and enjoyed for the experience of the temporary performance.

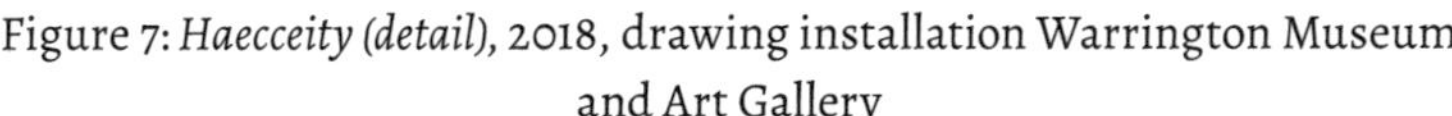

Figure 7: *Haecceity (detail)*, 2018, drawing installation Warrington Museum and Art Gallery

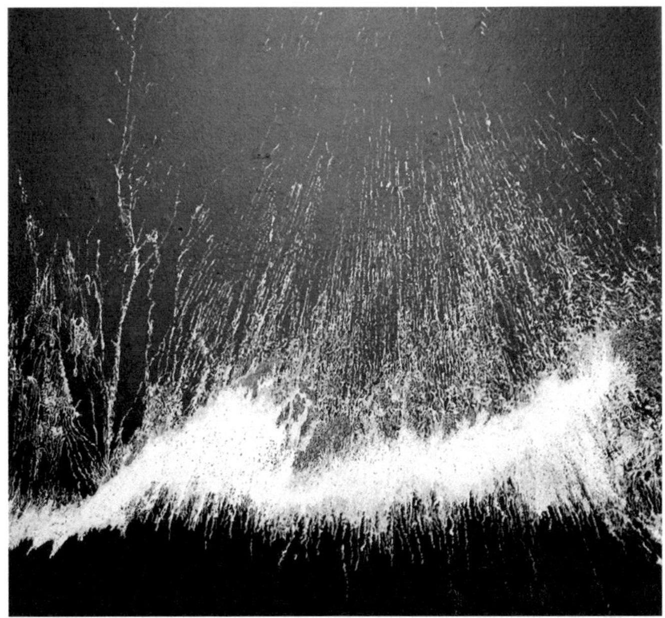

Haecceity provided the opportunity to combine drawing with sound. Interactive screenprints brought a new dimension into the gallery space. Images taken from the scan data were printed through silkscreens in a traditional manner but instead of using normal inks, conductive ink (electric paint) was used. This commercially available ink contains fragments of conductive material which, when dried, allows the conduction of electricity. The images printed with this ink responded to an electrical current, in this case the human touch which conducts electricity from the hand, triggering a sound recording to be played in the space: the visual transformed into a sonic experience.

Through a combination of multiple senses, my visual imagery and their personal memory, the viewer's normal line of vision and experience in the gallery was challenged. Viewpoints were disrupted requiring a visual and cognitive re-consideration in order to engage fully with the artwork. The sounds recorded while walking in the wetlands could only be activated through direct physical contact with the print surface; active participation and bodily movement was necessary in order for people to gain the sonic experience. A rich variety of captured sounds from the crackling of reeds to the roar of aircraft were played from various points around the gallery – not necessarily from a point closest to the trigger, challenging the perception of what is being seen and heard.

By exploring the creative potential between fine art practice and the capabilities of the developing digital era, I believe it is possible to explore a wider relationship between artist and technology. When working together they can inform, reimagine and challenge existing notions to give us a deeper understanding of the world around us. My aim is to show the beauty of walking and re-engaging with post-industrial landscapes; to question our interpretation of and to be cautious of the digital data sources upon which we are increasingly reliant to help us navigate. Above all I aim to invite personal encounters through walking. Through our personal encounters and multi-sensory experiences we observe moments; these moments build knowledge and through this knowledge we bestow value. The understanding that communities once had of these northern landscapes shaped our past; understanding their value today has the potential to protect our future.

Bibliography

Agnew, J (1987): Place and Politics: The Geographical Mediation of State and Society, London: Allen and Unwin.

Cresswell, T (2015): Place an introduction, Oxford: Wiley Blackwell.

Defoe, Daniel (1726) A tour thro' the whole island of Great Britain – (http://www.visionofbritain.org.uk/travellers/Defoe/34).

Defra, Understanding UK peatlands – (http://jncc.defra.gov.uk/page-5905).

Deleuze, G and Guattari, F (1980): A Thousand Plateaus, London: Bloomsbury Revelations.

Farley, P. and Symmons Robert, M. (2012): Edgelands: Journey into England's True Wildness, London: Vintage.

Giblett, Rod (1996): Postmodern Wetlands, Edinburgh: Edinburgh University Press.

Ingold, T. (2000): The perception of the Environment: essays on livelihood, dwelling and skill, Abingdon: Routledge.

Ingold, T. (2000): Being Alive, Abingdon: Routledge.

Macfarlane, R. (2007): The Wild Places, London: Granta Books.

Natural England, Carbon storage by habitat (2012) (publications.naturalengland.org.uk/file/1438141)

O'Rourke, Karen (2013): Walking and Mapping: Artists as Cartographers, Cambridge and London: MIT Press.

Stevenson, D (2018): Deciduous Drawings/Insoluble Ink: [Walking in Wetlands with Tracy Hill] An essay by Deborah Stevenson in response to Sensorium and Matrix of Movement. (https://issuu.com/tracyhill2/docs/tracy_hill_dd_ii)

Tuan, Y, (1977): Space and Place, London: Sage.

The North as a fantasy playground: re-evaluating the literary influences in the landscape photography of Raymond Moore

Tim Daly

Introduction

The photographer Raymond Moore (1920-87) who was born in Wallasey, studied painting at the Royal College of Art and in the mid-70s, taught photography at the influential Trent Polytechnic in Nottingham. In 1981, Moore was the first British photographer to have a retrospective at the Hayward Gallery, London. There are two published monographs of his work, *Murmurs at Every Turn* (1981) and *Every So Often* (1983). Although Moore's work drew influence from European and American sources, his work has a characteristically British undertone. Since his death in 1987, photography's expanded field of practice has emerged, freeing artists and photographers to explore themes and concerns beyond the established silos of practice of documentary and landscape. Moore's photographic career overlapped several significant points in the history of the medium, yet his highly individualised practice sat outside both established and emerging conventions. Despite this rich complexity, a continuing legal uncertainty over the legacy of Raymond Moore's archive has prevented a critical reevaluation of his work–his work is no longer accessible and as such, has not been exhibited or republished like many of his contemporaries. The following essay is based on an interview I made with the photographer in the last year of his life–a conversation in which Moore shared many thoughts and ideas that he'd otherwise kept to himself during a long career rejecting requests to elaborate on his work. In many ways revelatory, Moore's responses identify his own ruminations on photography and in particular loss, memory and the politics of representing the North. The aim of this chapter therefore is to re-examine Moore's work with particular reference to the influence of literature and the pull of the Northern landscape. I suggest that we should recognise in his work a richness and complexity and celebrate his hitherto unacknowledged influence on a generation of European photographers that were to follow, working with a detached, narrative distance. It was not possible to secure permission to reproduce examples of Raymond Moore's work for this essay, the ongoing legal issues that continue to make his work unavailable are well documented elsewhere. However, the following illustration is my own photograph, taken from a project called Conversations with Raymond Moore.

Figure 1: Tim Daly, *Gorstella, Cheshire,* 2019

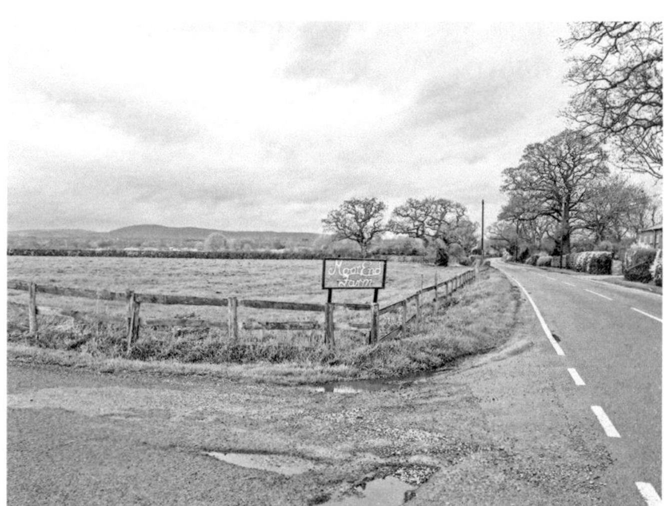

Literature infused praxis

Moore was a complex artist who was not given to writing about his work and rarely spoke of his motives. He was also skeptical about the perceived proselytizing tone of many of his contemporaries in the post-rationalisation of their output. Whilst erudite and highly knowledgeable, Moore felt unequipped to write about his subject matter and was wary of compromising his work through written explanation. However, he sometimes ventriloquised his motives through quotes and passages from a wide range of literary sources in exhibition catalogues and interviews. Indeed as Gerald Woods (1972: 152) observed, "Moore, although an articulate man, feels that words dissipate the imagery." This stance ensured that Moore's following statement was repeatedly used to contextualise his work:

> Confronted by the myriad relationships between objects in the visual world, I am impelled to choose or select those happenings that most accurately reflect or mirror a state of being at that one moment in time. This choice is governed by an instinctive awareness of the medium's essential power of translating and recreating in photographic terms. A new world is magically presented in the form of marks

made by the optical chemical process, related to the world of everyday visual contact and yet quite apart from it. From this map of experience, hopefully something of value may be revealed (1981a: 9).

The dilemma of documentary

Moore worked within a period of British photography dominated by independent documentary practitioners. Working outside the long-term project format common amongst his peers, Moore operated without a brief or an overtly narrative intent and was wary of being categorised as a documentary, or any other kind of photographer. In the 70s and 80s, documentary photography was still associated with observational gathering, as perceived by Barthes (1978: 18) as "a mechanical analogue of reality" and very much viewed as a kind of second-tier practice in comparison with painting and sculpture. The tension between documentation and equivalence, fictional or indexical representation underpins the complexity of the documentary terrain, while narrative-driven work by other British photographers at that time including Martin Parr and Paul Graham, sat firmly within rather than extending the genre. Moore's own approach however was more influenced by European and American practitioners. The work of Walker Evans and Eugene Atget both impacted on Moore in different ways. When Evans resided in Paris in the 1920s, his interest in Baudelaire's exploration of the vernacular and of the fleeting existence in a modern, urban environment would enrich his later work with the sensitivity of a cultural commentator rather than a purely pictorial storyteller. Evans' later collaboration with James Agee in *Let Us Now Praise Famous Men* (1941) also raised the status of a literary-infused documentary photography beyond a purely indexical remit. Evans' interest in Eugene Atget–the prototype solitary, existential wanderer–led him to review the posthumously published book Atget–*Photographe de Paris* in 1931. The very open-ended nature of Atget's work struck a chord with Evans (1931: 126) who observed, "It is possible to read into his photographs so many things that he may never have formulated in it himself." While Atget was wandering around Paris, Arthur Machen was writing *The Hill of Dreams* which was published in 1907. Cited by Moore as a seminal influence, Machen too celebrated the urban space as a fantasy playground, where repeated meanderings amongst a familiar terrain were a source of revelation for the artist. This kind of urban wandering situates Atget, Machen and Moore very much as proto-flâneurs, albeit with their own personal agendas of abandonment, fantasy and loss. Indeed, as Moore

(1987)[1] stated, "I'm a great believer in returning to the scene of the crime, living it again and letting it work on you… These places have much more than one could exhaust in one lifetime."

Moore and formalism

Moore's work can be divided into two periods loosely linked to different geographical territories. The first phase, from the early 60s to the late 70s, saw Moore explore the Pembrokeshire coast as well as Ireland, Cyprus and the US. This early period saw Moore photograph with a formal approach that stemmed from his earlier career as a painter. Sadly, there's only one image of his painting in circulation today–a dry landscape study in the style of Lawrence Gowing. Yet, as Mark Haworth-Booth (1981: 13) noted, Moore began as an experimental abstract painter in the 1950s and as a student at the Royal College of Art would have been aware of the British painters Roger Hilton, William Scott and Patrick Heron. Although no examples of Moore's abstract paintings survive, his earlier photographic work explores a flattening of the picture plane, a concern that is typical of abstract painting of this era. With a keen interest in contemporary sculpture, Moore (1987) reflected on his awareness of formal space: "Abstract relationships of a certain kind might lead you towards a lamppost and a fence or something, making you see a significance there you hadn't possibly seen before". In this sense, Moore's early work wasn't documenting place or narrating a social condition, it was shaping his environment into a series of optical refinements that challenged viewers to look again and see something else beyond the purely descriptive. Moore (1987) stated:

> One is drawn towards the things that mean something to you and the place is not really of any significance. So therefore one is after a certain kind of thing, which for me is found in this kind of environment more than anywhere else. It seems to me that I can go to place like Silloth on the Cumbrian coast and go back and back and back again to it because it seems to contain the kinds of elements that fascinate me and also you discover so many more new things.

Yet this early work and Moore's association with Minor White, Harry Callahan and the MIT scene sent early critical appraisal in one direction from which it took some time to emerge. Although distanced from such practice, Moore's work was often located as late Modernist, especially his use of formal elements of line,

1 Quotations from Moore dated 1987 are from an interview I conducted with the photographer, published for the first time in this essay. Subsequent quotations from this source will not therefore, have the usual page number citations.

form, shape and tone–and also of his fine printing. While this is indeed accurate of his early phase, Moore's unique awareness of formalism enabled him to discard symbolism, metaphor or any narrative intent for an abstract painter's outlook of a purely graphic and geometric sensibility. As Moore (1987) recounted:

> I think of a picture being essentially a kind of visual structure. Putting it simplistically is saying it's like having a beautiful architectural conception and building it knowing full well it won't be structurally stable enough to remain standing. The photograph has to be just as strongly felt so it will stand looking at and relooking at and you aren't irritated by a weak comprehension of the actual visual shapes and structures and relationships within the image.

Post-formalism

A second phase of work from the late 70s onwards saw Moore move on from this purely formal image making. At this turning point in his work Moore stated:

> I soon exhausted myself. The places didn't seem to ring true to my complete self. I moved from the coastline to Milford Haven where there were more traces of man, and sometimes took pictures in the more run-down coastal area. I was drawn to the edge of civilization (1981b: 24).

Here, Moore developed an additional element in his work repeatedly visiting the 'unpicturesque' North of England including Allonby, Maryport, Silloth, Flimby and Harrington, exploring man-made environment in complex, overlapping contexts. The north as Moore (1987) recalled, offered the chance to explore a social landscape:

> I like the kind of atmosphere that one finds on the English side of the Solway and as you've noticed yourself on the Wirral. It's a sort of limbo land, looking almost as if life had past it by. I can't quite explain why but it seems to symbolise an awful lot of what life in this country seems to be about.

Moore's attraction to the bleak Cumbrian coast at this time ran parallel to Chris Killip's and Markéta Luskačová's work in the North East, chronicling the economically cut adrift, yet Moore's representations were of an unpeopled terrain. Like the 1930s artist and photographer Paul Nash, Moore revealed his vision of the North through the depiction of inanimate objects in the quasi-surreal landscape of concrete, tarmac and pebbledash. Here, the more immediate personal poverty crystallised in Killip and Luskačová's images was mediated by Moore as a detached landscape of aftermath, loss and decline.

While Moore's own public statements about his practice were fundamentally non-committal, they played down other, more private aspects of his work. A later evaluation of Moore acknowledged the complexity of this second phase of his career. Graham Clarke (1997) noted the open meanings and movement between the sublime and the banal, making the commonplace both recognised and mysterious. Moore too, in later years talked about more personal motives, recounting to Ian Jeffrey:

> In recent photographs I have been making some kind of a return to Wallasey where I grew up in the 1930s. Whole tracts of the Cumbrian coast where I work nowadays remind me of those childhood areas. They also provide me with structures and images which allow me to comment on life in general (1981:220).

Moore and the New Topographics

Moore's interest in the banalities of the man-made landscape demonstrated his willingness to move away from late Modernism's pioneers of art photography intent on capturing exquisite moments in the natural wilderness, namely Minor White and to a lesser extent, Harry Callahan. Indeed as Moore moved further north, his work took on a deadpan and poignant undercurrent that coincided with the pre-occupations of a younger group of American photographers. While Moore never totally rejected the formalism gleaned from his early career as a painter, his work became cooler in tone, distant and more visually sophisticated. Moore's own unique approach connects with the seminal show New Topographics: Photographs of a Man-Altered Landscape in 1975 and the work of participants including Robert Adams, Frank Gohlke, Stephen Shore and Lewis Baltz. Like Stephen Shore who defined his practice as "interested in producing images that were generated by a conceptual framework, but at the same time, allowed for visual articulateness" (Lange 2002: 48), Moore's work was not descriptively documentary in the accepted sense of the word, but mediated by his own ruminations on loss, abandonment and dereliction. While Baltz and Adams' exploration of encroaching urbanism is set within the epic tracts of developing America, Moore comes closest to Stephen Shore and his noticing of the extraordinary in the everyday, most evident in his Uncommon Places (1982) project. Moore's lifelong curiosity with street furniture evidences a humbler, more reductive version of Walker Evans' and Stephen Shore's highway-centred imagery. Here was a more introverted man-made landscape of Northern Britain, more demure than the American highway-as-habitat, but no less evocative.

Moore's diffidence in relation to existing norms and practices set him apart from his British contemporaries but also from his craft-infused American contemporaries. Instead, Moore (1987) advocated a distanced, nuanced approach to technique and darkroom craft stating:

> I like images where the idea is presented without people looking at it and thinking "that's a fabulous shot, I wonder what telephoto lens he used". It's not the point, you should be unconscious of the means. I'm not very interested in ultra–sharp prints or bad prints; the quality should disappear and you're left with the image.

In this respect, Moore's rejection of romantic visions of the landscape and the alchemy of the darkroom, places his practice closer to conceptual artists using photography. In the UK, Moore's work is closest to Keith Arnatt, a conceptual artist who later worked exclusively with photography. Arnatt's own projects AONB (Area of Outstanding Natural Beauty (1982-84) and Forest of Dean (1986) use a Moore-like deadpan framing and narrative distance to capture the bleakness of an inhabited and somewhat tourist defiled wilderness. In AONB, Arnatt plays off the notion of an approved landscape against an alternative reality of dereliction, car parks and rubbish bins, puncturing the picturesque with pithy, Moore-like humour.

In the US, Ed Ruscha's photographically led artist's books of the 60s were prescient of the later cool, detached deadpan style which surfaced in the mid-70s. Alongside the late Modernism of White and Callahan, Ruscha's work appeared mechanical and rejected the accepted notions of photographic practice of the time. As Philpott (1999: 77) records, Ruscha described his intent as "What I was after was a no-style or non-statement with a no-style."

While Moore's work does not contain the usual preconceived temporal strategies of conceptualism, or the radical reductionism described by Lippard (1973: xiv) as "a cult of neutrality and a ferocious erasure of emotion and conventional notions of beauty," his rejection of a materially aestheticized intent, together with Keith Arnatt places their work partially in that field. As Hirsch (2009: 459) speculated, the legacy of the New Topographics show was the invention of a visual style–"A literal, deadpan style" and of a social landscape physically and spiritually depleted, released from romantic and picturesque concerns. Moore (1981b: 23) alluded to this: "I am also interested in visual humour, in shapes that relate in odd ways. Photography's peculiar deadpan face suits the subject."

Moore and literature

Tantalisingly, Moore was exploring notions of sequence and the grouping of photographs in the final phase of his working life. At a time when the self-publishing of an authored photography book was prohibitively expensive, Moore was unable to realise this in the book form, yet the thought of how he would have synthesised a sequence of image and text, remains an intriguing prospect. In the two published anthologies of his work, Moore employed a conventional epigraph to set the context of his images. In *Every So Often* (1983: 3) Moore quotes Paul Valéry–"To look is to forget the name of the things you are seeing."

Moore also framed his work using classical Chinese and Japanese poetry, which on occasion could appear gnomic but in other times set the context for his highly personal approach to his work. In the accompanying essay for Every So Often, Clive Lancaster briefly described how Moore had sent him a copy of a 17th century Japanese poem–Matsuo Basho's *The Narrow Road to the Deep North*. Intended as helpful background reference, Lancaster chose not to explore and expand on Moore's prompt further. The poems however, describe the poet Basho's northern meanderings, who, like Moore, attempts to connect with his past and renew his own creative practice. Surprisingly one of Basho's early lines states, "Last year I spent wandering along the seacoast"–a link no doubt spotted by Moore as he made his own autobiographical journey along the Cumbrian coastline. Moore's richly personalised work was enriched by his curiosity for literature and an interest in how localism could reveal greater, more universal themes. A further clue to Moore's thinking can be found in Arthur Machen's *The Hill of Dreams*, mentioned by Moore in an interview with Ian Jeffrey, where he stated:

> I remember thirty years ago or so coming across and feasting on the writing of Arthur Machen, author of *The Hill of Dreams*. His writing may seem stilted and archaic now, but I was fascinated by his attention to penumbra and to the half-tones around a shadow–seemed to be describing meeting places between two ways of being. He helped focus that sort of thing in myself (1981b: 24).

For Moore, reading Arthur Machen's fantasy novel *The Hill of Dreams* was an epiphany–yet it is hard to think of a more unlikely source of inspiration. Machen's text gives further clues to Moore's broad assimilation of literature bridging and connecting with his own work. Indeed, Moore's use of these unexpected references suggests an artist seeking to build a contextual framework outside the recognised practice silos of his day. While contemporary landscape practitioners such as Fay Godwin in collaboration with poet Ted Hughes was in a largely illustrational capacity, Moore's work instead embodied complex, philosophical awakenings gleaned from his knowledge of 7th century Chinese and medieval Japanese poetry,

Baudelaire, Rimbaud and Valéry and Jonathan Williams of the Black Mountain Poets.

For Moore enthusiasts, reading *The Hill of Dreams* can provide additional insights into his work. Although the book is remembered as a late Victorian drug-fuelled dream fantasy, there are many parallels between Machen's would-be writer protagonist and Moore's own response to his immediate environment. There's a common sense of striving to practice, but the most interesting connection between Moore and Machen is the use of the landscape as a fantasy playground. In *The Hill of Dreams*, Machen's writer protagonist Lucian Taylor wanders and yearns in a grey, bleak unnamed city suburb. The writer seeks out triggers from these local wanderings, conjuring sophisticated outcomes from banal, repetitive experiences. There are passages in *The Hill of Dreams* which read as if the protagonist is walking within a Raymond Moore photograph:

> [The landscape was] full of hidden meanings and the sense of matters unintelligible to the uninitiated.....The fact that sensations are symbols not realities hovered in his mind, and led him to speculate as to whether they could not actually be transmuted one into another....[Ancients] had mistaken the symbol for the thing signified. It was not the material banquet which really mattered, but the thought of it (Machen, 1907: 108).

In the novel, Lucian Taylor has an epiphany when he realises he could make literary works that appeal to the subconscious, a literature borne out of his own internal dialogue rather than purely from observation. This duality, I suspect, was a practical stance that Moore shared too. It wasn't the place or indeed the symbols that were important for him to transmit, it wasn't about technique either–but it was about a social landscape for his own personal reflection and purposes. As Moore (1981a: 12) stated, "For me, the no-man's land between the real and the fantasy–the mystery in the commonplace."

Moore and the optical unconscious

The suggestive otherness to which photography can allude, has been the subject of much speculation since the first critical writings on the medium. While no doubt enjoying the narration of his own successes through his textual accompaniments in The Pencil of Nature, William Henry Fox Talbot (1844-46:40) poses a prescient reflection on the serendipity of the medium:

> It frequently happens, moreover–and this is one of the charms of photography–that the operator himself discovers on examination, perhaps long afterwards, that he has depicted many things that he had no notion of at the time.

Later, Walter Benjamin's (1927) notion of optical unconscious–the circumstances when images refer to hidden, universal geometric universalities also impact on Moore's own keen interest in happenstance and is evident in this reflection on his working processes:

> There are some [photographs] which one seems to have shot and then suddenly realised, maybe it's your subconscious registering something you're not entirely aware of at the time. I'm a great believer in the subconscious, I have great faith in it. I find that even things of significance in the structure of the picture, relationships of form and shapes etc, one's subconscious more often than not proves to be an unerring guide for when to pull the trigger. Looking at the final print one is amazed to see that there are certain things that relate uncommonly. It's only after the event that you are able to see what I believe your sort of optical subconscious had registered (Moore, 1987).

Conclusion

Moore used the Northern Landscape as a fantasy playground to project his internal narrative onto the bleak, grey sites of his Solway towns. Formalism, the optical unconscious and memory are all elements found in his later work. Drawn to liminal spaces and deserted edgelands, Moore (1981b: 22) had a fascination with the nondescript in a social landscape, overlayed with his own sense of entropy, stating, "I'm a loner, a reflective pessimist, and I look for signs of finality and the end of time, impending departure and desperation." His banal, distanced and reductive view of the North was his way of recapturing a sense of the place of his childhood. Unlike his contemporary Roger Palmer whose bleak landscape text and image works forefronted his conceptual conceit, Moore demonstrated a more oblique, unrevealed conceptualism, yet this was equally embodied in the work. Moore's astute visual humour is similarly withheld and perhaps only intended for an audience of like-minded photographers. Like artist polymath Ian Breakwell, Moore's acutely observed details drawn from isolated incidents, reveal unexpected collisions of people, places and things, legitimising the mundane and the ordinary as a fertile ground for observation. Like Breakwell, Moore's approach could equally be described as "the epiphany of momentary alignment and juxtaposition" (Hammond, 1983: 22).

In conclusion, Moore was a mute chronicler of the mundane and an unrecognized proponent of the detached observational genre so familiar today. Whilst not part of the original New Topographics, Moore's work developed parallel concerns to his American counterparts albeit in the smaller, less developed British north. As Haworth-Booth alluded (1985: 115), Moore was compelled by "the phase of aftermath; ideas of loss, poetic reconstruction...." Perhaps a more rounded reading of Moore's later work is to view it as a literary infused practice–a pleasure in ruins shot with a late photography-style of distance and detachment; a bleak lust that had found its Shangri-La in the Solway Firth. A key concept developed by Rose Macaulay (1953: 48) in *Pleasure of Ruins*, could easily describe why we find Moore's later work so compelling. Macaulay suggests when confronted with decay, absence and loss, we build the ruin in our own minds, "The deserted spaces and ruins provide but a partial story, yet their incompleteness allow us to speculate and project our own personal narratives upon them."

Author Note

Like many art students in the 1980s, I first encountered the work of Raymond Moore in London's Art's Council bookshop, buying an exhibition catalogue of his work whilst visiting from Corsham where I was studying Fine Art. Later, I was fortunate to meet Moore when he visited Corsham to give a guest lecture. After a brief correspondence by postcard, (these were of course, pre-Internet days) Moore very kindly invited me to visit his home in Chapelknowe, north of the Solway Firth in the spring of 1987. Moore consented to be interviewed on tape, but sadly died some months later.

Moore was a generous man who took a shine to me because we were from the same part of the UK and also because of a picture I'd taken to show him. By chance I'd shown Moore a picture of a curvy, 1930s public toilet block that I'd shot and Moore was delighted to tell me that his father had been the architect of the same building. From 1985 onwards and fully under Moore's influence, I've been documenting the empty coastal features of the Thames Estuary, North Wales and the Wirral Peninsular, so familiar to Raymond Moore including New Brighton, Moreton, Leasowe and West Kirby.

Transcript of Interview

Interview with Raymond Moore, Chapelknowe 1987. While the questions I posed to Moore during this conversation stem inevitably from an undergraduate perspective, their naïvety perhaps disarmed the normally reticent Moore who did not as a whole comment on his work or his motives. I've resisted the temptation to edit either my questions or Moore's responses and as such our conversation is reproduced verbatim.

TD: I can't remember seeing a lot of people in your photographs. How do you account for this?

RM: I find that I'm naturally drawn to places, situations and the atmospheres of places. If people loom too large in a picture then I don't take it. There are in fact a number of pictures which contain people but they are usually small. I'm not really concerned with taking portraits because once a person looms too large in an environment your attention is drawn to that, which completely sidetracks the issue sometimes.

TD: To me these figures seem to have no more importance in the landscape than a tree or a lamppost.

RM: Yes. What interests me is that human beings really are brought down to size. They probably are no more significant than a tree growing or as you say a lamppost. They are all part of the visual scene. I guess that–some people will be absolutely horrified by this.

TD: I think the thing I connect with most in your images is this quietness and stillness. Is this important to you?

RM: Yes. I suppose basically I am a rather quiet person. I suppose it's reflected in the kind of music I like listening to, which tends to be more towards single instruments or a quartet rather than vast symphonies. Also I think that in making a good photograph or painting it isn't necessary to go miles in search of particularly exotic landscapes or situations.

TD: What do you think about contemporary landscape photography, like Fay Godwin for instance who hikes up to remote places.

RM: It's interesting that you should talk about Fay Godwin, I know Fay a little and I have a respect for her work and she works extremely hard, but I find it very difficult to get into her work otherwise. Have you seen the film on her?

TD: Yes: I remember all that equipment she seemed to lug around.

RM: Oh God yes. There was a part in which she was flicking through some postcards she had bought and she was saying how particularly picturesque they made the landscape look and then she went and did the self same thing herself. I couldn't understand this at all. But it's the concept of the landscape that seems to me, and I'm not trying to dig at her because I think it applies to a lot of other photographers and I've done the same thing myself sometimes, that worries me. It seems to be quite clear that she's got her eye on the market. So if you photograph a battlefield, some people and I suggest a minimal number will buy it because of its photographic qualities. But lots of people will buy it for its historical standpoint. They couldn't give a damn whether it's a good or bad photograph. It's a record of a battlefield and that's all that counts. The same goes for castles and other famous monuments for which this country is noted. Providing you do that and I'm not trying to deny it requires some skill, you can make some useful sales and feed some publishers as well, because I suppose you can always match it with a bit of Old English poetry stuck underneath. A few dozen of these and you've got the beginnings of a book.

TD: What do you think about photographers or artists working with text and image?

RM: I personally don't do that kind of thing because I own up to being possibly not good enough with words and secondly, I feel that if the camera and the photograph doesn't put the point across then I don't think you can bolster it with words which I think some people try to do, though not all of them. Roger Palmer thinks always in terms of word and image which is fine. But it's not my sort of country.

TD: I saw a show of Hamish Fulton's the other week in London and I was amazed how similar his work looked to Richard Long.

RM: Well, I'm sorry but I get terribly suspicious of a lot of this. They think they've cornered a certain kind of market for themselves with their galleries and publishers. There's very little more room for anybody else. In trying to creep in on the act maybe quite sincerely, they are going to be gently edged aside.

TD: It seems to me that this kind of work is a fusion of conceptual art and contemporary photography.

RM: I think, certainly as Hamish Fulton's work is concerned, I don't know an awful lot about Long, I think the fast that he went to India and completed that 10,000 mile walk or whatever, that sets people on edge straight away. You score instantly by putting people in a sort of empty environment immediately and then you flick images in front of them and these images acquire a sort of intensity and significance which I would submit, would not otherwise have acquired. If for instance you had said 'this guy had a luxury flight out to India and he was driven by Rolls Royce to these locations', I'm exaggerating again, but it would lose a mass of significance. I saw the Roger Palmer show of his work taken in South Africa and I thought that was good.

TD: Do you find when you've developed your film and you're looking at a contact print…

RM: I don't make contact sheets. 35mm contact sheets I can't tell anything from. The things which I'm interested in which is dependent on the quality of the atmosphere, I can't see in a contact print. So I end up having to make a lot of small test prints.

TD: Do you find then, better images in your test prints than that you'd expected?

RM: Sometimes. But mostly it's fair to say that on occasions one presses the button and one knows one's got it. Soon as I've developed the film I'm nosing for that image, hoping to Christ I haven't shaken the camera or done something daft. But it doesn't always work that way. There are some which one seems to have shot and then you've suddenly realised, maybe it's your subconscious registering something you're not entirely aware of at the time. I'm a great believer of the subconscious, I have great faith in it. I find that even in things of significance in the structure of the picture, relationships of form and shapes etc, one's subconscious more often than not proves to be an unerring guide when to pull the trigger. Looking at the final print one is amazed to see that there are certain things that relate uncommonly, whereas when you are actually faced with the subject, you just had some vague sense inside, well not vague, perhaps more intense than that, that this had to be taken, without being able to analyse it and say why. Its only after the event that you are able to see what I believe your sort of optical subconscious had registered.

TD: Do you find yourself drawn to particular objects as well as places?

RM: Yes I suppose so. It's difficult for me to verbalise too much on this. I like the kind of atmosphere that one finds on the English side of the Solway and as you've noticed yourself in the Wirral. It's a sort of limbo land, looking almost as if life had past it by. I can't quite explain why but it seems to symbolise an awful lot of what life in this country seems to be about. I'm sure if I were sent to Los Angeles for a summer, I'd probably come back without having taken anything. I wouldn't be able to contact it. Does that make sense?

TD: Yes. I've seen some pictures you took in Cyprus and I was amazed because they...

RM: Probably looked like Britain?

TD: Well yes.

RM: Ha! Well one is drawn towards the things that mean something to you and the place is not really of any significance. So therefore one is after a - certain kind of thing, which for me is found in this kind of environment more than anywhere else. It seems to me that I can go to place like Silloth on the Cumbrian coast and go back and back and back again to it because it seems to contain the kinds of elements that fascinate me and also you discover so many more new things. I'm a great believer in returning to the scene of the crime, living it again and letting it work on you. I don't mean going back and looking for the tripod marks saying to yourself " I'm going to take this again only better", it's just going back and allowing it to work on you and having the inner faith to believe that this place contains elements which you are more likely to find with patience rather than endlessly hunting or walking miles in search of something a bit significant. These places have much more than one could exhaust in one lifetime.

TD: It seems to me that people actually go out looking for 'successful photographs' as if they existed hidden away somewhere.

RM: Yes. Maybe it's true of today, I think it's always been true. This bloody recipe business.

TD: I find with looking at a lot of prints that there's an emphasis on technique and skill which seems of primary importance when it shouldn't even be secondary.

RM: Yes.

TD: It's almost like a display of virtuosity and it doesn't seem important to me at all.

RM: No it isn't. I strive for an image which is acceptable print wise and then that's it. One is then free to explore the nature of the image.

TD: Do you use a range of lenses?

RM: No. I do most of my work with a standard 50mm and 55m lens. Quite a lot of images, which I'd say are maybe my best, have been taken with a 28mm lens. It has a spacial strength about it because of the perspective convergence. Had I used a longer lens and flattened it out, I would have lost it. With the wide-angle you are sucked into the ambience of the set up. I hate wide-angle shots which obviously look like wide-angle shots, where you have converging verticals etc., and I'm afraid some of Harry Callahan's stuff irritates me a little.

TD: I think the wide-angle lens gives you a deeper arena to look into.

RM: Yes, I think if you can handle it and you're not snap happy with it–it can be quite useful. I like images where the idea is presented without people looking at it and thinking 'that's a fabulous shot, I wonder what telephoto lens he used.' It's not the point, you should be unconscious of the means. Also I'm not very interested in ultra–sharp prints or bad prints; the quality should disappear and you're left with the image. Sometimes ultra-sharp or in detail prints are equally as irritating as blurred or out of focus ones.

TD: I've noticed that in a few of your pictures you have a foreground occupying two thirds of the space instead of the normal half and half. How do you account for this?

RM: Well I don't know. I hear you saying this but I'm not conscious of it, I don't plan anything, it's just the way I see it. I automatically move in that direction. I don't know why.

TD: What about structuring your photographs? Do you consciously think about composition?

RM: I don't like the word composition actually, but that's just a personal thing of mine. I think of a picture being essentially a kind of visual structure. Hopefully you set up a kind of visual mood within the limits of the photographic process. Working within those limits one is still concerned with qualities and relationships, tensions between the images–that's half the fascination for me. Those things which are not evocative or provocative enough to compel some degree of attention are not worth talking about. This is the same thing that Cartier-Bresson was talking about when he said that the visual elements within the picture must stand on their own two feet and relate. Putting it simplistically is saying it's like having a beautiful architectural conception and building it knowing full well it won't be structurally stable enough to remain standing. The photograph has to be just as strongly felt so it will stand looking at and relooking at and you aren't irritated by a weak comprehension of the actual visual shapes and structures and relationships within the image. This is something difficult and obviously something which cannot be affected by any great extent by the approach of a photojournalist. I mean if you're in Vietnam with bullets whistling around you, you just point the camera and hope for the best.

TD: Don't you find with a lot of Third World photographs and famine reportage that we have seen so many photographs of this kind, we've developed a very high threshold preventing any kind of impact or effect on us anymore?

RM: Oh I think you're right there. I feel very strongly about that and it's a great shame that looking through colour supplements, whether the photographs are of some terrible happening in Beirut or the Chelsea flower show, I get an awful feeling that people don't look at the images at all, they end up like postage stamps ceasing to have any real impact. I think photojournalism to me, seems in a way dead. I'm sure if they heard that they'd all lynch me, but I just don't think there's any future in it. We have seen it over and over and over again.

TD: I don't think it's worked at the best of times, political art doesn't change anything.

RM: No I agree. I think people have said that my work was political but in a different sort of way. I suppose I couldn't understand this at first, then by and large these rather decrepit areas of the country producing images with this forlorn, empty, rather hopeless feel–that's why they don't get bought–is a kind of political statement which comes across almost sub-consciously.

TD: I think every move you make is political.

RM: It must be in that sense if you take the word at its broadest meaning. But, as you say, I don't think any of this does anything to me at all. I cannot quite remember the photographers name–he's quite well known, some kind of pictures for the colour supplements. It was a black and white shot of a couple of West Indian guys working on the railway in this country, standing on the track outside this station and I thought, well what the hell is this image supposed to mean. I just get a statement of a lot of irrelevant detail and I start to become interested in the buttons on his coat. I just don't see what it's doing, it didn't do anything.

TD: It's not as if you haven't seen it before.

RM: Yes, but I could not understand it at all. At the time a friend of ours who better be nameless, who is a very good photographer, had a discussion with us on her criteria for evaluating a good photograph. This turned out to be the amount of detail. In other words if you took a photograph of roofs which in one you could count 50,000 tiles and only 40,000 in the other pictures, then the 50,000 one had it. I thought then, what's the bloody point in this at all. I think if you want to tackle this thing then the word well written is much more potent than the visual image. I don't agree with this old Chinese thing about a picture being worth so many thousand words.

TD: What do you think about sequencing images?

RM: I think there's a lot to this. I never go out with the idea of using a sequence though...

TD: Things always happen afterwards?

RM: They do. In retrospect one flicks through images and pairs them off, finding that one heightens the intensity of the other and vice-versa, I think there's a lot in that. And when you're hanging a show you tend to group things together, I do anyway, which is a kind of sequencing.

TD: Do you take a lot of interest in contemporary art?

RM: I enjoy very much on the rare occasions when I get to see it, lots of contemporary sculpture. Don't ask me to say why, but the forms that arise from the sculptor have an affinity with the way I react to the outside world. You can't get away from influence and I'm not worried by it like some people are, it settles with time and it adds to your development. By looking at contemporary sculpture it doesn't mean that one has the same concerns, but the final forms that are evolved by the sculptor somehow sets one's own imagination working on other tracks. You can often suddenly realize situations outside one in the everyday world that have certain sorts of affinities and make some kind of sense which you wouldn't have recognized had you not seen a sculptor relate certain abstract shapes. Abstract relationships of a certain kind might lead you towards a lamppost and a fence or something, making you see a significance there you hadn't possibly seen before.

TD: Yes. Do you think then that it's important to work from within? I mean make a form of art that relates to your own personal situation in a visual way rather than juggling around with ideas and concerns all the time.

RM: Oh yes. I think that because I think there's too much of this stuff around now and I think we've got into a situation which has probably been there for a long time, where the important people are the critics and the artists seem like a lot of bloody sheep following on. They know if they do this or pay homage to that, then it's likely to gain them recognition. But there's not many of them that seen prepared to go their own way, which is a great shame because it fosters a kind of phony art environment. To think that the history of art has gone from A to B to C to D and then try and guess what E is going to be is a bad way of working. It doesn't happen like that. It means that you're not really feeling anything about anything except pushing your conceptual ideas, e.g. putting yourself into the next position on the chess board, and I don't think art is a game of chess. And if you're not caught up, and now I'm talking about photography, with the outside world then you shouldn't be taking photographs. You may not agree but we've not suddenly become devoid of passion and metaphor and a way of saying "look at this". You know if you lose that sense then it's time to pack up. I would certainly pack up if I realised this. Frequently I do, like a lot of photographers my age, maybe thinking to themselves "have I anything more to say?" You get sort of really frightened.

TD: But there's always more out there to see and to find.

RM: There's more out there but one's powers of recognition may be so depleted.

TD: I tried the other day to write down what I was interested in, photographically, what I was looking for in my pictures. When I finished, I was left with a few recurring objects and situations which seemed banal and a bit ridiculous.

RM: It does in away but I think that's what it's largely about; there may be other extra visual communicative qualities within the picture which may be important as well, but I think the basic thing is to compel some kind of attention and if you don't do that you haven't even started on the bottom rung.

References

Agee, J. & Evans, W. (1941): Let us now Praise Famous Men. Boston: Houghton & Miflin.

Barthes, R (1978): Image, Music, Text. New York: Hill and Wang.

Benjamin, W. (1927): Little History of Photography. In Jennings, M. Ed (1999): Walter Benjamin Selected Writings Volume 2 1927-1934. Cambridge: Harvard University Press.

Clark, G (1997): The Photograph. Oxford: Oxford University Press.

Evans, W (1931): The Reappearance of Photography. In Hound and Horn magazine issue 5, November 1931.
Fox Talbot, W.H. (1844-46): The Pencil of Nature. London: Longman, Brown, Green & Longmans.
Hammond, P (1983): Ian Breakwell's Witness: Love Among the Pork Scratchings. In Art Monthly, February (1983).
Haworth-Booth, M (1981): Murmurs at Every Turn: The Photographs of Raymond Moore. London: Travelling Light.
Haworth-Booth, M (1985): Josef Koudelka. In Creative Camera, March, 1985.
Hirsch, R (1999): Seizing the Light: A Social History of Photography. New York: McGraw-Hill
Jeffrey, I (1981) Photography: A Concise History. London: Thames and Hudson.
Lange, S (2002): A Conversation with Stephen Shore in Bernd and Hilla Becher, in Festschrift, Erasmuspreis. Munich: Schirmer/ Mosel.
Lippard, L (1973): Six Years: The dematerialization of the art object from 1966-1972. Los Angeles: University of California Press.
Macauley, R (1953): Pleasure of Ruins. London: Weidenfeld and Nicolson.
Machen, A (1907): The Hill of Dreams. London: Grant Richards.
Moore, R (1983): Every So Often. London; BBC/ Phaidon Press
Moore, R (1981a): Murmurs at Every Turn. London: Travelling Light.
Moore, R and Jeffrey, I (1981b) Ray Moore Talking. In Creative Camera March/April 1981. London: Creative Camera.
Philpott, C (1999): Sixteen Books and Then Some. In Edward Ruscha: Editions 1959-1999. Minneapolis: Walker Arts Center (1999).
Woods, G (1972) Art without Boundaries. New York. Henry Holt.

Rethinking space in the landscapes of Nordic cuisine

Darcy White

Introduction – space and its representation

In her book *For Space*, of 2005, Doreen Massey advocates unpacking our approach to thinking about and, importantly, "imagining" space not as "a surface continuous and given" but instead as "a meeting-up of histories", where an accretion of numerous trajectories contribute to how a given space *is* – certainly not singular nor even merely plural but where fluid and multivalent elements continually produce a space. In other words where space is in a constant state of being made (Massey 2005: 9).

Massey's object is to offer a new way of thinking about space, one that departs from the established 'habit' that conceives of space in relation to place, as counterpoised each to the other (Bergson 1911, Tuan 1977, Cresswell 2002). Here, 'place' is typically understood as "closed, coherent, integrated, as authentic, as 'home', a secure retreat", as meaningful, lived and everyday, generally taken to refer to somewhere real and bounded and with identifiable material and cultural characteristics; while 'space' is taken to be fairly vague, open and even abstract, and therefore implicitly meaning-less (Massey 2005: 6). As such, space and place have typically been framed in terms of an opposition: "the abstract versus the everyday, and so forth" (ibid). In an important intervention into the conception of space, Massey asks: "What then if we refuse this imagination?" (ibid).

Massey's core motivation appears to be pivoted around issues of social justice in a globalised and uncertain world, insisting on the recognition of the role and rights of Others, who are often not visible within representations. She argues that the tendency to hold a fixed, still, closed idea of a given space denies the richness and reality of all that has gone into, and continually goes into, creating that space – for Massey it is especially important to register the shifts, movements, people and social relations within a given space. Furthermore, the locality of any given geographical space is "implicated in the global" (Massey 2005: 102). In short she advocates a new approach to space where the vitality and dynamism of real life, together with social justice, are brought back into the picture.

> Space then cannot be a static slice orthogonal to time and defined in opposition to it. If movement is reality itself then what we think of as space is a cut through all those trajectories; a simultaneity of unfinished stories.' … 'space has time / times within it" (Massey 2003: 111).

This necessarily brings us to the 'problem' of the visual representation of space where, for photography in particular, the epistemological limits of the medium pose a problem, as Laura Mulvey has expressed it: "The still photograph represents an unattached instant, unequivocally grounded in its indexical relation to the moment of registration" (2006: 13). Perhaps less obvious is the degree to which the selected representation "asserts the moment at which one frame was recorded" (14). In this sense it fixes time in a continuous present, as in Barthes' well-rehearsed argument (1980). But in addition there is another way in which fixing occurs. The 'framing' of the photograph also insists upon or suggests a bounded-ness to the location in which it was taken and therefore landscape photographs may "play out a romance of detachment" (Massey 2005: 103).

For Massey, the fixity of such images is significant for the ways in which we conceive of space. She argues that through a historical connotation, (particularly following Bergson 1911) the very "conceptualisation of space" has been reduced to a "dimension for the display / representation of different moments in time", and this, she suggests, is not only long-established but "implicit" (Massey 2005: 7). Moreover, that this might lead us to imagine space as "static, closed, immobile, as the opposite of time" (18). Instead, Massey cautions that "time and space must be thought together", that they are "implicated in each other" (ibid), hence her proposition that we must "refuse that distinction … between place (as meaningful, lived and everyday) and space (as what? The outside? The abstract? The meaning*less*)?", in order fully to acknowledge the life, vitality and dynamism of any given space (6). In summary:

> it is not space that takes the life out of time, but representation. The real trouble is that the old equation of representation with spacialisation has taken the life out of space (Massey 2003: 113).

At the heart of this chapter lies an interest in the contribution made by contemporary landscape photography to the ways in which geographic spaces are conceptualised, envisioned, thought about – in others words – *imagined*. Here, I attempt to approach the representation of space in the spirit proposed by Massey – refusing the conventional notion that an abstract, or open, space is implicitly a meaning*less* space.

Massey is on record for saying that the discipline of geography fascinates her, because it is "a very multidisciplinary discipline" (2013), bringing together physical geography – topography geomorphology, biogeography, meteorology, climatology – with elements of the social and economic. The same might be claimed for landscape as a genre of photography – except, I argue, that all too often the social is absent, or indeed absented, by the selections, choices, framings, interests and tastes of the photographer – strongly influenced by the conventions of the genre, of course, and the function of the given landscape image – particularly within commercial and applied photography.

Here, I mean to refer to photographic representation, not so much as mimesis (Bryson 1983) rooted in an indexical trace of particular places and spaces, but as part of a discourse producing ideas about the North. More specifically, I am interested in examining how landscape photography is implicated in the process of constructing ideas about Nordic or Scandinavian space, through an investigation of a particular genre of commercial landscape photography; that used in the illustration of contemporary cookery books centered on this region. This focus enables me to think about some of the ways in which the Nordic region has been imagined in recent times and the role this plays in ongoing constructions of the North in the context of globalisation.

Through a study of examples of photographic landscape illustrations used in Nordic cookery writing, I explore the representation of a particular geographic and cultural space. The chapter therefore draws on Massey for the purposes of, in her words, "prising open" the "often hidden, ways of conceiving" of space (2005: 6).[1] The idea of the "hidden" interests me, particularly the ways in which attitudes and ideas – myths in Barthes' terms – lie quietly concealed within particular types of landscape photography found in everyday cultural products such as illustrated books, magazines and marketing materials of various kinds (Barthes 1957).

For this analysis of examples of landscape photography of the Nordic region, my intention is to "question the habit of thinking" about this particular space, "as a surface" – or more accurately as an array of surfaces, as visualised through photography (Massey 2005: 4). I aim to create a dialogue between two ideas of 'space' offered by Massey; the abstract intellectual space intended to facilitate an opening-up of thinking; and the dynamic geographical and social space, considered through the examples of landscape photography purposefully created to play a supporting role to cookery writing from the Nordic region. In-so-doing, I invite reflection upon what happens to "our implicit imagination" of the Nordic if we do this (Massey 2005: 4).

The cookbook genre is perhaps an unlikely focus for an analysis of landscape photography. However, in recent years there has been a proliferation of publications on Nordic (and Scandinavian) cuisine, most of which are richly illustrated with photographs of landscape and nature and other kinds of imagery. Within

1 Note Massey's work was largely focused on London and on South/Latin American.

the pages of such regional cookery books different histories are brought together around identifiable themes and characteristics, where old ideas about the region may be perpetuated and new ideas may be ignited. Following Anderson (1983), Appadurai (1988) and Massey (2005), it is argued that such books play a part in the creation of ideas about the North; in a continual process of making and unmaking.

Some narratives about the Nordic, as evidenced in two important books on its regional cuisine, are revealing of attitudes to the effects of globalisation. Firstly, I will argue that in one key example of Nordic cookery writing and photographic illustration, *NOMA: Time and Place in Nordic Cuisine*, published in 2010, some effects of globalisation are addressed and critiqued by an approach to locally produced food that challenges our thinking about the Nordic in relation to global issues. In the context of thinking about Massey, *NOMA* has an interesting subtitle: 'Time and Place in Nordic Cuisine' – I will return to this evocation of 'time' and of 'place'.

By way of contrast, I consider a second example, *The Nordic Cook Book* (Nilsson 2015). This, I will argue, evidences a resistance to change, achieved through the absenting or denial of the presence of any cultural Other, despite the de facto influence of people from within the Nordic population who originate from other parts of the world. The idea of time evoked here is that of timelessness.

The argument here is underpinned by a wider interest in the ways that landscape photography, and the landscape genre more generally, influences our ideas about particular kinds of geographic, cultural, and social space; an interest in the representation of the spaces (and places) of landscape and how they come to shape our imaginative world. However, my particular curiosity has been sparked by what I will call the 'stripped-out' landscape image; by which I mean simplified, with extraneous detail removed, left out of the frame or avoided by the compositional choices made by the photographer. Often these are almost abstract landscape images of a kind that, I would argue, play into the notion of a 'pristine', 'wilderness' image of Nordic regions. Examples of such 'air-brushed', fictive images can be found in applied / commercial landscape photography and have co-opted an aesthetic first cultivated by high-end landscape photographic art – for example that of Richard Misrach (b. 1949), Hiroshi Sugimoto (b. 1949), Axel Hütte (b. 1951) – and of Andreas Gursky (b. 1955) particularly with images such as *Düsseldorf Flughafen II* (1994). However, for all these artists the landscape genre has been employed in a critical relation to its subject matter. This is especially apparent in Gursky's work – for example in *Rhein II*, (1999) – in this example the artist has purposefully stripped-out particular elements of the geographical space, thereby encouraging the viewer to notice and question the absences – the human impact for example.

A 'stripped-out' form of landscape image may be thought about in relation to Massey's ideas on 'space as a dimension' – an abstract sense of space without the particularities of 'place' (Massey 2006). The role that such images play in our individual and collective consciousness is of interest when we imagine Nordic regions, particularly when they may signify as timeless and pristine landscapes. In such instances, and in the context of neoliberalism and globalisation, these 'stripped-out', supposedly 'pristine' landscapes can have a cultural, political and market value. My argument is that such images in their embodiment of the pristine have a role in the functioning of the neoliberal, late capitalist world order.

Ideas on the North

To study the cookbooks of a given country or region is to gain access to a wider set of factors than its food heritage and contemporary cuisine. Carol Gold, in her 2007 account of the history of Danish cookbooks, observes that we tend to "delve" into a cookbook but "very few people actually read" them, instead, they appear to function as "documents of desires, fears and hopes" (11).[2] In 1988, 21 years before Gold's work on Danish food culture, Arjun Appadurai published an influential study of Indian cuisine: *How to Make a National Cuisine: Cookbooks in Contemporary India*. In it he suggested that cookbooks offer the kinds of "vicarious pleasures" associated with the "literature of the senses" (3). Furthermore, in a design related context, Adrian Forty's important thesis in *Objects of Desire* (1986) demonstrated that the impulse driving the demand for a given product is determined by the ideas and values embodied by it. The two contemporary case studies under discussion here – *NOMA* and *The Nordic Cook Book* – are examples of highly popular products that appeal both to the "senses", and to particular "desires", ideas and values. The attraction of such books appears to be located in the promise of sensory delights, a connection to 'authenticity' (although experienced vicariously), and to ideas of sociability where good, simple food can be shared with friends and family. All this is conveyed by the descriptions of the raw ingredients for the type of food under discussion, its preparation and presentation. However, hopes and fears, ideas and values, and promises of sensory pleasures, are also evoked through an abundance of photographic images – many of which are landscapes – created and selected on the basis of the ideas and values they embody and the appeal they have for us as readers, viewers and consumers.

The signifiers and aesthetics found in the kinds of landscape images utilised in cookbooks associated with the Nordic region draw upon ideas about the North that have been developed over centuries, and were famously explored by Peter Davidson, in *The Idea of North*, first published in 2005, and the subject of much discussion and academic work since. Here, Davidson suggests that "everyone carries their own idea of north within them"; a phrase repeated several times, for em-

2 Gold, 2007, p11 quoting Nicola Humble from: 'A Touch of Boheme: Documents of Desires, Fears and Hopes', *Times Literary Supplement*, June 1996, p15.

phasis one assumes (Davidson 2016: 10). Indeed, the vastness and vagueness of the imagined area encompassed by the North is associated with so many different ideas and imaginaries that "a choice has to be made of a few points of focus" (172). The same is true for the purposes of this discussion, for which a few familiar characteristics and tropes will have to suffice. According to Davidson the North is typically perceived as a "harder place, a place of dearth: uplands, adverse weather, remoteness from cities … a region of austere marvels … a shadowless, treeless place" (11). This is also borne out by Ysanne Holt who, writing about northern England and Scotland, says remoteness is often sought out for its suggestiveness of "an intense and immediate authenticity" (2013: 218). Holt notes that ideas about the North often point to the "untamed and unruly", sometimes linking these with "an elemental purity" (ibid). Many related ideas, such as: clean, pure, simple and wild – can be found in abundance in food writing on the characteristic pleasures of Scandinavian and Nordic food, all typically connoting freshness, authenticity and the merits of a modest way of life.

Davidson noticed that images of Scandinavia are often imbued with the "colours of twilight, … the early winter dark" and of the "protracted summer evenings", observing that films by Knut Erik Jensen "return again and again to the cobalt-blue of the last of the light" (2016: 185). He also notes a "crepuscular grey" recurring in interior shots of painted rooms and in the depictions of autumn landscapes and of "numinous twilight houses" found in archetypal paintings of the 18th, 19th and even early 20th century, such as those by Nils Kreuger and Vilhem Hammershøi; "the painter of light fading in rooms" with their "balance of serenity and melancholy" (ibid). Davidson suggests that such images "speak powerfully to every element in the spectator that would play with the idea of renouncing the metropolis – presence, activity, movement – for remoteness, absence, stillness"; concluding that, essentially "these images are about pastness" (ibid).

However, it is not only the representation of topographies and interiors that shape our ideas; the weather of a given place is often imbued with loaded characteristics where it may be "enlisted to heighten an effect; to typify" and "to establish a … characterization" (Massey 2003: 109). Thus, the depiction of the elements can be instrumental to the establishment of what has been described as a "moral climatology" (Livingstone, 2002), where weather and climate are "mobilised as culturally inflected categories to reinforce particular political geographies" (Massey 2003: 109). In the case of the Nordic region, the association of harsh weather conditions and long, dark winters, combined with remote and austere landscapes, have been employed to connote the worthiness of struggle and endurance.

Nordic identity

Just as ideas about the North have been created and reinforced over time, the idea of an identifiable and coherent 'Nordicness' should also be understood as a construction. In his groundbreaking study of 1983, *Imagined Communities*, Benedict Anderson demonstrates that imagination is central to the construction of community identities, defining nations as 'imagined' communities; "imagined as both inherently limited and sovereign" (6). Following Gellner (1964), he argues that 'nationalism' is not simply there ready to be awoken, but has to be created and that visual representation has played a central role in the creation of ideas about nationhood; literally making a nation imaginable. According to Anderson, "almost all serious scholars" agree that national identities have only been extant in any meaningful way since the late eighteenth century, yet "all nations imagine themselves ancient". He describes the ways that such nations successfully construct a belief in a shared ancient history, as a "puzzle"; wondering "how new things could be imagined so old" (Anderson 1991). Anderson observes that the rise of nationhood coincided with a decline of the major religions, but that the mechanism for nations coming into existence originated in the widening availability of print media, where a shared language and common interests were disseminated in books and newspapers, where "mass produced reading" was inscribed with a "grammar and syntax" of national identity, fundamental to the establishment of national imaginaries (1991).

This new situation was also connected to a changing sense of time; a new mechanical, industrialised time. Moreover, Anderson cites Benjamin's idea of "Messianic time" (1973: 265),[3] where there exists "a simultaneity of past and future in a instantaneous present" which Anderson describes as of "such fundamental importance that, without taking it fully into account we will find it difficult to probe the obscure genesis of nationalism" (Anderson 1983: 24). Through literature and newspapers, people become aware of the existence of one another and of life going on in different places at the same time; meaning that while the members that make up a given nation will "never know most of their fellow-members ... yet in the minds of each lives the image of their communion" (Anderson 1983: 6). However, this process necessitates that the complexities of a given 'national' history are distilled into a few key dates and events, which are then repeated in an apparently endless account that narrates the nation's supposed ancient history. Furthermore, details, and even substantial factors that do not sit comfortably in the narrative are "reinterpreted to make them seamless" (Anderson 1991).

The Nordic region is made up of several national and community identities brought together under a combined regional identity. The terms 'Nordic' or 'Scan-

3 Quote reprinted in Anderson 1983: 24

dinavian' are frequently used as synonyms for a small group of countries in northern Europe, located on or near the Scandinavian Peninsula, and in the North Atlantic. However, the interchangeable use of these terms – for example in the titles of books on the region's food culture – is at best misleading; their histories and roots are complex to an extent that is beyond the scope of this discussion. So, let the following suffice: the term 'Scandinavia' is generally used as a collective noun for Denmark, Sweden and Norway – largely, but not exclusively, based on cultural and linguistic links – while 'Nordic' also includes Finland, Iceland, Greenland, the Faroe Islands and Aaland Islands, and was to some extent coined as a matter of political expediency. A key milestone in the establishment of the term 'Nordic' came in 1952 when the Nordic Council was founded to develop cooperative transport and administrative systems and was responsible for enabling distribution and travel across the region without need of a passport. It continues to play a central role in enabling these countries to work together effectively in matters such as transport, communication, education and other cultural and economic activities.

Since the early 2000s there has been a systematic effort from a variety of local and national authorities within the Nordic region to brand local identities for a "global public", but as Reestorff et al observe, this has been concurrent with efforts to create safeguards against globalisation (2011: 14). Any meaningful understanding of the region needs to incorporate an appreciation of demographic shifts in terms of migration both within the region and from further afield. Rural areas have experienced significant levels of depopulation due to internal migration into cities where labour markets are stronger, creating shortages in the agricultural workforce. As a result regional authorities have encouraged transnational migrants to fill labour gaps in the countryside.

Anderson's purpose in identifying the mechanisms for producing national identity was based upon his wish to understand what drives people to be prepared to die for their country, arguing that nationalism is fuelled by feelings of love rather than incitement to hatred (1983: 142). However, in the context of globalization, anxieties about national identity flourish. For Massey, this is why the re-imagination of place and space is crucial. She argues that where the specificities of a given notionally bounded area – a "local place" – is the site of "the everyday, the real and valued practices, the geographical source of meaning," the effects of globalisation can fuel anxieties that result in "a retreat to place" (Massey 2005:5).

One manifestation of this emerged in 2004 when the Danish Government set up a "canonisation project" – to define and construct lists of cultural practices and products that are identifiably Danish – in order to project a common national culture as a "safeguard against globalization" (Reestorff et al 2011: 14); an example of what Anderson calls an "official nationalism"; a "conscious, self-protective policy ...emanating from the state" (1983: 159). In this context the term 'globalisation' appears to refer to the frequency, ease and speed by which cultural products and practices are exchanged across regional, as well as national, borders – including of course cooking practices, cookery books and landscape photography. However, globalisation involves more than this. Massey argues that the "particular form of neoliberal capitalist globalization" (2005: 4) that we are experiencing, is not a "natural" or inevitable development, but a "duplicitous combination of the glorification of the (unequally) free movement of capital on the one hand with the firm control over the movement of labour on the other" (ibid).

In their 2011 study of the impact of globalisation on contemporary Nordic art, *Globalizing Art: Negotiating Place, Identity and Nation in Contemporary Nordic Art*, Bodile Marie Stavning Thomsen and Kristin Ørjasæter set out to move beyond the perspective of the "self-sufficient nation-state" and are at pains to point out that the region "cannot be thought of as self-contained" (Reestorff et al: 10) and neither should it be understood as a coherent unit (11). Moreover, they stress that the assertion of an identifiable "Nordicness" must be understood as a construction, where cultural products such as contemporary art are the result of an "intertwining of the national, regional, and global", and where the "Nordic" is a negotiated concept and "always in transformation" (ibid); essentially agreeing with the ideas of Anderson, Appadurai and Massey who see culture as in a continual process of production:

> In this way globalization fuels an ongoing process of negotiating Norwegian, Danish, Swedish, Finnish, Icelandic, Faroese, and Greenlandic national cultures and a common understanding of a specific Nordic culture (Reestorff et al 2011: 14).

Globalizing Art demonstrates that one of the effects of globalisation is that "the movements of 'flows' of different symbolic forms, objects, subjects simply transcend national borders with an unprecedented intensity" – in a "complex connectivity" (Reestorff *et al* 2011: 15).[4] I am particularly interested in the extent to which *NOMA* and *The Nordic Cook Book* openly acknowledge the interplay of 'other' cultural influences on 'Nordic' cuisine. I consider the work of two highly influential 'Nordic' chefs – one with an agenda for preserving what he takes to be identifiably Nordic cooking traditions – appearing to deny the influence of the global, whilst the other invites a fresh approach to the Nordic when it comes to food – but one that very much acknowledges the impact of globalisation through its very assertion of locality.

4 Following John Tomlinson, 1999.

The cookbooks

Food writing about Scandinavian and Nordic cuisine is long-established and far-ranging.[5] In the English speaking regions alone there is a long tradition; in the USA and more recently in the UK, and across Australasia too. Although collections of handwritten recipes from the Nordic region survive from the thirteenth century, the first published cookbooks date from the early seventeenth century. These publications tended not to be illustrated; a practice that largely continued up until the early 20th century – and, on the occasions when they were, it was with tiny pen and ink drawings. However, this slowly changed with an increase in black and white as well as colour photography and other illustrations; at a time when the print quality of mass-produced books was of a markedly lower standard than we are now used to. Then from the early/mid 1960s substantial books on Scandinavian cooking were written and published in the UK and USA (Johnson 1964, Hazelton 1965, Brown 1968),[6] often by those with close family or professional links to the region.

From this period such books typically gave accounts of Scandinavian customs and the contexts in which they originated; describing the short and cool growing season that led to a limited range of ingredients and a great dependency on preserving – for example Hazelton describes a cuisine that was "very monotonous" (Hazelton 1965: 6) but where good food was characterised as "pure" and "fresh tasting" (8). They emphasised the degree of care taken in their approach to hospitality which was based on "simple pleasures", where flowers on the table were "a necessity of daily life", the art of arranging food was "taught in every household course" and "every Scandinavian cookbook has illustration upon illustration of beautifully presented foods to guide the housewife" (6).

Then from the 1970s photographic illustration became commonplace. Images of ingredients, cooking procedures, finished dishes and tables spread ready for the meal became widespread. During this period writers on Scandinavian cuisine took a pragmatic approach; one emphasising that her book "does not offer exotic dishes such as roast reindeer" (Frank 1978: 4). However, the significance of the photography grew with the inclusion of increasing numbers of images of food, plus a few contextualising shots began to accompany the food writing. This continued through to the recent past when from around 2010, with the release of the publication of *NOMA: Time and Place in Nordic Cuisine* (Redzepi 2010), the design

---

5 Note: for most of this history of cookery writing the titles and content of cookbooks from this region reflected specific nations or used the term Scandinavian, only in the 21st century has the term Nordic been widely used.

6 See Hardisty, Jutte (1970) for a comment in the Introduction that suggests that the British have 'recently become interested in food', n.p.

and layout of publications on Nordic cookery writing has undergone a noticeable change with the inclusion of significant numbers of photographs of landscapes and the 'natural' world. On initial consideration these appear to support and give a wider context to the accounts of food and recipes, however the two books under discussion have moved so far towards the visual that they are effectively a hybrid genre – where the cook book and photo book meet. The general increase in photographic illustration, placed alongside recipes in books on cuisine and food traditions, can perhaps be understood in the wider context of writing on food and lifestyle, for in the age of the internet we are more likely to use our laptop or mobile phone to find a recipe. This new style of cookbook offers a sensory appeal: visual, olfactory and haptic in a new "literature of the senses" (Appadurai 1988: 3). Such books promise a palpable experience that vicariously transports us to the places of our imagination.

My own research suggests that this increasing tendency appears to have been given additional momentum by the publication of *NOMA* in 2010; a highly acclaimed book written by René Redzepi (b.1977). Redzepi is the head-chef at *noma* – an innovative restaurant based in Copenhagen. He was pivotal to its conception and development, and has been in-post since it opened in 2003.[7] With this venture Redzepi has been credited with 'reinventing Nordic cuisine'.[8] The multi award-winning restaurant was voted the "World's Best Restaurant" in 2010, 2011, 2012 & 2014,[9] attracting huge attention across the food writing media. The original restaurant closed in 2017 in order to relocate elsewhere in the city the following year. There have been further temporary manifestations of *noma* 'popping-up' in a number of cities around the world – in each case the emphasis is on the local availability of ingredients.[10] Redzepi's reputation, and the associated MAD Academy,[11] continue to flourish. It is also important to note the early involvement of Icelandic / Danish artist Olafur Eliasson (b.1967), who worked closely with Redzepi and his team in the development of the approach to food.

The title '*NOMA*' is based on an abbreviation of the two Danish words 'nordisk' (Nordic) and 'mad' (food) – Nordic food – however, the innovative approach and style of the food have given rise to the epithet the 'new Nordic cuisine'. The second clause of the title – *Time and Place in Nordic Cuisine* – points to the deeper concerns

7 Note *NOMA* (capitals) is used for the book title and *noma* (lower case) for the restaurant – this follows the established practice.

8 Co-founded with Claus Meyer, food writer however they parted company soon after.

9 As voted by Restaurant magazine's World's Best Restaurants in 2010, 2011, 2012 and 2014.

10 For example London 2012,Tokyo in 2015, Sydney 2016 and Mexico 2017.

11 MAD Academy is an educational venture, based in Copenhagen, set-up by Redzepi in 2011 to support the global food industry – at the time of writing Magnus Nilsson has just been appointed director of the new MAD Academy.

of the book which has been designed to set out the food philosophy and creativity of Redzepi, around which the cuisine is based. Fundamental to the approach is a belief in the importance of seasonality and locality in the production of, and foraging for, quality ingredients. Here Redzepi engages in what he calls "The Perfect Storm"; a term he uses to encapsulate "the maelstrom of operating at the cutting edge of international gastronomy using only locally sourced ingredients" (Redzepi 2010: 'Frontispiece' n.p.). Therefore, the notion of 'time' promoted by the ethos underpinning *NOMA*, is the present. It is based entirely upon what is locally available; in season. The time of *NOMA* is 'now'.

Commentators typically note the way that the approach is based on "clean flavours" and an emphasis on "purity, simplicity and freshness".[12] Such characteristics have long been associated with the Nordic, leading me to suggest that while the cuisine might be 'new' the tropes of Nordicness are well established – all of which are signified in the photography that almost dominates the book. Indeed, from the outset photography was to play an important role. A statement by Redzepi in the frontispiece explains that around 200 "specially commissioned" photographs, by Ditte Isager, are included showing Redzepi's "dishes, his suppliers and ingredients" and significantly for this discussion – "the Nordic landscape" – for perhaps most surprising is the way in which the photographs operate, in that they are not merely illustrative of the food under discussion. Although most depict ingredients or plated food, the ingredients appear in their original state, recently harvested or foraged and the finished dishes are often presented with raw, freshly gathered leaves, moss, flowers, berries or grasses – in this way a strong connection to nature is established visually. Interspersed are numerous shots of land and seascapes, and of nature – these make rather oblique reference to the food under discussion – for example a photograph of a large field of "Fennel growing on the West Coast of Zealand" (48); a pine forest in "Zealand Woods" (109); the autumn branches of a "Beech Tree" (170); a seascape and a coastline in Arctic Norway, each with the title – "Norwegian Fjord" (132 and 138-9). Some depict specific people associated with *noma* – actively gathering ingredients or posing motionless for portraits in the landscape – as in "Hanne Letoft from South Zealand" (44) and "Susanne Grefberg from Gotland" (181) – each pictured standing beneath a huge sky; "K.S. Møller from Zealand" collecting fungi in woodland (211); and "Tage Rønne from Hareskovby" pictured on the wooded banks of a lake gazing upward (234) – in all such shots the landscape dominates. Through its use of photography the book presents the food under discussion as very firmly connected to the season and to the land or sea; to the time and the place.

12 See also "The New Nordic Food manifesto", 2004, (http://www.newnordicfood.org) accessed February 10, 2020

These are just a few examples. There are almost two hundred full-page photographs, including one double-page spread – landscape in format in other words. I suggest that the emphasis on photography – but particularly the way in which landscape and nature photography is used – is almost as radical in approach as the cuisine itself. The scale, quality and quantity of the photography suggests that for some readers this publication functions much like a coffee-table book – to be enjoyed visually – and in many instances it is difficult to believe that the recipes will be attempted, for they depend upon highly obscure ingredients and are largely intended to demonstrate an approach that can be adapted according to the specifics of any given locality and season.

However, its ambition goes beyond this. Its purpose is to feed and inspire the imagination. Presented here – in a kind of visual manifesto – is a new philosophy of cooking and eating, where the photography enables the reader to envision the approach despite its radicalism; and for Redzepi and his team to create "new ways to see the world" (Mirzoeff 2015: 297). As Nicolas Mirzoeff has identified for all kinds of activists, and which I now relate to food revolutionaries such as Redzepi and Eliasson, "visual culture is a way to create forms of change" (289). But whereas Mirzoeff advances the idea that in the contemporary world this is fundamentally about digital, networked culture – the use of pixels – this *NOMA* publication takes the form of a large format, hardback book. If the "medium is the message" (McLuhan, 1964), then *NOMA*'s message is embedded in, and carried by, the abundance of simple, palpable photographic images, printed on thick, heavy, high-quality paper – to enrich the experience and feed the imagination.

In this new 'literature of the senses', examples of carefully considered and well produced photography serve to compete with the internet – but, in addition to this, Eliasson insists that there is something fundamentally different about what Redzepi is doing; something experimental and bent upon making the connection between the "meal on the plate" and the environment. However, while "the *NOMA* environment is largely Scandinavian", Eliasson insists that "we should see the greater ecosystem too" (2010: 9) – from his position of both food revolutionary and artist, he likens the experience of food to that of art – and suggests that as with art "we should not separate form and content" (ibid). Eliasson argues that if "food can be political ... about responsibility, sustainability, geography and culture" then "maybe this knowledge can be made into a kind of flavour enhancer" (Eliasson 2010: 9).

Following the enormous success of this approach to photographic illustration, unparalleled in other regional cuisine, there has been a general increase in the use of photography in cookbooks but particularly those centered on the Nordic regions; the prime example being Magnus Nilsson's *The Nordic Cook Book* of 2015. Nilsson is a highly successful and sought after chef, his restaurant *Fäviken* in Sweden is routinely listed among the World's " 50 Best Restaurants". In addition, Nilsson is a keen photographer – all the landscape and portrait photography in this book is his, taken during the period of research, largely between 2012 and 2014.

The book includes large numbers of photographs – around 130 in total. About 45 of these are by Erik Olsson and relate to the recipes; mostly showing finished dishes and plated food. Each of these have been set in the centre of the given page, and 'framed' by a generous white boarder. The rest are by Nilsson and they are larger – filling the full size of the pages – these include pictures of the natural world, interiors and portraits. Interspersed among all these are over 40 large landscape photographs – 35 of which are reproduced as full, double-page spreads. It is the latter in particular that shifts the genre of the book from a standard cookbook to a hybrid cookery/photography book. These landscapes typically depict sparse and remote places – and at times the framing renders them almost abstract. Of particular interest are those forming the title-pages for the various sections that provide an organising structure for the book's 768 pages. First, a double-page image forms the title-page for the "INTRODUCTION" (n.p.) – a seascape entirely dominated by an empty sky – sets the tone for the sea and landscape photography in the book overall. The photographs for the title-pages for other sections rarely have an obvious link to the particular subject matter – examples include: a section on "EGGS" carries an almost abstract image of a "Vast view and moody sky, about to start raining, Iceland, early May 2013" (38-39); for "PORK" – "Powerlines and vast view, snow, close to North Cape, Norway May 2014" (294-295), another almost abstract image which despite the powerlines appears pristine; for "BEEF AND VEAL" – "Iceland Spring, 2013 (310-311)", showing a wide expanse of stark rocky ground against a high mountain scene obscured by misty cloud; for "PASTRIES, BISCUITS AND SWEETS" – "Atlantic Ocean, April 2013" (528-529); for "BASICS AND CONDIMENTS" – "Melting glacier and volcanic ash, Iceland Spring 2013" (640-641) and for "GLOSSARY" an untitled seascape, obscured by fog (724-725). These are but a few.

In addition to those filling the numerous title-pages, double-page landscape photographs are interspersed throughout the book – such as "Fog and puffins in flight, Faroe Islands, end of July 2013" (282-283) – an empty image but for a few ethereal birds almost lost in the mist. Also included are a number of near abstract images based on natural forms – one example is an extreme close-up of a rock – entitled "A really beautiful stone surface by the Norwegian coast ... Norway, May 2014" (620-621).

Nilsson took around 8,000 photographs during his research trips. All landscapes included in this book appear to have been taken in Norway, Iceland, the Faroe Islands and Sweden – particularly Jämtland – Nilsson's homeland. Only occasionally is there a gentler agricultural scene – such as that on the title-page for "VEGETABLES & LEGUMES" – "Fields and hills close to my home, Jämtland, Sweden, June 2014" (76-77). None of the landscape images is from Denmark – which has an altogether tamer topography and fewer remote and uncultivated places, and none is from Finland. In 2016, the year following the publication of his cookbook, he brought out a book of photography on Nordic "landscapes, food and people".[13]

Both heritage and modernity are signified – photographs of ancient utensils, still in use to this day in some cases. One photograph brings the reader's attention to the longevity of the processes and utensils used; in this case the date of 1774 marked on "the upper handle of the milk sieve" (60-61). Heritage is also established by a return to traditional line illustrations to demonstrate traditional techniques, for example "how to clean a Baltic herring" (192). Other photographs show modern clean and bright surfaces and serving dishes. The old and the new are brought together across the range of illustrations used in the book overall – in one particular case within a photograph showing a computer key pad alongside an aged and cured leg of mutton "having been nibbled ... photographed on a desk in an Oslo home" (410). This should remind us of Anderson's idea that the genesis of a national identity requires the establishment of "a simultaneity of past and future in an instantaneous present" (1983: 24).

I consider this to be a beautiful book, lovingly researched and crafted. With genuine integrity Nilsson worked to document and preserve the deep heritage of the cooking practices of this vast region through the fastidious collection of recipes and contextual knowledge. As he explains: "We can theorize how people ate in the old days, but we can't recreate it, so it's important to document and keep the transfer of food knowledge going" (Rob, 2015). His thorough approach was rewarded when in the year of its publication it was winner of BBC Radio 4's 'Food Programme'; a programme that has earned respect for its serious approach to food and cooking with over 40 years of regular broadcasting. However, I am concerned that there is a sense in which the food, and therefore wider culture, of the Nordic region is represented here as fixed and bounded, through its selection of photographic and other imagery.

Arjun Appadurai argues that: "We need to view cookbooks in the contemporary world as revealing artifacts of culture in the making" (1988: 22). This approach whereby cookery books are understood as fundamentally revealing of, but importantly also contributing to "culture in the making", is an idea that sits well alongside Massey's notion of space as dynamic, continually in the state of being "made", and is not just a central concern of this chapter but also for Redzepi and Eliasson, in the 'now' of NOMA's approach. Both Appadurai and Gold demonstrate that "cookbooks tell stories" but, moreover, they are of academic value because of what they "tell us about the society in which they were written" (Gold 2007: 13); the

13 Nilsson, Magnus (2016): Nordic: a Photographic Essay of Landscapes, Food and People, London & NY, Phaidon.

unwitting testimony of the writers who draw on and reveal a far wider range of factors than mere ingredients and culinary skills. For example: levels of literacy, levels of numeracy, changes in the economy, "structures of class and hierarchy", the growth of bourgeois consciousness, or of "domestic ideologies"(Appadurai 1988: 3), the evolution of nationalism and national identity. And importantly – as shifts that occur as a "country … encounters the rest of the world from within the boundaries of the … state"(Gold 2007: 13). In this way changes in what we see in cookbooks relate to what is happening in the real world – and are not merely reflective. Arguably, far more interesting, are the ways in which cultural products such as images, including those in cookery books, are productive – acting as catalysts of change in society by leading on new ways of seeing, understanding and negotiating the world, contributing to the acceptance of ideas and to the construction of identity. Gold points to the ways in which cookery writing can "open up worlds" and "allow our imagination to wander freely across the globe"(177). As already suggested, today an unprecedented emphasis is put upon not simply illustrating cookbooks with photographs of ingredients or finished dishes but on the geographical context from which they originate – so much so that such books are designed to stimulate the imagination.

However, they are potentially also productive of negative and defensive attitudes. Much like Appadurai's (1988) work on the construction of national identity in India through an analysis of its food culture, Gold's 2007 study of Danish cookbooks, produced in and for their country of origin, revealed "clear statements of nationalism and debate over nationalist issues" (176). However, while the books on regional cuisine under discussion here purport to be recipe books about a region, they have largely been produced for audiences outside of that region – primarily for English speaking readers.[14] Therefore, if like Gold, I am to suggest that they reveal something "about the society in which they were written", then I will also need to consider how they function for the 'reader' of these books in the English speaking world. (13)

The Nordic landscape 'as a surface'

As already established, Massey set out to challenge the habit of thinking about space "as a surface" and this is particularly applicable to the still (two-dimensional) photographic image. In examples of landscape photography the spaces of the Nordic region have been characterised through a small number of different tropes;

14 For example there appears to be a wide appeal outside of Denmark – in UK and Germany in particular – note effects of easier travel – globalisation – Thomsen, B.M.S. notes the emergence of 'Nordic' contemporary art colonies' in Berlin for example p16-17.

images that evoke a severe wilderness, sometimes with dramatic topography but often featureless and austere, and appearing to be empty. The latter are typically captured in distant, pulled back shots. Such characteristics – whether dramatic or empty – are often combined with an impression of remoteness, perhaps fulfilling a desire that there are such places in existence, as yet unspoiled; an outsider's view of Nordic regions, because they know little of the human activities and stories that have played out across such landscapes. Often these depictions appear as empty, stripped-out, abstracted spaces – superficial in appearance – literally "a surface". Massey's concerns about the effects of space are rooted in a moral objection, where "the old chain of meaning (space-representation-stasis) continues to wield its power. The legacy lingers on" (2003: 113). What she brings to the discussion of space are the interests of communities at a global level in terms of their stories, their values, their priorities; ultimately their equal right to consideration in any encounter of a given space. Central to her argument is an unease that when we imagine space as a surface it "carries with it social and political effects" (2005: 4), the danger being that it can lead us to "conceive of other places, peoples, cultures simply as phenomena 'on' this surface" (ibid). But this, she argues, "is not an innocent manoeuvre, for by this means they are deprived of histories" (ibid).

I now return to my concern with the 'stripped-out' landscape image to consider the effects of this kind of photographic illustration with its particular ways of imagining Nordic space; as pristine, pure, clean, untouched. Following Massey I suggest that in order to change our habit of seeing this space we must consider what has been left out of the picture, for as Massey says, to imagine a given space simply as a surface may have the effect of producing a narrative that "obliterates the multiplicities, the contemporaneous heterogeneities of space" (2005: 5). This takes me back to Nilsson's book: *The Nordic Cook Book* – for despite its signifiers of history, heritage and authenticity there is little trace or evidence here of the cultural complexity that created the foods described and illustrated. Yet Nilsson has stated that "Nordic food culture is made up of influences from all over the world", which have been adapted to suit local circumstances and tastes, insisting that "Nordic cooking is not conservative, it is in fact open-minded" (2015: 36). But this claim is not adequately borne out in the experience of reading the book, and is entirely absent in its visual aspects – particularly through its photography – for despite the occasional suggestion that the recipes need not be dutifully adhered to, the overall message suggests a clinging onto a tradition (a narrow tradition), creating a strong impression of timelessness.

A chapter in *The Nordic Cook Book* written by Nordic food historian, Richard Tellström, explains that in a region that "allows policy and nation building to dictate food culture, minorities are necessarily marginalised and their influence on the food culture is overlooked" (2015: 25). He argues that this situation has been created by a lack of research on "the national position of minority cuisines … either in their own right, or in relation to the major food cultures" (ibid). Tellström cites the indigenous Sami minority, of over 100,000 people, and the fact that Roma people are also present in similar numbers. And he says, vaguely, that "there are other ethnic and religious minority groups whose food culture constitutes an indispensable part of Nordic culture", but again he explains that these have not been researched, either in their own right or in relation to the mainstream Nordic culinary culture, and says it is for this reason that it is "not possible to give a complete picture of the food culture that exists among the people in the Nordic countries" (ibid). This is a telling use of language – "a complete picture" – of course no picture is ever complete, the nature of representation is such that selections have to be made and as a result there will always be losses. However, like Massey, my concern is that we are not habituated to consider the absences within any given picture frame. And nowhere is this more relevant than in relation to the 'stripped-out' landscape image, to which Massey's ideas provide an important corrective framework.

Nordic artists have long explored for themselves this question of 'what has been left out of the picture'. The 2011 study by Thomsen and Ørjasæter, mentioned at the start of this discussion, considers the activities of contemporary artists whose work engages in negotiations and constructions of "new, less territorially bound communities, territories and social relations" and found that for these artists the experience of deterritorialisation transforms the "old national communities into anachronisms" (Reestorff *et al*: 29). More specifically, following Gayatri Chakravorty Spivak, whose work took the representation of the Other to be a site for ethical concern (Spivak 1983),[15] Ørjasæter asks "what it takes to make the audience look for the voices of the participating subalterns" (Reestorff *et al*: 29) – concurring with Spivak, she concludes that in the Nordic region, even with the knowledge of post-colonial theory and an awareness of globalised issues and interests, "ethnocentrism is not dead" (Ørjasæter 2011: 236).

It transpires that *The Nordic Cook Book* was in part a response to Nilsson learning that:

> the islands' sheep farmers and fishermen are now starting families with people not native to the region – from as far away as Thailand and the Philippines – and who weren't raised on classic recipes for puffin stuffed with cake, or boiled sheep's head (Rob 2015).

As a result Nilsson set out to "document" the food heritage of the entire Nordic region – to both "define" and "preserve". He explains that he was determined to

15 Spivak, Gayatri Chakravorty (1983): Lecture 'Can the subaltern speak', first published in the journal *Wedge*, 1985.

include all aspects of this heritage including photographs of pilot whales being butchered believing them to be necessary to the understanding of the region's food culture and is on record as saying: "I don't think its right to censor culture" (ibid). However, despite this, he and the book's publisher produced a highly selective view of the Nordic as unchanged, rooted in and dependent upon mainstream tradition – while the impact of globalisation and immigration are not visible in these supposed 'documents'. Furthermore, the media representation of this food-writer prefers to show him as an archetypal 'pure' Nordic male, typically picturing him against a remote landscape in the Faroe Islands and ignoring his cosmopolitan interests as a chef and apparent "love of tacos" (ibid), or the fact that he runs restaurants in many locations including popular Scandinavian ski resorts.

In *The Nordic Cook Book* Magnus Nilsson's purist visual representations appear to resist the potential to renegotiate what Thomsen and Ørjasæter describe as, "the frameworks constructing national identity ... in light of new transnational relations" (back-cover), in what amounts to a denial of the influences of the food cultures of indigenous peoples and of migrant communities. Conversely, *NOMA's* emphasis on the local calls attention to the global – mutually dependent terms – in so far as it highlights some of the more negative impacts of globalisation as they relate to the transport of food over vast distances and the resultant heavy use of fossil fuels and emissions of greenhouse gases to the detriment of the well-being of the planet and all its inhabitants – human and non-human. Moreover, the philosophy behind the approach articulated in *NOMA*, unlike that underpinning *The Nordic Cook Book*, does not become manifest as an anxiety about local identity, nor as a purist preoccupation with defending the historic characteristics of mainstream food traditions. Instead, it actively encourages an open and creative attitude to the availability and use of local, seasonal ingredients. However, while reinventing the local food culture – creating a new Nordic cuisine – with its determinedly 'open' approach to the use of locally and seasonally available ingredients, *NOMA* none-the-less perpetuates the tropes of 'Nordicness' and contributes to a continual making and remaking of the Nordic region in ways that are entirely recognisable. But, in insisting on local seasonal foods, the philosophy underpinning the approach to cuisine here refuses to "play out a romance of detachment" and instead takes responsibility for the resources used (Massey 2005: 103).

Concluding thoughts – Massey's gift of space

At the start of this chapter I set in motion a train of thought that drew from Massey's provocation to "question the habit of thinking" of space "as a surface" and instead to learn to think of it in terms of "a meeting-up of histories"(2005: 4). My aim was to consider what happens to our "implicit imagination" of the Nordic if we do this (ibid). Following Massey I set out to rethink the conventional notion that an abstract, or open, space is implicitly a meaningless space (2005: 6).

This discussion has sought to reflect upon whether *NOMA* and *The Nordic Cook Book* may be considered as sites of negotiated practices, where the 'Nordic' as a concept is "always in transformation" (Reestorff *et al* 2011: 11). Ultimately, I have found that the key difference between the two books lies in the producers of *NOMA* being willing to imagine "new types of communities", (Reestorff *et al* 2011:10) while Nilsson appears to want to document something as it is, or even as it was, – "to keep the transfer of food knowledge going" (Rob, 2015). In being protective of mainstream Nordic heritage Nilsson's approach has been to produce an account of the Nordic region as fixed and bounded. But, as Massey asserted, "You can't go back in space ... You can't hold places ... still" (Massey 2003: 111).

During the first two decades of the 21st century the Nordic region has increasingly been affected by globalisation through the movements of people and products from other parts of the world – particularly the Global South. However, photographic representations of Nordic landscapes and the wider cultural environment, as used in popular and widely available cooking and life-style publications, impose permanence and order, thereby negating the "possibility" of "imagining space as the sphere... of the existence of multiplicity" (Massey 2005: 10). In avoiding some important aspects of life in the region *The Nordic Cook Book* is an example of this. Here the myth of the Nordic as a single cultural entity is perpetuated, and the realities of global migration are rendered invisible. In representations of places and spaces, expunged of the details of the "contemporaneous heterogeneity" of human life (Massey 2005: 10), the apparent absence of Others is thus normalised in a manner that denies their contributions to an ever-transforming culture – the negotiated 'Nordicness' that comes of globalised interactions and influence. This reinforces anxieties about the presence of the Other and contributes to the production of xenophobia. The 'stripped-out' landscape is arguably, therefore, a site where uncomfortable factors are omitted in order to achieve, in Anderson's terms, a seamlessness that will facilitate the "imagined community" (Anderson 1991).

In some, though not all respects, the use of photography in *NOMA* is less problematic. The philosophy underpinning *noma* / *NOMA* is fiercely aware of the politics that underscore global food production and distribution. Its commitment to sourcing ingredients locally and seasonally is borne of a concern for the global. And in insisting on an entirely innovative – even experimental – approach to food, the whole project side-steps any need to engage with tradition or heritage. However, as with *The Nordic Cook Book*, there are no photographic references to the ethnic population or the global Other – therefore once again this registers as an absence. However, for a reader who is paying close attention, perhaps two photographs stand out (Redzepi 2010: 154 & 203). Each depicts a recipe that includes chocolate – nowhere else is such an 'exotic' ingredient called for. But its inclusion is conspicuous – making the reader sharply aware of the journey that such an ingredient will have undergone, in terms of production and transport, and therefore the lives it will have touched. Clearly such images are not "meaning*less*".

The place occupied by commercial landscape photography in shaping our ideas about the North, and the Nordic region more specifically, is also relevant to the formation of attitudes to the physical environment – the so-called 'natural' world. The Nordic imaginary feeds on the illusory documentary quality of much landscape photography, contributing to an everyday denial of the realities of climate breakdown and ecological catastrophe. While seemingly innocent, everyday abstracted landscape images serve to obscure the realities of environmental degradation, deny the effects of over-consumption, and facilitate our willingness to continue to consume, unchecked. In their refusal of the material realities of global capitalism such images representing Nordic space are, once again, certainly not "meaning*less*" (Massey 2005: 6), but they are negatively encoded – here the signification of an abiding natural wilderness serves to deny the scale of the effects of exploitation and over-consumption of the earth's resources, a form of denial central to the ideologies of global capitalism.

In *For Space*, Massey argues against the notion that space is static and unchanging, an idea based on an 'old' way of thinking in which there is a "conflation of the spatial with representation" (Massey 2005: 30). Such a way of conceiving space imposes permanence and order on "history/life/the real world", avoiding the complexities and dislocations of the living world; within such a conception "there is no multiplicity" and no "co-existence of difference" (2003: 113) – for these reasons the stripped-out landscape image may be understood as one example among many "Hegemonic geographical imaginations" (Massey 2003: 114).

The problem of reducing space to "stasis" resides in the way that the "very life, and most certainly the politics, are taken out of it" (Massey 2005: 30). Massey recalls that she developed these ideas slowly, in the context of observing the "perniciousness of exclusive localisms", understanding them to have been produced by the "grim inequalities of today's hegemonic form of globalization" but was at a loss to know how to respond (Massey 2005: 6). In a sense this study of Nordic cookbooks is my response to similar concerns. I have noted particular forms of visual representation that give expression to, and perpetuate, such 'localisms' – in this case a genre of landscape photography employed within an everyday commercial context. Here stripped-out and near abstract landscape images are central. Massey's "gift of space" offers a fresh strategy for reconsidering these kinds of representations, meaning that, ultimately, Massey's prerogative is a quietly optimistic one. Core to her thesis is a deeply held belief in the importance of being vigilant in the ways that we approach space. Indeed, for Massey, taking space seriously "opens up our minds" (2013) and creates the potential where "progressive politics can also be imagined" because invariably the "spacial is political" (Massey 2005: 9).

However, the world is in an even darker place than it was when Massey was working on these ideas. Drawn to geography for its possibilities as a multidisciplinary subject she never-the-less argues that there is a need to bring together the social and natural sciences, "more than we have historically done" particularly in an age burdened with "environmental problems ... which are *utterly* social too" (2013). Taking a lead from Massey, I would like to think that more is possible in relation to the ways in which we approach the representation of space through the genre of landscape photography; that social commitment and progressive politics find a stronger voice and critical distance in engaging with the representation of space; in its practice, reception and theorisation. In taking space seriously we come to understand that the 'stripped-out' landscape photograph was never "meaning*less*" and going forward into a future of harsh global turbulence, may cease to be tenable – for it will have entirely lost its veneer of innocence.

References

Anderson, Benedict (1983): Imagined Communities: Reflections on the Origin and Spread of Nationalism, First published 1983, second edition 2006, London & New York: Verso.

Anderson, Benedict (1991): Imagined Communities: On British Nationalism – YouTube 9 February 2016, introduced by Ali, Tariq, first broadcast in 1991, BBC.

Appadurai, Arjun (1988): "How to Make a National Cuisine: Cookbooks in Contemporary India" in Comparative Studies in Society and History 30, no.1.

Appadurai, Arjun (2010): "How Histories Make Geographies: Circulation and Context in a Global Perspective", Bhabha, Homi, ed. 1990. Nation and Narration. London: Routledge.

Barthes, Roland (1973): Mythologies, transl. Annette Lavers, Frogmore, St. Albans: Paladin; orig. pub. 1957.

Barthes, Roland, (1984) Camera Lucida, transl. Richard Howard, London: Fontana; orig. pub. 1980.

Benjamin, Walter (1973): Illuminations, London: Fontana.

Bergson, H (1911): Matter and Memory, London: George Allen and Unwin.

Brown, Dale (1968): Cooking of Scandinavia, New York: Time Life Books.

Bryson, Norman (1983): Vision and Painting: The Logic of the Gaze, Newhaven: Yale University Press.

Cresswell, Tim (2002): "Theorising place", in The SAGE Handbook of Human Geography, vol.1, ed. Roger Lee et al. London: Sage, pp. 7-25.

Cresswell, Tim (2015): Place. An Introduction, Oxford: Willey-Blackwell. Second Edition.

Davidson, Peter (2016): The Idea of North, London: Reaktion, first pub. 2005.

Davies, William (2015): The Happiness Industry. How the Government and Big Business Sold Us Well-Being, London & New York: Verso.

Eliasson, Olafur (2010): "Milk Skin and Grass" in Redzepi, René (2010): Noma: Time and Place in Nordic Cuisine, (with photography by Ditte Isager), London & NY: Phaidon, pp. 6-9.

Forty, Adrian (1986): Objects of Desire: Design and Society Since 1750, London & NY: Thames and Hudson Ltd.

Frank, Beryl (1978): Scandinavian Cooking, London & New York: Evans.

Gellner, E (1964): Thought and Change, London: Weidenfeld and Nicholson.

Gold, Carol (2007): Danish Cookbooks. Domesticity and National Identity, 1616-1901, Seattle: University of Washington Press. From the series: New Directions in Scandinavian Studies.

Hardisty, Jutte (1970): Scandinavian Cooking, Twickenham: Hamlyn.

Hazelton, Nika Standen (1965): The Scandinavian Cookbook, London & New York: Collier-MacMillan.

Holt, Ysanne (2013): "A Hut on Holy Island: reframing northern landscape," in Visual Studies 28/3.

Johnson, Alice, B (1964): The Complete Scandinavian Cookbook, London & New York: Collier – MacMillan.

Latour, Bruno (2019): Down To Earth Politics in the New Climatic Regime, Cambridge: Polity Press, translated by Catherine Porter; first published in French, Paris, Éditions La Découverte, 2017.

Massey, Doreen (1997): "A Global Sense of Place", in Reading Human Geography, ed. Trevor Barnes and Derek Gregory, London: Arnold, pp.315-323.

Massey, Doreen (2003): "Some times of Space" in May, Susan (ed) 2003, Olafur Eliasson The Weather Project, London: Tate, p.107-118.

Massey, Doreen (2005): For Space: London, Sage.

Massey, Doreen (2006): Serpentine Gallery, London, "24 Hour Interview Marathon" https://www.youtube.com/watch?v=BVl6AgmAW4k.

Massey, Doreen (2013): Podcast "On Space" – in interview with David Edmunds and Nigel Wharburton – Social Science Bites, 08-05-13 – https://www.youtube.com/watch?v=Quj4tjbTPxw.

McLuhan, Marshall (1964): Understanding Media: The Extensions of Man, New York: McGraw-Hill.

Mirzoeff, Nicolas (2015): How to See the World, London: Pelican.

Mulvey, Laura (2006): Death 24X a Second: Stillness and the Moving Image, London: Reaktion Books Ltd.

Nilsson, Magnus (2015): The Nordic Cook Book, London & New York: Phaidon.

Nilsson, Magnus (2016): Nordic: a Photographic Essay of Landscapes, Food and People, London & New York: Phaidon.

Ørjasæter, Kristin, (2011): "Art, Aid, and Negotiated Identity" in – Thomsen, Bodile Marie Stavning & Ørjasæter, Kristin (2011): Globalizing Art: Negotiating Place, Identity and Nation in Contemporary Nordic Art, Aarhus: Aarhus University Press.

Redzepi, René (2010): Noma: Time and Place in Nordic Cuisine, (with photography by Ditte Isager) London & New York: Phaidon.

Reestorff, Camilla Møhring; Stage, Carsten, Thomsen, Bodile Marie Stavning & Ørjasæter, Kristin, (2011): "Introduction" in – Thomsen, Bodile Marie Stavning & Ørjasæter, Kristin (2011): Globalizing Art: Negotiating Place, Identity and Nation in Contemporary Nordic Art, Aarhus: Aarhus University Press.

Robb, Adam (2015): "The Chef Preserving Nordic Cuisine (and Waffles). Magnus Nilsson discusses the importance of documenting uncensored culinary culture, why he refuses to give more interviews – and Tinder", New York Times Style Magazine, 26-10-2015 https://www.nytimes.com/2015/10/26/t-magazine/sweden-chef-faroe-islands.html.

Spivak, Gayatri Chakravorty (1983): Lecture "Can the subaltern speak", first published in the journal Wedge in 1985, as "Can the Subaltern Speak?: Speculations on Widow Sacrifice"; also in A Critique of Postcolonial Reason. Toward a History of the Vanishing Present, 1988 & revised 1999, Cambridge Mass. and London: Harvard University Press.

Tellström, Richard (2015): "A Brief History of Nordic Cuisine", in Nilsson, Magnus, 2015, The Nordic Cook Book, London & New York: Phaidon, pp.23-33.

Thomsen, Bodile Marie Stavning & Ørjasæter, Kristin (2011): Globalizing Art: Negotiating Place, Identity and Nation in Contemporary Nordic Art, Aarhus: Aarhus University Press.

Tomlinson, John (1999): Globalization and Culture, Oxford: Polity Press.

Illustrations

Nicky Bird

Figure 1: *Photograph by John Ross Polson*, late 1960s, courtesy of Margaret Polson and Timespan. Original in colour.

Figure 2: *Photograph by Graeme Dodd*, 1962, courtesy of Mrs S. M. Barnes and Timespan. Original in colour.

Figure 3: *Photograph by John Ross Polson*, 1970, courtesy of Margaret Polson and Timespan. Original in colour.

Figure 4: Oblique aerial view of bridge under construction and the site of Helmsdale Castle, June 1971 © HES (John Dewar Collection)

Figure 5: Photograph by Nicky Bird. *Untitled work in progress*, April 2017. Original in colour.

Figure 6: *Ghosting the Castle: A Map between Archive and Memory*, by Nicky Bird, 2017. This is documentation made by the Timespan archivist showing Nicky Bird's map work in situ in the Archive area; the image – announcing the map's arrival – was then sent to the Archive's Twitter feed. The image is therefore a smartphone Tweet-photograph courtesy of Timespan. Original in Colour.

Elizabeth Cronin and Jessica Keister

Figure 1: Tyndall Glacier, Whale Sound Drawn by H. Fenn, from a photography by Dr. Hayes, engraved by Kingdon and Boyd, in I[saac] I. Hayes The Open Polar Sea: a Narrative of a Voyage of Discovery towards the North Pole, in the Schooner "United States" New York: Hurd and Houghton, 1867, pp. 438 The New York Public Library, Astor, Lenox, and Tilden Foundations.

Figure 2: William Bradford, The Arctic Regions London: Sampson Low, Marston, Low and Searle, 1873, pp.63 (detail) The Miriam and Ira D. Wallach Division of Art, Prints and Photographs, Photography Collection, The New York Public Library, Astor, Lenox, and Tilden Foundations.

Figure 3: Improved positives: F. G. Jackson Mapping (top); And Planted a Bullet Behind the Left Ear which Bowled Him Over (bottom) in Arctic exploration, being a collection of photographs of Arctic regions and explorers, The Miriam and Ira D. Wallach Division of Art, Prints and Photographs, Photography Collection, The New York Public Library, Astor, Lenox, and Tilden Foundations.

Figure 4: Preliminary photograph In Difficulties in Arctic exploration, being a collection of photographs of Arctic regions and explorers, The Miriam and Ira D. Wallach Division of Art, Prints and Photographs, Photography Collection, The New York Public Library, Astor, Lenox, and Tilden Foundations.

Figure 5: *Situation of the Polaris* in *Arctic exploration, being a collection of photographs of Arctic regions and explorers,* The Miriam and Ira D. Wallach Division of Art, Prints and Photographs, Photography Collection, The New York Public Library, Astor, Lenox, and Tilden Foundations.

Figure 6: *View to the Westward from near the Flag-Staff on Cape Flora* in Frederic G. Jackson, *A Thousand Days in the Arctic* New York: Harper & Brothers, 1899, pp.464, The New York Public Library, Astor, Lenox, and Tilden Foundations.

Figure 7: *Fantastic Appearance of the Pack* in Sir Allen Young, *The Two Voyages of the 'Pandora' in 1875 and 1876* London: Edward Stanford, 1879, pp.35, The New York Public Library, Astor, Lenox, and Tilden Foundations.

Figure 8: Improved positives: *I Went Up to Within Eight Yards of Him and Killed Him with One Shot* (top); and *An Addition to Our Larder* (bottom) in *Arctic exploration, being a collection of photographs of Arctic regions and explorers* pp.108-109, The Miriam and Ira D. Wallach Division of Art, Prints and Photographs, Photography Collection, The New York Public Library, Astor, Lenox, and Tilden Foundations.

Tim Daly

Figure 1: Daly, T (2019) *Gorstella, Cheshire.* As a long-time admirer of Moore's work, I often spot Moore-like images during my own travels. This image is taken from my project Conversations with Raymond Moore.

Aileen Harvey

Figure 1: Aileen Harvey, *East River/Hudson 1405/151005032011*, 2011, watercolour on paper.

Figure 2; Figure 3. Rhona Eve Clews, *Certain bodies/subtle air* and *The air is not only an empty space*, 2015, silver gelatin prints from photograms.

Figure 4: Aileen Harvey, *Descending order*, 2011, watercolour on paper, nine parts.

Figure 5: Aileen Harvey, *In the shadows the groundwater stayed frozen*, 2016, collected water, sandstone, peat, pencil and acrylic medium on paper.

Figure 6: Figure 7; Figure 8. Ryan L. Moule, *War of the Ghosts*; *Torn Negative*; *Fog Variation* from Vessels and Vestiges, 2017, chemically unfixed silver gelatin photographs.

Figure 9: Aileen Harvey, *Mostly water 03062010*, 2010, ink and stamp on card.

Figure 10: Donald Urquhart, *Ornithology*, 1997, oil on canvas.

Tracy Hill

All Images: © *Tracy Hill, Artlab Contemporary Print Studios, University of Central Lancashire.*

Figure 1: *Cadishead Moss*, 2015, Irlam.

Figure 2: *The Boundary*, 2015, from the series Sensorium.

Figure 3: *Black Waters*, 2017, from the series Matrix of Movement.

Figure 4: *Temporal Wandering*, 2016, from the series Haecceity.

Figure 5: *Genius Loci*, 2017, from the series Matrix of Movement.

Figure 6. *Standing Ash*, 2017, from the series Matrix of Movement.

Figure 7. *Haecceity* (detail), 2018, drawing installation, Warrington Museum and Art Gallery.

Mikko Itälahti

Figure 1: *Map of the southwestern quarter of Finland*. The town of Kuopio is located in the north-east (top-right) corner. The railway network is indicated by bold line and major cities and towns by roundels. (Data sources: National Land Survey of Finland 2018, Finnish Transport Agency 2018)

Figure 2: *The area south from Kuopio on a topographic map (1938)*. The numbers refer to the locations of historical imagery and places mentioned in the material: 1) Nuolimäki cutting (fig. 5); 2) Lake Matkus embankment (fig. 4), 3) Vanuvuori Hill, 4) Pitkälahti station (fig. 7); 5) views onto Kallavesi and dark forest by the original Savo railway alignment, 6) Haminavuori Hill, viewpoint of Magnus von Wright's View from Haminalahti (Map image source: Timo Meriluoto)

Figure 3: *Another cluster of historical railway imagery slightly north from Kuopio,* on topographic military topographic map 1:20 000 (1938). Numbers refer to following locations: 1) An approximate viewpoint of Victor Barskevitsh's View from Puijo towards Kallansillat (fig. 6), 2) Kallavesi straits and the southern end of the Kallavesi overpass, combined swing bridge (figures 9 & 10.), 3) Semaphore (fig. 11.), 4) Villa Granit-Ilmoniemi, Kettulanlahti (fig. 8.). (Map image source: Timo Meriluoto)

Figure 4: Victor Barsokevitsch (c. 1890-1893): *Lake Matkus embankment* (Finnish Railway Museum)

Figure 5: Victor Barsokevitsch, (c. 1890-1893) *Rock cutting at Nuolimäki hill, approximately one kilometre south of the Matkus embankment*. The huge effort required to build the railway through this rough terrain again becomes evident (Finnish Railway Museum)

Figure 6: Victor Barsokevitsch (c. 1902-1909): *View from Puijo hill onto Kallansillat* (the Kallavesi overpass). (Kuopio Cultural History Museum)

Figure 7: I.K. Inha: *Pitkälahti Station*, c. 1894. From Finland in Pictures (Suomi kuvissa/Finland i Bilder/La Finlande pittoresque), 1896. (Finnish heritage agency)

Figure 8: Victor Barsokevitsch: *Villa Granit-Ilmoniemi, Kettulanlahti, Kuopio* 1902. Recently completed Iisalmi railway on the foreground. (Kuopio Cultural History Museum)

Figure 9: Gustav Rafael Roos: *Kallavesi overpass, new road and swing bridge arrangements,* Päiväranta, Kuopio, 1930s. (Finnish Railway Museum);

Figure 10: Gustav Rafael Roos: *Kallansillat swing bridge, opened for the lake steamer "S/S Maaninka" to pass through* (Finnish Railway Museum)

Figure 11: Gustav Rafael Roos: *A semaphore main signal preceding the Kallavesi swing bridge from the south,* 1930s. (Finnish Railway Museum)

Figure 12: Mikko Itälahti: *Pitkälahti transportation landscape, May 2017,* a re-photograph after I.K. Inha's Pitkälahti station (1896, figure 7.). The former station yard locates a depot of a construction company. The railway, in order to copy with demands of acceleration and competition pressure from road transport, was moved to a new straighter alignment and electrified in 1970s and early 1980s, skipping the scenic sections along Kallavesi Inha mentioned. Behind the railway roars the E5 main road through Kuopio, recently built to a motorway standard.

Julia Peck

All images by – and by courtesy of – Olaf Otto Becker

Figure 1: *705 Nuussuaq 07/2006.*

Figure 2: *Point 660, 2, 08/2008.*

Figure 3: *Deforestation of primary forest, Central Kalimantan, Indonesia* 03/2012.

Figure 4: *60 Minutes Dettifoss.*

Lena Quelvennec

Figure 1: *Still frame: 00:00:26.* Perboni, Alessio. Northern Lights in Iceland, in REAL TIME!!! YouTube: February 13, 2013. Courtesy of the artist.

Figure 2: *Still Frame: 00:01:36.* Perboni, Alessio, Northern Lights in Iceland, in REAL TIME!!! YouTube: February 13, 2013. Courtesy of the artist.

Figure 3: *Comment 01*, "Perboni's answers", accessed October 20, 2018. (https://www.youtube.com/watch?v=dGQ7EZs5xu8)

Figure 4: *Comment 02*, "Stay with the group", accessed October 20. 2018. (https://www.youtube.com/watch?v=dGQ7EZs5xu8)

Figure 5: Frederic Edwin Church. *Aurora Borealis* (1865), Oil on canvas, 142.3 cm × 212.2 cm © Smithsonian American Art Museum, Gift of Eleanor Blodgett.

Figure 6: Comment 03, "Buses full of tourists" accessed October 20, 2018. (https://www.youtube.com/watch?v=dGQ7EZs5xu8)

Figure 7: *Comment 04*, "Add to its beauty", accessed November 16, 2018. <https://www.youtube.com/watch?v=dGQ7EZs5xu8>

Figure 8: *Comment 05*, "Just perspective", accessed November 16, 2018. (https://www.youtube.com/watch?v=dGQ7EZs5xu8)
Figure 9: *Comment 06*, "Beautiful", accessed October 21, 2018. (https://www.youtube.com/watch?v=dGQ7EZs5xu8)
Figure 10: *Comment 07*, "Shaking camera", accessed October 21, 2018. (https://www.youtube.com/watch?v=dGQ7EZs5xu8)
Figure 11: *"The special camera"* Picture of Light (1994) dir. Peter Mettler, Canada/Switzerland: Andera Zuest/Grimthorpe Film, running time: 00:01:39. Reproduced with permission from Grimthorpe Film Inc.
Figure 12: *"Aurora Borealis"* Picture of Light (1994): dir. Peter Mettler, Canada/Switzerland: Andera Zuest/Grimthorpe Film, running time: 00:35:05. Reproduced with permission from Grimthorpe Film Inc.
Figure 13: *Comment 08*, "real time", accessed October 21, 2017 (https://www.youtube.com/watch?v=dGQ7EZs5xu8)

Anne Wriedt

All images by courtesy of: The Picture Collection, University of Bergen Library.
Figure 1: Knud Knudsen & Company, Stalheim Hotel and Naerødal Valley, 1888.
Figure 2: *Naerødal Valley from Stalheim*. Stereoscopic image, 1860s.
Figure 3: *Hornidalsrokken in Nordfjord*, 1881-82
Figure 4: *Bondhus Glacier in Mauranger, Hardanger*, 1890s.
Figure 5: *Kvinnherad brochure*, 1994.

Biographies of Contributors

Nicky Bird is an artist whose work considers the contemporary relevance of 'found' photographs and hidden histories of specific sites, investigating how they remain resonant. Her work incorporates new photography with oral histories and collaborations with people who have significant connections to the original site and its photographic archive. Alongside commissioned projects such as Ghosting the Castle (2017), she has exhibited nationally and internationally, with published essays on themes of erased place and digital exchange of photographs. Nicky is also a Reader in Contemporary Photographic Practice at The Glasgow School of Art.

Elizabeth Cronin is the Assistant Curator of Photography at the New York Public Library. She is the author of *Heimat Photography in Austria: A Politicized Vision of Peasants and Skiers* (Fotohof edition, 2015) and has published several articles on the topic. She has curated and co-curated such exhibitions as *Viewpoints: Latin America in Photographs* and *Public Eye: 175 Years of Sharing Photography*. Cronin is currently organizing an exhibition on how the Arctic has been visualized. She holds a PhD in Art History from the Graduate Center, City University of New York. She has an MA in German Studies from the Technical University of Dresden.

Tim Daly teaches photography at the University of Chester in the UK and has a research interest in the 'thingness' of photography and the materiality of the photographic print. Tim has written over twenty books on photography production and project development working with most US and UK publishing houses. As a photographer, Tim has exhibited his work widely, including at The Photographers' Gallery, London and at the NGBK in Berlin. In 2017, Tim established Fugitive Press to distribute artist's books that explore the materiality of the photographic print, unconventional materials and touch.

Chris Goldie is formerly Senior Lecturer, currently Honorary Research Fellow, in the Department for Media Arts and Communication, Sheffield Hallam University. He has a BA in history and an MA in cultural studies. His PhD thesis explored the culture and politics of space in 1960s Britain. Chris has taught at Sheffield City

Polytechnic/ Sheffield Hallam University since 1985. His teaching and research focus has been interdisciplinary, working with students in the fields of history, fine art and design, art history, film and media. Recent publications have appeared in the *Journal of Design History* (2011), *The Journal of International Relations, Peace Studies and Development* (2017), (2018), (2019), and the *Design Journal* (2019). Chris co-edited, with Darcy White, *Northern Light: Landscape, Photography and Evocations of the North*, published by transcript Verlag in 2018.

Aileen Harvey is an artist whose work engages with the experience of place. Her processes of walking, photography, drawing, and writing are used to inter-relate location, time and the body. Born in London, Aileen studied philosophy at Edinburgh (1998) and Cambridge (2000), and then sculpture at Wimbledon College of Art (2008); the one subject informing the other. Exhibitions include: Bernard Leach Gallery, St Ives; Customs House Gallery, Sunderland; Karussell, Zürich; An Lanntair, Stornoway; The Photographers' Gallery.

Tracy Hill was born in Birmingham studied Fine Art at Bournville School of Art, Birmingham, Sheffield Hallam University and The University of Central Lancashire, Preston. Currently a research associate and co-leader of Artlab Contemporary Print studios at The University of Central Lancashire, her practice investigates and reconsiders the relationship between our developing digital capabilities and the aesthetics of the traditional hand created mark. Her work creates a hybrid space allowing a cross over between technological control and the emotion of human experience, challenging and exploring print as a platform of multiple-dimensions.

Mikko Itälahti is a landscape researcher, a photographer and a doctoral candidate at the Aalto University School of Arts, Design and Architecture in Helsinki, Finland. His educational background is in human geography. Currently he is finalising a dissertation monograph on the environmental sensibilities in photographic landscape imagery related to the Finnish railways. Mikko thinks of landscape photography as a medium for an encounter with the non-human world; a form of aesthetic apprehension that also involves various multisensory, spatial and cultural imaginations. His approach – involving an arts-based element – thus seeks to span the traditional domains of representational, phenomenological and material-realist ontologies.

Jessica Keister, formerly the Associate Conservator for Photographs at the New York Public Library, is currently the principal conservator at Steel City Art Conservation in Pittsburgh, PA. Prior to that, she spent six years as Paper & Photograph Conservator at the Conservation Center for Art & Historic Artifacts in Philadelphia. Jessica received an M.S. in Art Conservation, with a primary concentration in Photographic Materials and a secondary concentration in Works on Paper, from the Winterthur/University of Delaware Program in Art Conservation. She is a Professional Associate of the American Institute for Conservation (AIC) and an active member of the AIC Photographic Materials Group.

Julia Peck is a photographer, writer and academic based at the University of Gloucestershire. Julia has had a long-standing interest in the landscape and the environment and is particularly interested in political ecology and philosophies that explore non-binary approaches to human/nature relationships. Her photographic work has been exhibited in the UK and she has contributed images, articles and reviews to *Next Level, Dandelion, Source, Visual Studies, History of Photography, Photographies* and *Journal of Australian Studies.*

Lena Quelvennec graduated from Lund University In 2018 with a Master's degree in Visual Culture. Her research focuses on visualities between human beings and extreme environments, peripheral space, political occupations and the relationship between art and activism in the context of environmental struggles. Working for cultural organizations in contemporary art (Muse'e d'art du Valais, Skissernas Museum, Galleri Pictura) and in documentary cinema and image education (Image'Est, Tënk Lussas, Nordisk Panorama), she previously obtained a Master's in Visual Arts in 2013 at the HEAD, Geneva, researching digital documents and art.

Darcy White is Principal Lecturer in Visual Culture in the Department of Media Arts and Communication, Sheffield Hallam University (SHU). Her interest in art began as a landscape painter and printmaker. Initially studying fine art she later gained a BA and MA in the history of art and then taught with the Workers Education Association before taking up a post at SHU, where she teaches the history and theory of photography. She is the founder of the 'Northern Light' Contemporary Landscape Photography research group and, with Chris Goldie, co-convener of its biennial conference. Recent publications include: (with Elizabeth Norman) *The Public Sculpture of Sheffield and South Yorkshire,* Liverpool University Press, and, co-edited with Chris Goldie, *Northern Light: Landscape, Photography and Evocations of the North,* transcript Verlag. An environmental and social activist, Darcy is, with Stephanie Hartle, co-convener of the 'Visual Activism' research group at SHU.

Anne Wriedt is research associate and assistant curator at Museum for Photography Braunschweig. She studied Art History and Visual Culture at the Universities of Copenhagen, Leipzig and Kiel. For her master thesis on Norwegian photographer Knud Knudsen she received the Utrecht Young Researchers Grant. She is co-author of the publication, *Faraway Focus. Photographers go travelling (1880-2015)* and was assistant curator of the exhibition Wanderlust and Idleness. Landscape, Tours and Detours in Leisure Culture at the Museum for Photography Braunschweig.

Cultural Studies

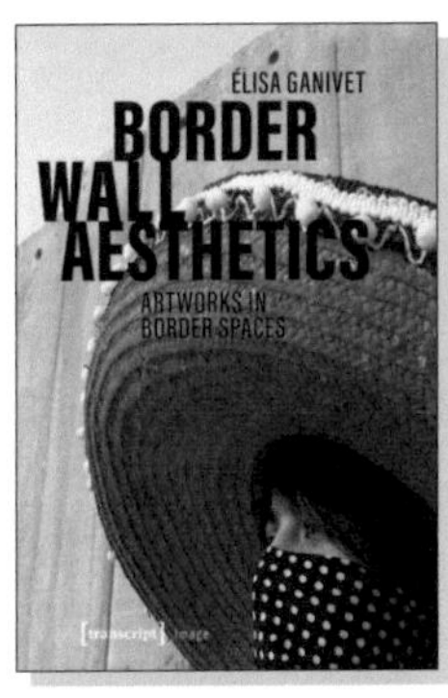

Elisa Ganivet
Border Wall Aesthetics
Artworks in Border Spaces

2019, 250 p., hardcover, ill.
79,99 € (DE), 978-3-8376-4777-8
E-Book: 79,99 € (DE), ISBN 978-3-8394-4777-2

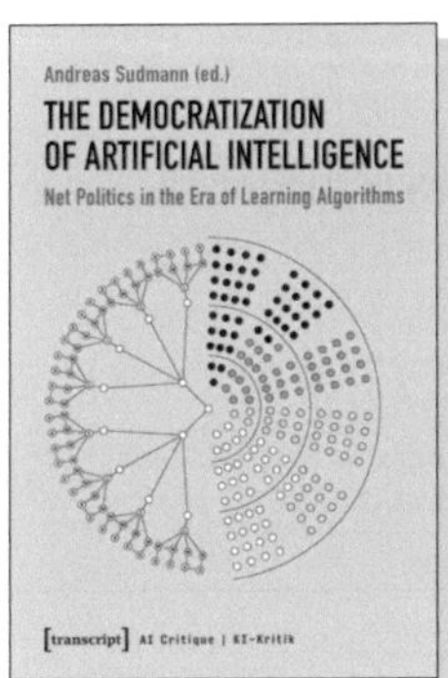

Andreas Sudmann (ed.)
The Democratization of Artificial Intelligence
Net Politics in the Era of Learning Algorithms

2019, 334 p., pb., col. ill.
49,99 € (DE), 978-3-8376-4719-8
E-Book: free available, ISBN 978-3-8394-4719-2

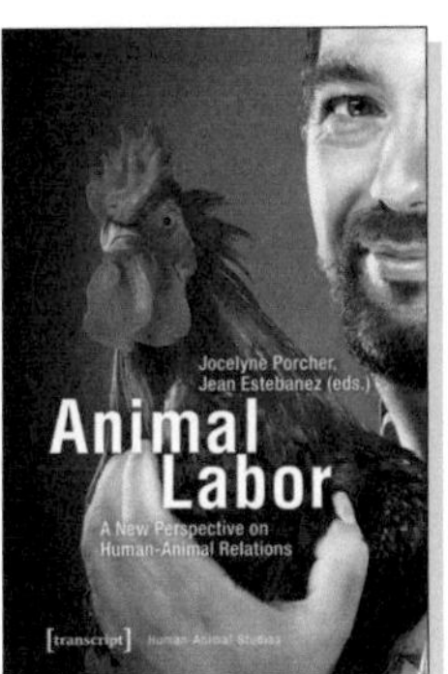

Jocelyne Porcher, Jean Estebanez (eds.)
Animal Labor
A New Perspective on Human-Animal Relations

2019, 182 p., hardcover
99,99 € (DE), 978-3-8376-4364-0
E-Book: 99,99 € (DE), ISBN 978-3-8394-4364-4

Cultural Studies

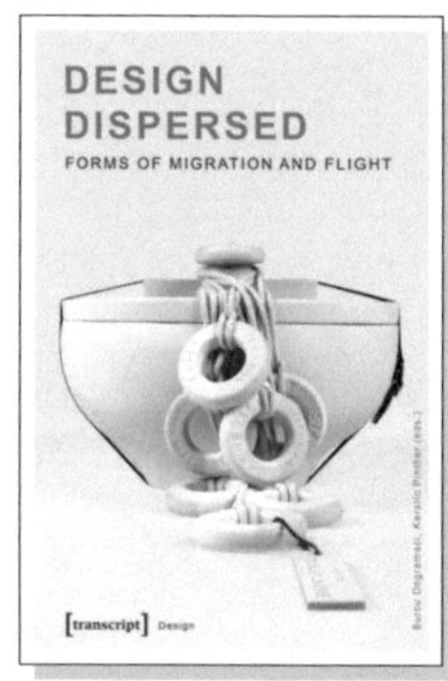

Burcu Dogramaci, Kerstin Pinther (eds.)
Design Dispersed
Forms of Migration and Flight

2019, 274 p., pb., col. ill.
34,99 € (DE), 978-3-8376-4705-1
E-Book: 34,99 € (DE), ISBN 978-3-8394-4705-5

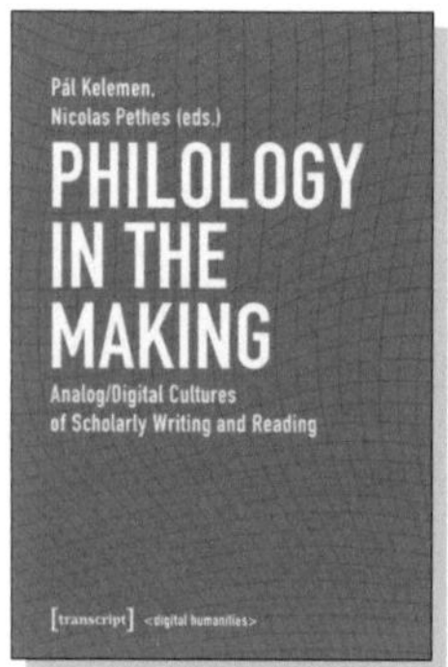

Pál Kelemen, Nicolas Pethes (eds.)
Philology in the Making
Analog/Digital Cultures of Scholarly Writing and Reading

2019, 316 p., pb., ill.
34,99 € (DE), 978-3-8376-4770-9
E-Book: 34,99 € (DE), ISBN 978-3-8394-4770-3

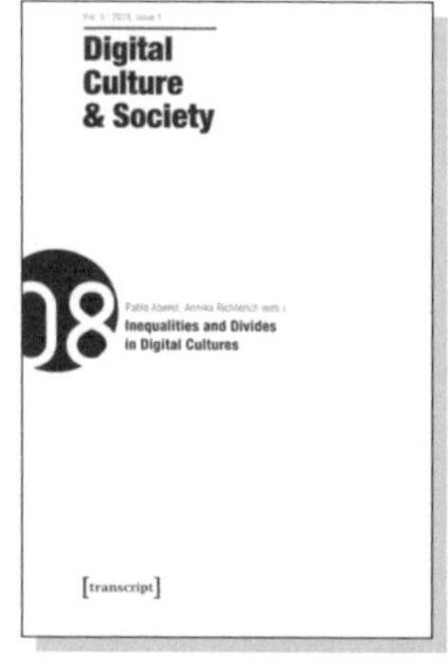

Pablo Abend, Annika Richterich,
Mathias Fuchs, Ramón Reichert, Karin Wenz (eds.)
Digital Culture & Society (DCS)
Vol. 5, Issue 1/2019 –
Inequalities and Divides in Digital Cultures

2019, 212 p., pb., ill.
29,99 € (DE), 978-3-8376-4478-4
E-Book: 29,99 € (DE), ISBN 978-3-8394-4478-8

All print, e-book and open access versions of the titles in our list are available in our online shop www.transcript-verlag.de/en!